Journal of Moral Theology

Volume 12, Special Issue 2
October 2023

Guns in the United States

Edited by
Michael R. Grigoni
and
Cory D. Mitchell

JOURNAL · OF MORAL THEOLOGY

Journal of Moral Theology is published semiannually, with regular issues in January and July. Our mission is to publish scholarly articles in the field of Catholic moral theology, as well as theological treatments of related topics in philosophy, economics, political philosophy, and psychology.

Articles published in the *Journal of Moral Theology* undergo at least two double blind peer reviews. To submit an article for the journal, please visit the "For Authors" page on our website at jmt.scholasticahq.com/for-authors.

Journal of Moral Theology is available full text in the *ATLA Religion Database with ATLASerials®* (RDB®), a product of the American Theological Library Association.
Email: atla@atla.com, www.atla.com.
ISSN 2166-2851 (print)
ISSN 2166-2118 (online)

Journal of Moral Theology is published by The Journal of Moral Theology, Inc.

Copyright © 2023 individual authors.

Pickwick Publications, An Imprint of Wipf and Stock Publishers, 199 W. 8th Ave., Suite 3, Eugene, OR 97401
www.wipfandstock.com. ISBN: 979-8-3852-0754-1

JOURNAL OF M·O·R·A·L THEOLOGY

EDITOR EMERITUS
Jason King, *St. Mary's University, San Antonio, TX*

EDITOR
M. Therese Lysaught, *Loyola University Chicago Stritch School of Medicine*

SENIOR EDITOR
William J. Collinge, *Mount St. Mary's University*

ASSOCIATE EDITORS
Mari Rapela Heidt, *Notre Dame of Maryland University*
Alexandre A. Martins, *Marquette University*
Mary Doyle Roche, *College of the Holy Cross*
Matthew Shadle, *Window Light*
Kate Ward, *Marquette University*

MANAGING EDITOR
Jean-Pierre Fortin, *St. Michael's College, University of Toronto*

EDITORIAL ASSISANT
Aaron Weisel, *Ave Maria University*

EDITORIAL BOARD
Christina Astorga, *University of Portland*
Jana M. Bennett, *University of Dayton*
Mara Brecht, *Loyola University Chicago*
Jim Caccamo, *St. Joseph's University*
Carolyn A. Chau, *King's University College at Western University, Ontario Canada*
Meghan Clark, *St. John's University*
David Cloutier, *The Catholic University of America*
Christopher Denny, *St. John's University*
Julia Fleming, *Creighton University*
Joseph Flipper, *University of Dayton*
Nichole M. Flores, *University of Virginia*
Craig Ford, *St. Norbert College*
Matthew J. Gaudet, *Santa Clara University*
Natalia Imperatori-Lee, *Manhattan College*
Kelly Johnson, *University of Dayton*
Andrew Kim, *Marquette University*
Warren Kinghorn, *Duke University*
Leocadie Lushombo, *Santa Clara University*
Ramon Luzarraga, *St. Martin's University*
William C. Mattison III, *University of Notre Dame*
Christina McRorie, *Boston College*
Cory D. Mitchell, *PeaceHealth*
Suzane Mulligan, *Catholic Theological Ethics in the World Church Liaison, St. Patrick's Pontifical University, Maynooth, Ireland*
Anna Perkins, *University of the West Indies*
Joel Shuman, *King's College*
Christopher P. Vogt, *St. John's College*
Paul Wadell, *St. Norbert College*

JOURNAL OF MORAL THEOLOGY
VOLUME 12, SPECIAL ISSUE 2
OCTOBER 2023

CONTENTS

Moral Theology and Guns in the United States: Staging an Encounter
    Michael R. Grigoni 1

Gun Laws and Gun Deaths: An Empirical Analysis and Theological Assessment
    Conor M. Kelly 9

Natural Law's Return: Uncovering the Roots of Intractability on Guns as Prelude to New Growth
    John E. Carter 33

Concealed Carry, Agency, and Attention in a Technocratic Context
    Luis G. Vera 58

Guns, Construction of Threat, and Lived Ecclesiologies
    Katie Day 84

The Christian Handgun Owner and Just War
    Michael R. Grigoni 108

Christian Arguments for Gun Violence Prevention: Reflections on Moral Claims in the Context of Advocacy
    Ellen Ott Marshall 133

Gun Culture, Free Riding, and Nothing Short of Conversion
    Gerald W. Schlabach 158

Firearms and Moral Theology: A Response
    Tobias Winright 185

Moral Theology and Guns in the United States: Staging an Encounter

Michael R. Grigoni

GUNS HOLD A VEXINGLY UNIQUE PLACE IN THE UNITED STATES. The US has, by far, the highest prevalence of private firearm ownership among high-income nations in the world. Current estimates place the number of guns in private hands between 350 and 400 million.[1] The United States also has the highest prevalence of firearm-caused death among high-income nations, enduring from 2016 to 2019 an average of forty thousand firearm-caused deaths per year.[2] Over 2020 and 2021, this number has begun to approach the 50,000 mark.[3] Further, the polarization that marks public discourse on guns shows no signs of easing despite the tragic recurrence of mass shootings in contexts formerly considered immune to such violence, from school classrooms to houses of worship and beyond.[4]

---

[1] For the lower estimate, see Jennifer Mascia and Chip Brownlee, "How Many Guns Are Circulating in the US?," *The Trace*, updated August 28, 2023, originally published March 6, 2023, www.thetrace.org/2023/03/guns-america-data-atf-total/. For the higher estimate, see Small Arms Survey, "Estimating Global Civilian-Held Firearms Numbers," June 2018, www.smallarmssurvey.org/sites/default/files/resources/SAS-BP-Civilian-Firearms-Numbers.pdf, 4. Mascia and Brownlee discuss the challenges of developing an accurate estimate given that there is no national firearm registry in the United States. See also Philip J. Cook and Kristin A. Goss, *The Gun Debate: What Everyone Needs to Know*, 2nd ed. (Oxford: Oxford University Press, 2020), 2–4.

[2] See "Firearm Deaths in the US: Statistics and Trends," *USAFacts*, accessed September 10, 2023, www.usafacts.org/data/topics/security-safety/crime-and-justice/firearms/firearm-deaths/, which draws from Centers for Disease Control and Prevention data.

[3] *USAFacts* reports 45,222 firearm-caused deaths in 2020, and 48,830 firearm-caused deaths in 2021. See "Firearm Deaths in the US," *USAFacts*. For an analysis of 2021 firearm-caused death data, see John Gramlich, "What the Data Says about Gun Deaths in the US," Pew Research Center, April 26, 2023, www.pewresearch.org/short-reads/2023/04/26/what-the-data-says-about-gun-deaths-in-the-u-s/. Provisional CDC data indicates that gun deaths decreased in 2022 compared to 2021. See Jennifer Mascia, "Gun Deaths Dropped Slightly in 2022—But Were Still High," *The Trace*, July 10, 2023, www.thetrace.org/2023/07/gun-deaths-cdc-data-suicide-homicide/.

[4] An April 2021 Pew Research Center poll found that partisan divisions on most gun policy proposals "have grown wider over the last few years," including "even

Given this, it is no wonder that scholars are increasingly turning their attention to guns. For decades, analyses of guns and their effects in the United States have largely been carried out in the fields of criminology and public health via quantitative modes of analysis.[5] Unsurprisingly, such approaches have failed to account holistically for the social and cultural reasons for firearm prevalence in the United States. Contemporary approaches to gun scholarship, particularly in the domains of sociology and cultural studies, have made significant inroads into correcting this trend. Often interdisciplinary in nature, this research has improved our ability to articulate why guns remain an entrenched feature of our social landscape, showing that guns do not exist abstractly but are incorporated into particular forms of life;[6] that "American gun culture" is not a monolithic entity but is composed of various subcultures that have evolved over time;[7] that guns are not

---

on whether gun violence is a serious national problem" (Carroll Doherty, Jocelyn Kiley, Nida Asheer, and Calvin Jordan, "Amid a Series of Mass Shootings in the US, Gun Policy Remains Deeply Divisive," Pew Research Center, April 2021, www.pewresearch.org/politics/2021/04/20/amid-a-series-of-mass-shootings-in-the-u-s-gun-policy-remains-deeply-divisive/). See also Harry Enten, "The US Has Never Been So Polarized on Guns," *FiveThirtyEight*, October 4, 2017, fivethirtyeight.com/features/the-u-s-has-never-been-so-polarized-on-guns/, which cites 2017 Pew Research Center data much to the same effect. On school shootings, see John Woodrow Cox, Steven Rich, Linda Chong et al., "More than 356,000 students have experienced gun violence at school since Columbine," *The Washington Post*, updated June 11, 2023, originally published April 20, 2018, www.washingtonpost.com/education/interactive/school-shootings-database/. For a journalistic overview of shootings at houses of worship from the 2007 New Life Church shooting to the present, see John Blake, "One of the Most Dangerous Hours in America is Now 11 o'clock on Sunday Morning," *CNN*, June 10, 2023, www.cnn.com/2023/06/10/us/faith-violence-security-blake-cec/index.html. See also Katie Day, "Guns, the Construction of Threat, and Lived Ecclesiologies," in this special issue.

[5] See Jennifer Carlson, Kristin A. Goss, and Harel Shapira, "Introduction: New Approaches to Research on Guns," in *Gun Studies: Interdisciplinary Approaches to Politics, Policy, and Practice*, ed. Jennifer Carlson, Kristin A. Goss, and Harel Shapira (Abingdon, UK: Routledge, 2019), 1; David Yamane, "The Sociology of US Gun Culture," *Sociology Compass* 11, no. 7 (2017): 1–10.

[6] See Abigail Kohn, *Shooters: Myths and Realities of America's Gun Cultures* (New York: Oxford University Press, 2004), a pioneering volume in the ethnographic study of guns which finds a variety of gun cultures existing in the San Francisco Bay area. Upholding Kohn and many of the ethnographic studies cited below as models, Yamane calls for the increased use of qualitative methods to study the "social practices" of gun owners and the "social worlds" they inhabit. See Yamane, "The Sociology of US Gun Culture," 7.

[7] Yamane distinguishes between "Gun Culture 1.0" (which centers on hunting and recreation) and "Gun Culture 2.0" (which centers on armed self-defense), writing that "the center of gravity of US gun culture has shifted over the course of the past half-century from recreational shooting to armed self-defense." See Yamane, "The Sociology of US Gun Culture," 5. See also David Yamane, "Gun Culture 2.0: The

simply material but social objects that house meaning relative to the social worlds they occupy;[8] and that within these worlds, guns can be put to a variety of different uses, whether to navigate economic and societal precarity in contexts of civil decline,[9] perform projects of nationalist recovery in the US-Mexico borderlands,[10] or reinforce hegemonic masculinity in states like Texas,[11] among others. These studies indicate not only the diversity of American gun cultures, but also how guns become integrated into particular communities and tethered to particular ways of being in the world. They also indicate the challenge before moral theologians and Christian ethicists seeking to do work on this topic. Such work cannot proceed in abstraction from these lived dynamics. If moral theology and Christian ethics requires attention to the embeddedness of the human person in specific social worlds, and consideration of the moral dimensions of everyday life, then those seeking to reflect normatively upon the place of guns in the United States will find this research indispensable to their efforts.[12]

Evolution and Contours of Defensive Gun Ownership in America," *The ANNALS of the American Academy of Political and Social Science* 704, no. 1 (2022): 20–43, which describes the evolution of Gun Culture 1.0 and Gun Culture 2.0 in greater historical detail, highlights the diversity of subcultures that fall under "Gun Culture 2.0," and speculates about the possible emergence of a gun culture centered around Second Amendment activism which he calls "Gun Culture 3.0."

[8] See Jonathan Obert, Andrew Poe, and Austin Sarat, eds., *The Lives of Guns* (New York: Oxford University Press, 2019); Jonathan M. Metzl, ed., "What Guns Mean: The Symbolic Lives of Firearms," special issue of *Palgrave Communications* (2019): www.nature.com/collections/jdiffcfjba.

[9] See Jennifer Dawn Carlson, *Citizen-Protectors: The Everyday Politics of Guns in an Age of Decline* (New York: Oxford University Press, 2015), an ethnography of handgun owners in Detroit and Flint, Michigan, in which the practice of concealed carry manifests what she describes as a form of "armed citizenship." Her more recent work continues in this qualitative vein. See Jennifer Dawn Carlson, *Policing the Second Amendment: Guns, Public Law Enforcement, and the Politics of Race* (Princeton, NJ: Princeton University Press, 2020); Jennifer Dawn Carlson, *Merchants of the Right: Gun Sellers and the Crisis of American Democracy* (Princeton, NJ: Princeton University Press, 2023).

[10] See Harel Shapira, *Waiting for José: The Minutemen's Pursuit of America* (Princeton, NJ: Princeton University Press, 2013), an ethnography of the Minutemen in the US-Mexico border region.

[11] See Angela Stroud, *Good Guys with Guns: The Appeal and Consequences of Concealed Carry* (Chapel Hill: University of North Carolina Press, 2016), a qualitative interview-based study carried out in Texas that attends to the lived experience of male and female concealed carriers and which demonstrates, among its findings, that female concealed carry reinforces rather than undercuts patriarchal gender roles (see, in particular, her chapter titled, "Men and Guns," in *Good Guys with Guns*, 28–54).

[12] For additional volumes, see Jennifer Carlson, Kristin A. Goss, and Harel Shapira, eds., *Gun Studies: Interdisciplinary Approaches to Politics, Policy, and Practice* (Abingdon, UK: Routledge, 2019); Craig Hovey and Lisa Fischer, eds., *Understanding America's Gun Culture*, 2nd edition (Lanham, MD: Lexington, 2021);

Regrettably, there exist few sustained treatments of guns in the United States by moral theologians and Christian ethicists. This is especially unfortunate given the intricate link sociologists have established between Christianity and gun ownership in the United States.[13] Guns are not simply an entrenched feature of US American life but of US American Christian life. Among the treatments that have appeared, many have been written by pastors and activists. Presbyterian pastor James E. Atwood has authored three volumes, *America and Its Guns: A Theological Exposé*, *Gundamentalism and Where It Is Taking Us*, and *Collateral Damage: Changing the Conversation about Firearms and Faith*, all of which offer wide ranging reflections on guns from a Christian perspective.[14] In *Common Ground: Talking about Gun Violence in America*, Newtown, Connecticut, native and Disciples of Christ minister Donald Gaffney combines personal narrative with reflections on scripture, firearms-related statistics, and American history to facilitate conversation about guns in church communities.[15] Activists Shane Claiborne and Michael Martin's *Beating Guns: Hope for People Who are Weary of Violence* similarly presents reflections on guns for lay audiences.[16] There is

---

Benjamin Dowd-Arrow, Terrence D. Hill, and Amy M. Burdette, eds., "Guns and Society," special issue of *Sociological Inquiry* 91, no. 2 (2021): 245–504; Trent Steidley and David Yamane, eds., "Sociological Perspectives on Guns in America," special issue of *Sociological Perspectives* 65, no 1. (2022): 5–235.

[13] See, for example, Andrew L. Whitehead, Landon Schnabel, and Samuel L. Perry, "Gun Control in the Crosshairs: Christian Nationalism and Opposition to Stricter Gun Laws," *Socius: Sociological Research for a Dynamic World* 4 (2018): 1–13; Stephen M. Merino, "God and Guns: Examining Religious Influences on Gun Control Attitudes in the United States," *Religions* 9, no. 6 (2018): 189; David Yamane, "Awash in a Sea of Faith and Firearms: Rediscovering the Connection between Religion and Gun Ownership in America," *Journal for the Scientific Study of Religion* 55, no. 3 (2016): 622–636. These studies correlate "Christian nationalism" (Whitehead et al.), "white evangelical Protestants" (Merino), "Evangelical Protestant affiliation," and "theological conservatism" (Yamane) with higher rates of gun ownership and/or resistance to gun control compared to other religious groups and theological orientations.

[14] James E. Atwood, *Collateral Damage: Changing the Conversation about Faith and Firearms* (Harrisonburg, VA: Herald, 2019); James E. Atwood, *Gundamentalism and Where It Is Taking America* (Eugene, OR: Cascade, 2017); James E. Atwood, *America and Its Guns: A Theological Exposé* (Eugene, OR: Wipf and Stock, 2012).

[15] Donald V. Gaffney, *Common Ground: Talking about Gun Violence in America* (Louisville, KY: Westminster John Knox, 2018). As a child, Gaffney attended Sandy Hook Elementary, the scene of the deadliest mass shooting at an elementary school in US history in 2012.

[16] Shane Claiborne and Michael Martin, *Beating Guns: Hope for People Who Are Weary of Violence* (Grand Rapids, MI: Brazos, 2019). Michael Martin is director of RAWtools, an organization that, among its practices, aims to build a network of "Disarming Locations" that refashion guns into garden tools. See "Swords to Plowshares," RAWtools, www.rawtools.org/swords-to-plowshares/.

thematic overlap between the texts. Atwood and Claiborne and Martin, for example, use the metaphor of the gun as idol to suggest that firearms function as a "false god" that seduces their owners with bogus promises of security.[17] Both Atwood and Gaffney draw from their experience as gun owners to build rapport with their readers. All of the books have in common a desire to engage communities on the ground.[18]

Taken together, these books indicate the need for resources that address the place of guns in the United States from a Christian theological perspective. Treatments by theologians and ethicists can complement and complicate the arguments developed in such resources. A handful of texts have recently appeared that do precisely this. Edited by Christopher B. Hays and C. L. Crouch, *God and Guns: The Bible against American Gun Culture* brings together biblical scholars to weigh in on the place of guns in American life.[19] Significantly, the volume acknowledges that there exists "a tension between texts in the Bible that seem to suggest that Christians are not always to refrain from violent means, though nonviolence seems to be the norm."[20] The volume's essays wrestle with this fact, from engagements with the conquest narratives in Joshua (Brent Strawn) to New Testament passages often used to justify gun ownership (Shelly Matthews), bringing penetrating biblical scholarship to bear on this timely issue. In *God and Guns in America*, ethicist Michael Austin draws on virtue ethics, just war, and just peacemaking, among other frameworks, to develop a multilayered consideration of guns in the United States.[21] Also a gun owner, Austin seeks to develop a third way between the status quo and a pacifist rejection of guns to mitigate polarization. Written in response to the 2012 slaying of Trayvon Martin, Kelly Brown Douglas's *Stand Your Ground: Black Bodies and the Justice of God* offers a trenchant critique of Stand Your Ground laws and what she names as a broader "stand-your-ground

---

[17] Atwood, *America and Its Guns*, 19–32; Claiborne and Martin, *Beating Guns*, 165–80.

[18] There also exists an innumerable set of resources other than books that treat guns from a Christian perspective, from pdfs, brochures, and blog posts, on the one hand, to statements issued by religious leaders and social organizations, on the other. For a survey of these materials, see Ellen Ott Marshall, "Christian Arguments for Gun Violence Prevention: Reflections on Moral Claims in the Context of Advocacy" and Tobias Winright, "Firearms and Moral Theology: A Response," both of which appear in this special issue.

[19] Christopher B. Hays and C. L. Crouch, eds., *God and Guns: The Bible against American Gun Culture* (Louisville, KY: Westminster John Knox, 2021).

[20] Stanley Hauerwas, "Foreword," in *God and Guns: The Bible against American Gun Culture*, ix–x.

[21] Michael W. Austin, *God and Guns in America* (Grand Rapids, MI: Eerdmans, 2020).

culture" in the United States that renders life more precarious for persons of color.[22] Douglas draws attention to the racialized dimensions of gun violence in America, which must be centered as theological treatments of this issue continue to be developed. While each of these books have helped advance the conversation, they are painfully few.[23] More scholarship is needed as the place and effects of guns in our common life becomes simultaneously more devastating and banal.

This special issue of the *Journal of Moral Theology* (JMT) seeks to build upon these volumes and further stimulate theological reflection on the topic of guns in the United States. It features essays by moral theologians and Christian ethicists from a variety of ecclesial backgrounds who approach this topic from a broad range of areas of expertise. It does not aim to issue a final, conclusive word on the place of guns in the United States, but to advance conversation about the place guns *should* take in our common life.

The issue opens with Conor Kelly's "Gun Laws and Gun Deaths: An Empirical Analysis and Theological Assessment," which surveys the place of gun violence in the United States and what Catholic moral commitment requires regarding this sign of the times. Kelly consults a broad range of studies which suggest that limiting access to guns results in a decrease in gun deaths, highlighting the "growing consensus" that there indeed exists a relationship between firearm availability and firearm mortality. He concludes that, given their commitment to the common good, Catholics should make a prudential judgment to support gun legislation that reduces firearm prevalence, despite challenges to establishing this relationship as causal.

In "Natural Law's Return: Uncovering the Roots of Intractability on Guns as Prelude to New Growth," John Carter proposes a return to natural law discourse as a means of countering the predominance of originalism (and legal positivism, more broadly) in shaping the gun debate in the United States today. His article provides a valuable

---

[22] Kelly Brown Douglas, *Stand Your Ground: Black Bodies and the Justice of God* (Maryknoll, NY: Orbis Books, 2015).
[23] While space does not permit commentary, see also Mark Ryan, "Guns and Practical Reason: An Ethical Exploration of Guns and Language," *Journal of Moral Theology* 11, no. 1 (2022): 85–106; John T. Noonan, Jr., "Cooperation in the Culture of Death," *Theological Studies*, 82 no. 1 (2021): 55–68; Benjamin D. Utter and Tarris Rosell, eds., "Bullets, Baptists, and the Bible," special issue of *Review & Expositor* 117, no. 3 (2020); Michelle Byrne, Virginia McCarthy, Abigail Silva, and Sharon Homan, "Health Care Providers on the Frontline: Responding to the Gun Violence Epidemic," in *Catholic Bioethics and Social Justice: The Praxis of US Health Care in a Globalized World*, ed. M. Therese Lysaught and Michael McCarthy (Collegeville, MN: Liturgical Press Academic, 2018), 31–45; Lyndon Shakespeare, "Friendship, Love, and Mass Shootings: Toward a Theological Response for Gun Control," *Anglican Theological Review* 95, no. 4 (November 2013): 607–625.

overview of the eclipse of natural law in US American legal history and the detrimental effects of this eclipse on Second Amendment interpretation and legislation. Echoing recent calls for a broader recovery of natural law in Christian ethics, Carter views contemporary approaches to natural law as providing a basis upon which the impasse of political polarization about guns in the United States might be mitigated.

In the articles that follow, Luis Vera and Katie Day each consider a specific firearms-related practice—concealed carry and armed church security, respectively—through a particular theological lens. Vera's "Concealed Carry, Agency, and Attention in a Technocratic Context" evaluates concealed carry in light of Pope Francis's critique of the technocratic paradigm in *Laudato Si'*. In applying Francis's critique to the practice of defensive gun carry, Vera argues that we must situate existing analyses of the ethics of guns within a broader consideration of how guns are expressive of our technological condition. In "Guns, the Construction of Threat, and Lived Ecclesiologies," Day considers armed church security, drawing on sociological surveys and her ongoing qualitative research (with David Yamane) regarding the use of guns in ecclesial spaces. She resources Dietrich Bonhoeffer's ecclesiology to argue that armed church security generates a fortress ecclesiology that counters the church's call to hospitality. Both articles creatively demonstrate how specific theological frameworks can be used to advance reflection on the uses to which guns are put in everyday contexts.

The remaining articles can be seen as charting a pathway from just war to just peacemaking regarding guns in US American life. In "The Christian Handgun Owner and Just War," Michael Grigoni draws upon the just war tradition to reflect on his ethnographic research with Christian handgun owners in central North Carolina. He indicates the benefits and limits of just war for doing so, finding just war helpful, on the one hand, for illuminating the lived experience of his interlocutors, but unable, on the other, to attend to contextually significant factors such as race, which he demonstrates through consideration of the Deacons for Defense and Justice, a civil rights era African American self-defense group. He concludes by gesturing toward just peacemaking as an alternative framework.

Ellen Ott Marshall's "Christian Arguments for Gun Violence Prevention: Reflections on Moral Claims in the Context of Advocacy" begins by identifying moral confusion about the role of vulnerability in gun violence prevention materials and activism. The failure of such materials to distinguish between "existential," "statistical," and "virtuous vulnerability" undercuts their ability to speak clearly and prophetically about the scourge of gun violence in America. She argues that gun violence prevention activism can address this confusion by centering the vulnerability of those most at-risk to firearm-caused violence, finding the practice of vigil keeping for gun violence victims and survivors clarifying in this regard.

If Marshall turns to a particular practice of peacemaking, Gerald Schlabach, in "Gun Culture, Free Riding, and Nothing Short of Conversion," turns to a just peace ethic to issue a call for conversion among those who privilege their own good over the common good with respect to guns. Framed in terms of the "free-rider problem," Schlabach wrestles with the challenge presented by gun owners who may recognize the collective benefits of reducing the number of guns in circulation but will not give up their guns for personal reasons. Drawing upon just peacemaking, he argues that the only way out of our moral morass may be "nothing short of conversion."

The issue closes with Tobias Winright's "Firearms and Moral Theology: A Response," which offers reflections on the contributions to this special issue. A leading moral theologian in the ethics of war and peace and criminal justice ethics, Winright brings not only his expertise but his lived experience to bear on the question of guns in the United States. His response opens with a dramatic and disturbing account of the 2022 Central Visual and Performing Arts High School shooting as experienced by Winright from Ireland, where he had relocated for an academic appointment, and his daughter, who had remained in St. Louis, Missouri to finish her senior year of high school, and who survived the shooting. Winright's account indicates our collective vulnerability to gun violence in our contemporary landscape, and I am grateful for his own vulnerability in sharing this personal account with us. In the remarks that follow, Winright offers helpful insights, commentary, and criticism to the essays contained herein. He concludes with a provocation—that moral theologians and Christian ethics aim for "accessibility" in their writing on the "life-and-death-matter" of guns in the United States. May we heed his call.

Michael R. Grigoni, PhD, is Assistant Professor in the Department for the Study of Religions at Wake Forest University.

Cory D. Mitchell, DBe, is System Director of Ethics for PeaceHealth.

Gun Laws and Gun Deaths: An Empirical Analysis and Theological Assessment

Conor M. Kelly

IN THE UNITED STATES, THE QUESTION OF HOW (AND WHETHER) to regulate firearms is a perennial debate that circles around the same issues without resolution or progress. Much of this is the result of increased partisan polarization around gun control.[1] With partisan positions more ossified, people are quick to make reflexive judgments about gun policy based on their political allegiances without thinking about other values. While this short-circuited analysis helps prevent decision fatigue, an assessment based entirely on default assumptions and political tribalism is more in line with the "remarkable superficiality in the area of moral discernment" (*Evangelii Gaudium*, no. 64) that Pope Francis lamented than with the "serious attempts to make sound moral judgments based on the truths of our faith" that the United States Catholic Bishops insist are the responsibility of the faithful as they engage in political life.[2] A better response from Catholics requires more sustained engagement of various gun control policies in light of the theological convictions that are supposed to inform a Catholic way of life. This article provides the foundation for such an analysis, drawing on empirical data about the role of firearms in lethal violence to assert that Catholics have good reasons to advocate for tighter restrictions on access to guns as a result of their faith commitments.

The article proceeds in three parts. The first discusses the nature of gun violence in the United States today and explains why the current situation is untenable for those who profess the Catholic faith. The

---

[1] "Amid a Series of Mass Shootings in the US, Gun Policy Remains Deeply Divisive," *Pew Research Center*, April 20, 2021, www.pewresearch.org/politics/2021/04/20/amid-a-series-of-mass-shootings-in-the-u-s-gun-policy-remains-deeply-divisive/. For further analysis of the development of this trend and its impact, see Harry Enten, "The US Has Never Been So Polarized on Guns," *FiveThirtyEight*, October 4, 2017, fivethirtyeight.com/features/the-u-s-has-never-been-so-polarized-on-guns/.

[2] United States Conference of Catholic Bishops, *Forming Consciences for Faithful Citizenship: A Call to Political Responsibility from the Catholic Bishops of the United States* (Washington, DC: United States Conference of Catholic Bishops, 2019), no. 17.

second examines the ways gun policies affect gun deaths, evaluating existing research on the connections between firearm availability and gun deaths to describe how less access to guns can yield the kind of reductions in lethal violence Catholics should hope to see as a result of their concerns for the common good. Finally, the third part identifies concrete gun policies most likely to achieve the positive ends at which a Catholic approach to gun violence should aim. The result is a clearer account of how Catholic theological convictions can yield a more critical reflection on gun control debates, opening avenues for a more faithful form of citizenship for Catholics navigating a heavily contested but extremely consequential feature of contemporary political life.

GUN VIOLENCE IN THE UNITED STATES: AN UNACCEPTABLE STATUS QUO

According to the Centers for Disease Control and Prevention, the United States had 39,707 gun-related deaths in 2019, the most recent year to have been thoroughly evaluated by scholars. On a population basis, this translates to 12.09 gun deaths per 100,000 people in the United States.[3] While these numbers might seem small—particularly in comparison to the more than 1 million deaths attributed to the COVID pandemic—the totals for gun deaths are hardly inconsequential.[4] First, the 2019 numbers are consistent with an alarming rise in firearm-related deaths (the nearly identical 2017 numbers represented the highest total in nearly four decades), which has now made firearm-related deaths more common than motor vehicle fatalities.[5] Meanwhile, both the absolute numbers and the per capita death rate place the United States among the nations with the most firearms deaths globally, significantly outside the ranges typical

---

[3] Centers for Disease Control and Prevention, "Web-Based Injury Statistics Query and Reporting System (WISQARS): Injury Counts and Rates; All Intents Firearm Deaths and Rates per 100,000," accessed May 24, 2023, www.cdc.gov/injury/wisqars/fatal/index.html. Data from subsequent years show even more troubling trends (45,222 deaths or 13.64 per 100,000 in 2020 and 48,830 or 14.71 per 100,000 in 2021), but these data are too recent to have been subjected to the scholarly analysis the 2019 data has received. I therefore focus on the 2019 statistics to keep the comparative analyses as consistent as possible.

[4] Centers for Disease Control and Prevention, "Trends in United States COVID-19 Hospitalizations, Deaths, and Emergency Visits by Geographic Area," *COVID Data Tracker*, May 18, 2023, covid.cdc.gov/covid-data-tracker/#trends_totaldeaths_select_00.

[5] Jiaquan Xu, Sherry L. Murphy, Kenneth D. Kochanek, and Elizabeth Arias, "Deaths: Final Data for 2019," *National Vital Statistics Reports* 70, no. 8 (July 26, 2021): 14. To understand the trend by way of comparison, see Kenneth D. Kochanek, Sherry L. Murphy, Jiaquan Xu, and Elizabeth Arias, "Deaths: Final Data for 2017," *National Vital Statistics Reports* 68, no. 9 (June 24, 2019): 13.

of its high-income peer countries in the Global North.⁶ In international terms, the impact of gun violence in the United States is a disheartening manifestation of American exceptionalism, exemplified by the fact that in 2019 the United States, which had approximately four percent of the world's population, was home to forty-four percent of the planet's firearm suicides.⁷ This comparison with other countries therefore not only reveals a damning portrait of gun violence in the United States but also indicates that a less tragic outcome is indeed possible.

When considering this data in light of Catholic theological commitments, this final point is crucial, for the fact that the current level of gun deaths in the United States is not foreordained underscores the violence these statistics represent. Firearms are not merely another cause of death like heart disease or cancer, which reflect the finite nature of the human condition—what Brian Davies (following Thomas Aquinas) would call an unfortunate but unavoidable form of "evil suffered." On the contrary, firearms cause unnecessary deaths, representing a much less inevitable manifestation of "evil done," which can only occur as a result of a misuse of human freedom.⁸ The misuse is amplified by the fact that the Catholic Church emphasizes "the incomparable value of every human person" (*Evangelium Vitae*, no. 2) and has insisted that "whatever is opposed to life itself, such as any type of murder, genocide, abortion, euthanasia or wilful self-destruction ... [is a] supreme dishonor to the Creator" (*Gaudium et Spes*, no. 27). From this vantage point, each gun death is a personal tragedy that represents a sinful usurpation of God's authority over life and death, cutting somebody's life short through a direct violation of what the Catholic Church considers to be the human person's most fundamental right—the right to life (see *Compendium*,

---

⁶ The Global Burden of Disease 2016 Injury Collaborators, "Global Mortality from Firearms, 1990–2016," *JAMA* 320, no. 8 (August 28, 2018): 792–814. This study determined that firearm deaths generally had an inverse relationship with a country's income profile (809), and an earlier study comparing firearm mortality rates in 23 "populous, high-income countries" found that the United States had a total death rate 10 times higher than its comparable peers. Erin Grinshteyn and David Hemenway, "Violent Death Rates: The US Compared with Other High-income OECD Countries, 2010," *American Journal of Medicine* 129, no. 3 (March 1, 2016): 269. For more recent data comparing "high-income countries and territories" beyond just the Organization of Economic Cooperation and Development, see Katherine Leach-Kemon and Rebecca Sirull, "On Gun Violence, the United States is an Outlier," *Institute for Health Metrics and Evaluation*, May 31, 2022, www.healthdata.org/acting-data/gun-violence-united-states-outlier.

⁷ Kara Fox, Krystina Shveda, Natalie Croker, and Marco Chacon, "How US Gun Culture Stacks Up with the World," *CNN*, April 10, 2023, www.cnn.com/2021/11/26/world/us-gun-culture-world-comparison-intl-cmd/index.html.

⁸ Brian Davies, *The Thought of Thomas Aquinas* (Oxford: Clarendon, 1992), 92–97.

no. 157). Given that the Catholic community avers that all human rights, including this most fundamental one, are "*inalienable* insofar as 'no one can legitimately deprive another person, whoever they may be, of these rights, since this would do violence to their nature'" (*Compendium*, no. 153), gun deaths of any number must remain a significant issue for all Catholics looking to assess the state of social life according to their faith commitments. Indeed, given the Catholic Church's expectation that Catholics have "an absolute imperative to respect, love, and promote the life of every brother and sister" (*Evangelium Vitae*, no. 77), the dramatic numbers of gun deaths in the United States are not merely a matter of which Catholics should take note; it is also a serious concern that demands a proactive response in order to fulfill the Christian disciple's responsibility to love one's neighbor as oneself.

In addition to concerns about the right to life, there is also another reason for which Catholics in particular should not dismiss the problem of gun violence out of hand in the way that a comparison to other leading causes of death or reliance on political alignments might prompt them to. Specifically, the Catholic commitment to the common good and the church's emphasis on the preferential option for the poor help highlight the fact that the damage gun violence does to the inviolable dignity of the human person in the United States is even more dramatic than an initial glance at the data might suggest. After all, the national statistics are generic averages, and so can only provide a comprehensive picture if all gun deaths are distributed more or less evenly which, of course, is not the case. Instead, gun deaths tend to concentrate in certain areas and among certain populations, creating a maldistribution of lethal violence in the United States that leaves some communities disproportionately affected by the heartbreaking reality of gun violence while giving others the luxury of imagining that firearm deaths are not a social problem. Some of these differences may seem benign. For instance, the fact that New York had 3.9 gun deaths per 100,000 residents in 2019 while Massachusetts had 3.4, does not by itself indicate that some gross injustice has been committed against all New Yorkers.[9] When the variations become dramatic, however, they begin to have moral significance because no one should have to live with the near constant risk of firearm death in their daily life that the high concentration of lethal violence in certain communities entails. These circumstances deprive people of the "sum of those conditions of social life which allow social groups and their individual members relatively thorough and ready access to their own

---

[9] Centers for Disease Control and Prevention, "Firearm Mortality by State: 2019," *National Center for Health Statistics*, last modified March 1, 2022, www.cdc.gov/nchs/pressroom/sosmap/firearm_mortality/firearm.htm.

fulfillment" (*Gaudium et Spes*, no. 26), thereby violating the common good the Catholic Church insists belongs to "all and [to] each individual" (*Sollicitudo Rei Socialis*, no. 38). Unfortunately, a closer analysis of the data on gun deaths reveals that these sorts of deprivations are indeed occurring for many people and in many places.

To begin with geography, the uneven distribution of gun deaths across states results in some stark numbers across the spectrum, as thirty states had firearm-related death rates higher than the national average in 2019, and Alaska, the state with the highest firearm mortality rate, had more than double that average with 24.4 deaths per 100,000 people.[10] While no single explanation accounts for every state's experience, at the highest end, state-level numbers typically reflect the outsized role firearms play in suicide. For example, Alaska had the second highest rate of suicides per capita in 2019, and the states with the four highest rates of suicide that year were all in the top ten when sorted by firearm-related deaths per capita.[11] The concentration of gun deaths in certain states therefore raises important questions about society's ability to aid the vulnerable individuals who are most at risk for suicide, revealing that the dramatic variation between states raises morally salient issues insofar as these "deaths of despair" often have complex structural roots.[12]

When one considers homicides separately, another geographic variation in the distribution of gun violence emerges, the rural-urban divide. Thus, one comprehensive analysis of gun homicides, which used 2015 data, found that a handful of cities containing less than a quarter of the US population accounted for half of all gun homicides.[13] Much like the suicide rate, these numbers point to larger structural problems. In urban contexts, the highest rates of gun homicides are further "clustered" in a small number of neighborhoods "marked by intense poverty, low levels of education, and racial segregation."[14] These areas, which have gun homicide rates nearly sixteen times higher than the national averages and roughly 400 times higher than

---

[10] Centers for Disease Control and Prevention, "Firearm Mortality by State: 2019."
[11] Centers for Disease Control and Prevention," Suicide Mortality by State: 2019," *National Center for Health Statistics*, last modified February 15, 2023, www.cdc.gov/nchs/pressroom/sosmap/suicide-mortality/suicide.htm, see also Centers for Disease Control and Prevention, "Firearm Mortality by State: 2019."
[12] Although their evaluation involves more than just suicide, Anne Case and Agnus Deaton's recent research has made much of the complex structural forces influencing what they have identified as "deaths of despair." See Anne Case and Agnus Deaton, *Deaths of Despair and the Future of Capitalism* (Princeton, NJ: Princeton University Press, 2020).
[13] Aliza Aufrichtig, Lois Beckett, Jan Diehm, and Jamiles Lartey, "Want to Fix Gun Violence in America? Go Local," *The Guardian*, January 9, 2017, www.theguardian.com/us-news/ng-interactive/2017/jan/09/special-report-fixing-gun-violence-in-america.
[14] Aufrichtig, Beckett, Diehm, and Lartey, "Want to Fix Gun Violence."

the rates typical of high-income countries across the globe, represent structural manifestations of the "failure to bother to love" that the moral theologian James Keenan has described as the crux of sin.[15] The concentration of gun violence in these areas is therefore not a statistical fluke but a pronounced symptom of collective moral failure that demands a collective moral response.

Meanwhile, the role of racial segregation in urban homicides points to another way in which deadly gun violence disproportionately affects certain communities and not others. "The nation's number one victims of violence," the public policy researcher Thomas Abt observes, "are disadvantaged and disenfranchised young African American and Latino men," with homicide the second most common cause of death among Latino men and the leading cause of death for black men, "account[ing] for more deaths *than the nine other top causes combined.*"[16] Research from the Giffords Law Center determined that Black men, who constitute less than 6 percent of the US population, account for 52 percent of all gun homicide victims, with the result that Black Americans are more than 10 times more likely than their White compatriots to die as a result of firearm homicides (20.3 deaths v. 1.8 deaths per 100,000).[17] Women of color similarly bear a higher burden of gun violence than their white peers in domestic violence contexts.[18] These statistics underscore the United States Catholic Bishops' insistence "that racism is a life issue" and point to the profound importance of tackling the segregation and inequality that persist in the United States today with "a genuine conversion of heart, a conversion that will compel change, and the reform of our institutions and society."[19] With respect to gun violence, this conversion must start with a recognition of the outsized effects of gun violence on communities of color, a reality that should then stimulate a vigorous response from Catholics, called to recognize that "'the love of Christ impels us' to see others as our brothers and sisters (2 Cor 5:14). For, 'if [one] part suffers, all the parts suffer with it…'

---

[15] Aufrichtig, Beckett, Diehm, and Lartey, "Want to Fix Gun Violence"; James F. Keenan, *Moral Wisdom: Lessons and Texts from the Catholic Tradition*, 2nd ed. (Lanham, MD: Rowman and Littlefield, 2010), 55–58.

[16] Thomas Abt, *Bleeding Out: The Devastating Consequences of Urban Violence— And a Bold New Plan for Peace in the Streets* (New York: Basic Books, 2019), 2 (emphasis in original).

[17] "Gun Violence Statistics," *Giffords Law Center*, accessed May 24, 2023, giffords.org/lawcenter/gun-violence-statistics/.

[18] "Domestic Violence," *Giffords Law Center*, accessed May 24, 2023, giffords.org/issues/domestic-violence/.

[19] United States Conference of Catholic Bishops, *Open Wide Our Hearts: The Enduring Call to Love; A Pastoral Letter against Racism* (Washington, DC: United States Conference of Catholic Bishops, 2018), 30, 7.

(1 Cor 12:26)."[20] There can be no dismissiveness of the depth and breadth of suffering the current state of affairs inflicts on men, women, and children of color. On the contrary, Catholics must confront the status quo on gun violence in the United States.

Beyond place and race, there are further demographic characteristics that affect the distribution of gun deaths in specific circumstances. For instance, although men are more likely than women to be victims of homicide overall, "more than two-thirds of intimate partner homicides involve a male perpetrator and a female victim."[21] Unfortunately, these statistics speak directly to the uneven distribution of gun violence because research indicates that guns increase the lethality of family violence by a factor of 12.[22] The numbers also highlight a broader social injustice, as scholars note that feminicide emerges from patterns of cultural oppression and social exclusion that get reified in institutional forms.[23] Meanwhile, children face more acute risks of gun violence than other demographic groups. According to the Giffords Law Center, firearm injuries were the leading cause of death for all children in the United States in 2020.[24] Boys have historically had the highest risk, accounting for more than four-fifths of all children's gun deaths between 2002–2014.[25] Some of these deaths were related to homicides, resulting in a significant discrepancy between races, but many of the children's gun deaths resulted from accidental injuries and suicides.[26] Much like the issues of race and place, these disparities demand a Catholic response as a result of the Catholic Church's affirmation of the equal dignity of all who have been made in the image and likeness of God (*Compendium*, no. 144).

While each of these disparities poses a problem for Catholics because of the ways the concentration of lethal firearm violence puts a greater number of lives at risk in certain circumstances, they also

---

[20] United States Conference of Catholic Bishops, *Open Wide Our Hearts*, 18.
[21] Emma E. Fridel and James Alan Fox, "Gender Differences in Patterns and Trends in US Homicide, 1967–2017," *Violence and Gender* 6, no. 1 (2019): 32.
[22] Linda E. Saltzman, James A. Mercy, Patrick W. O'Carroll, Mark L. Rosenberg, and Philip H. Rhodes, "Weapon Involvement and Injury Outcomes in Family and Intimate Assaults," *JAMA* 267, no. 22 (June 10, 1992): 3043–3047.
[23] Marianne Tierney Fitzgerald, "Vulnerability and Development: Reading *Populorum Progressio* in Light of Feminicide," *Journal of Moral Theology* 6, no. 1 (2017): 83–84, 89.
[24] "Kids and Guns," *Giffords Law Center*, accessed May 24, 2023, giffords.org/issues/kids-and-guns/.
[25] Katherine A. Fowler, Linda L. Dahlberg, Tadesse Haileyesus, Carmen Gutierrez, and Sarah Bacon, "Childhood Firearm Injuries in the United States," *Pediatrics* 140, no. 1 (July 2017): e20163486, 4.
[26] Fowler, Dahlberg, Haileyesus, Gutierrez, and Bacon, "Childhood Firearm Injuries," 4.

reveal the problematic power of the "structures of sin" the Catholic Church emphatically condemns (*Sollicitudo Rei Socialis*, no. 36). These structures, which "always" involve the "falsification or the oppression of some human beings by others," capture the influence of collective forces, like systemic forms of racism, that manage to shape the decisions of individual moral agents and then inform the experience of all in the world around them.[27] As a form of social sin, these structures of sin represent "sin committed against the justice due in relations between individuals, between the individual and the community, and also between the community and the individual," functioning as a "sin against the common good and its demands" (*Compendium*, no. 118). Given that the uneven distribution of gun deaths tracks so neatly with the communities and demographic groups routinely excluded from the greatest benefits of social life in the United States—for instance, the mentally ill, the economically disenfranchised, the racially minoritized, and those denigrated by gender or age—there is a significant dimension of injustice to the unequal burden of gun violence in this country. Indeed, considering the biblical notion of justice as "right relationship" with God and neighbor, there is an immediate violation of justice not only in the disparities themselves but also in the tendency to dismiss these disparities and their impact.[28] Right relationship with one's neighbor requires recognizing her or his hardships, particularly when those hardships reflect broader social problems and are not equally shared.

Finally, Catholics have been called to counteract the pernicious effects of structural sin by embracing a radical solidarity shaped by the preferential option for the poor (*Sollicitudo Rei Socialis*, no. 38; *Compendium*, no. 193).[29] To ignore the tremendous impact that the current approach to guns has on certain communities is to deny the very "mindset which thinks in terms of community and the priority of the life of all over the appropriation of goods by a few" (*Evangelii Gaudium*, no. 188), at the heart of this solidarity. Catholics must therefore reject the status quo, even when the effects of gun violence seem minimal in their own immediate contexts, because for many of

---

[27] José Ignacio González Faus, "Sin," in *Mysterium Liberationis: Fundamental Concepts of Liberation Theology*, ed. Ignacio Ellacuría and Jon Sobrino (Maryknoll, NY: Orbis Books, 1993), 538. For more on the causal influence of structures of sin, see Daniel K. Finn, "What Is a Sinful Social Structure?," *Theological Studies* 77, no. 1 (March 2016): 136–164.

[28] John R. Donahue, "Biblical Perspectives on Justice," in *The Faith that Does Justice: Examining the Christian Sources for Social Change*, ed. John C. Haughey (New York: Paulist, 1977), 69–70.

[29] For more on the importance of solidarity as the basis of the Catholic response to structural sin, see Daniel J. Daly, "Structures of Virtue and Vice," *New Blackfriars* 92, no. 1039 (May 2011): 348.

their brothers and sisters this is quite literally the difference between life and death. Significantly, this conviction must translate into action if it is to have any real impact, for "one of the key distinguishing factors of solidarity is that it is a state of being that demands that people who are in a relationship of solidarity be willing to act on behalf of one another as a result of the bond that they share."[30] One of the most important ways to accomplish this goal is to consider how political policies could help reshape the distribution of lethal violence, something empirical research has recently illuminated by evaluating the relationship between firearm availability and firearm deaths. By examining this empirical data and considering its implications, Catholics can take active steps to combat the violations of the common good evident in the unjust distribution of firearm lethal violence in the United States, demonstrating their commitment to solidarity and their pursuit of justice as right relationship.

GUN POLICIES AND THE DISTRIBUTION OF LETHAL VIOLENCE: EMPIRICAL INSIGHTS

Although there might be a degree of skepticism regarding how much can be done to change the status quo on gun violence, there is good reason to believe that an intentional reevaluation of gun policies could in fact lead to a positive transformation of the dismal state of affairs. The basis for this hope lies in the fact that a significant factor in the current variation of firearm mortality are differences in the legal regulation of gun ownership. The exact relationship between gun policies and gun deaths is a complicated connection to establish precisely, in part because information about this link has important implications for polarized debates about gun control laws. Nevertheless, there is a growing consensus that gun laws can and do affect the distribution of lethal violence in ways that ultimately point toward positive contributions for the common good from tighter legal restrictions on firearm availability. By relying on empirical data rather than anecdotal assumptions, one can arrive at a nuanced understanding of the ways gun policies affect gun deaths. Conscientious Catholics can then use this information to identify concrete opportunities to combat the gun violence epidemic in the United States through the pursuit of the most impactful policy changes.

The simplest way to appreciate how different gun policies could counteract the unjust distribution of lethal firearm violence is to recognize how greater access to firearms translates into more gun deaths. Thanks to studies involving both international comparisons and interstate analyses in the US context, this has become a well-

---

[30] Rebecca Todd Peters, *Solidarity Ethics: Transformation in a Globalized World* (Minneapolis, MN: Fortress, 2014), 65.

documented empirical conclusion, albeit one that deserves nuanced consideration. For instance, an early influential article examined the correlations between firearm access and overall homicide rates among high-income countries after noting that the United States had the highest homicide rate and the highest rates of civilian gun ownership among its peers.[31] Using a well-established proxy for gun ownership (a necessary concession in all gun studies because few places have comprehensive registries of gun owners or other consistent data on ownership rates), the study's authors found a statistically significant link between firearm availability and overall homicide rates across the sample of economically developed nations.[32] A comprehensive review of multiple studies on the links between firearm availability and homicide rates found "a strong association of firearm availability with firearm homicide, but not with nonfirearm homicide."[33] One outlier study suggested that firearm availability in high-income countries did not correlate at a statistically significant level with homicide rates, but by the authors' own admission, this reflected a lack of data rather than evidence disproving the possibility of a connection.[34] Significantly, that same study found that gun availability did relate to suicide rates, however, concluding that "the proportion of households owning a firearm was significantly related to the proportion of suicides committed with a gun and the rate of suicides carried out with a gun."[35] Since gun suicides are far more lethal than suicide attempts relying on other methods, the increased prevalence of gun suicides in countries with more firearms amounts to another way in which firearm availability affects the distribution of lethal violence, beyond homicide rates in isolation.[36]

---

[31] David Hemenway and Matthew Miller, "Firearm Availability and Homicide Rates across 26 High-Income Countries," *Journal of Trauma: Injury, Infection, and Critical Care* 49, no. 6 (December 2000): 985. International comparative studies on the effects of firearm availability tend to focus on high-income countries because data from lower- and middle-income countries is sparse. Lisa M. Hepburn and David Hemenway, "Firearm Availability and Homicide: A Review of the Literature," *Aggression and Violent Behavior* 9, no. 4 (July 2004): 425.

[32] Hemenway and Miller, "Firearm Availability and Homicide Rates," 986–987.

[33] Hepburn and Hemenway, "Firearm Availability and Homicide," 429.

[34] Tony R. Smith and Bradley R. Stevens, "A Cross-National Investigation of Firearm Availability and Lethal Violence," *European Journal of Psychiatry* 17, no. 1 (January-March 2003): 34–37. This study also had a smaller sample size, which contributed to the authors' judgment that the minimal correlation had only limited significance.

[35] Smith and Stevens, "Cross-National Investigation," 34.

[36] E. D. Shenassa, S. N. Catlin, and S. L. Buka, "Lethality of Firearms Relative to Other Suicide Methods: A Population Based Study," *Journal of Epidemiology and Community Health* 57, no. 2 (February 2003): 120–124.

These international studies are informative, but they all have their limits, beginning with the "serious problem" of "the quality and comparability of the data."[37] Not only is actual data on firearm ownership hard to come by, but mortality rates are not established uniformly across countries, and nations with fewer resources often have less ability to monitor statistics regularly. Consequently, international studies tend to restrict their samples to countries with readily available firearm death data, meaning that most of these studies are based on samples of convenience rather than completely representative groupings.[38] Although this gap might mean that certain broader trends are masked in the existing studies, there is still room to draw meaningful conclusions from the current research. For instance, studies acknowledging the lack of comprehensive international data are able to sort through the convenience samples to arrive at a subset of comparable countries—like the populous high-income countries surveyed in one of the aforementioned articles—that can be used to identify robust correlations. Still, even in these best-case scenarios, the limited sample sizes make it difficult to introduce a wide range of control variables, creating a genuine challenge for international comparisons.[39]

As a result of these limitations, international studies helpfully point toward a strong correlation between firearm availability and firearm mortality, but they typically fail to offer the kinds of data that would allow researchers to determine the causal direction of this relationship. The one exception to this rule is a single study that used a broad sample of countries at varying stages of economic development and controlled for several variables in order to rule out the prospect of reverse causality (that is, that higher homicide rates prompted an increase in gun ownership). This study found no basis to support the reverse causality hypothesis, leaving the theory that more guns have a causal impact on gun deaths intact. In fairness, however, this study relied on much earlier data, so it is difficult to guarantee that an actual causal trend from increased firearm availability to increased firearm deaths remains persistent.[40] One team of scholars has used this ambiguity to assert that without a clear causal correlation between increased firearm availability and a country's homicide and suicide rates, there is no sufficient rationale to promote legal interventions

---

[37] Hepburn and Hemenway, "Firearm Availability and Homicide," 425.
[38] T. S. Richmond, R. Cheney, and C. W. Schwab, "The Global Burden of Non-Conflict Related Firearm Mortality," *Injury Prevention* 11, no. 6 (December 2005): 351.
[39] Hepburn and Hemenway, "Firearm Availability and Homicide," 429.
[40] Anthony W. Hoskin, "Armed Americans: The Impact of Firearm Availability on National Homicide Rates," *Justice Quarterly* 18, no. 3 (September 2001): 569–592, esp. 587–588.

designed to restrict firearm availability.[41] This assertion, however, both overstates the certainty required for empirical data to influence policy judgments and understates the conclusions from existing research.

To begin, those who would challenge the import of international data seem to operate with unrealistic expectations about how to draw conclusions from empirical evidence. By suggesting that policies should not shift until there is complete certainty about a particular connection, advocates of this restrictive approach establish a threshold that empirical data, especially empirical data from social scientific research, will almost never be able to cross. By adopting something analogous to the "precautionary principle," which says that every new course of action should be rejected until it can be *conclusively* proven that the change will do no harm, these authors create the conditions for an almost absolute maintenance of the status quo because it is much more difficult to rule out every counterfactual than it is to demonstrate the likelihood of some success.[42] Given the damaging nature of the status quo on gun violence, however, Catholics cannot hew to this set of presuppositions. Rejecting this view is not just a matter of pragmatism, though; there are also theological reasons for a more accepting approach to policy reform because Catholics insist that "decisions about political life are complex and require the exercise of a well-formed conscience aided by prudence."[43] To close off virtually all possibility of change by establishing an unattainable evidentiary threshold does not reflect the kind of "prudential judgment" attuned to "the art of the possible" Catholics are supposed to employ in their evaluation of "specific policy choices."[44] Instead, Catholics must use prudence to work through the insights that emerge from the experts, doing their best to draw the most reasonable conclusions from the available data while always being mindful of the fact that they may need to modify their judgments as circumstances change and new evidence appears. When one refuses to overstate the certainty that prudence demands, the current data on the links between firearm availability and gun violence can in fact provide a sufficient basis for reevaluating existing policies and challenging the status quo, an observation that becomes all the more apparent when one considers

---

[41] Don B. Kates and Gary Mauser, "Would Banning Firearms Reduce Murder and Suicide: A Review of International and Some Domestic Evidence," *Harvard Journal of Law and Public Policy* 30, no. 2 (March 2007): 649–694.

[42] On the precautionary principle, see Kevin Kelly, *What Technology Wants* (New York: Penguin, 2010), 246–251.

[43] United States Conference of Catholic Bishops, *Faithful Citizenship*, no. 31.

[44] United States Conference of Catholic Bishops, *Faithful Citizenship*, nos. 32–33.

the second problem of understating the conclusions these data currently provide.

With respect to the understatement issue, although there are variations in the size of the correlations between firearm availability and gun deaths in the existing international studies, it does not follow that no such correlation exists. On the contrary, studies have not produced sufficient evidence to reject this connection. Thus, not only have the majority of international comparative studies shown at least some correlation, but the most carefully designed studies have also shown the most significant relationships. The variation, then, stems mostly from differences in the groups of countries sampled, which can have a profound effect on conclusions in this international research, where the inclusion or exclusion of individual countries can shift the data profile dramatically, skewing the sample.[45] Studies that address these limitations by selecting the most similar countries have established the most statistically significant links between firearm prevalence and firearm homicides, whereas those studies yielding a positive correlation at a statistically nonsignificant level have less comparable samples.[46] To suggest that there is no empirical evidence for a link between firearm availability and firearm mortality at the international level is therefore inaccurate. At best, there is room for disagreement, but only because of the way some studies were constructed. When considering the big picture by taking stock of the trends that emerge across studies and focusing on the studies using the strongest methods, the actual message from the empirical data is that a correlation between firearm availability and gun deaths is far more likely than not.

Even if one were inclined to question the certainty of the picture arising from these international studies, there is no reason to assume that this needs to be the last word. In an effort to establish the correlation between firearm prevalence and firearm mortality more clearly, researchers have also examined the connections between these two things within the United States, closely studying how state, county, or even city-level variations on one side of the equation impact the other. Because these studies compare different communities within as similar a social context as possible, this "fertile area for research" provides an invaluable complement to the data that emerge from the international comparisons and ultimately further strengthens the conviction that Catholics can do something to interrupt the current distribution of lethal firearm violence through policy reforms.[47]

---

[45] Hepburn and Hemenway, "Firearm Availability and Homicide," 427.
[46] Hepburn and Hemenway, "Firearm Availability and Homicide," 425–429.
[47] Mark Gius, "The Effect of Gun Ownership Rates on Homicide Rates: A State-Level Analysis," *Applied Economics Letters* 16, no. 17 (2009): 1687.

As with the international comparative research, the precise results of the domestic studies have varied to a degree, but the general consensus is that greater availability of firearms correlates with higher rates of lethal violence, depending on the cause of mortality and the type of geographic areas compared. Thus, to begin with murders, a 2009 study determined that "gun ownership rates have a positive effect on homicide rates" in a state-by-state comparison.[48] As a result, the author argued that reductions in gun ownership would likely reduce murders overall, a conclusion consistent with the fact that firearms account for approximately two-thirds of all homicides in the United States.[49] These results were amplifications of earlier studies that had determined that owning a gun increased an individual gun owner's likelihood of being murdered in their own home, making this tragic outcome nearly three times as likely to occur as it was in households without a gun.[50] In the 2009 study, overall murder rates at the state level (rather than individual risks) were similarly elevated in connection with household gun ownership rates, but the effects were determined to be of a small magnitude.[51]

In contrast, a broad-based 2014 study of the relationship between gun ownership and homicide rates across all states between 1981 and 2010 found "a robust relationship between higher levels of gun ownership and higher firearm homicide rates" for which other control variables could not account.[52] The "substantial" correlation translated into a 12.9 percent effect on the firearm homicide rate for each standard deviation shift in gun ownership, as measured by a standard proxy statistic. The study's reliance on a proxy for gun ownership—again, a necessary concession to the limited data on actual gun ownership rates—led the authors to include a note of caution about the potential disconnect between their conclusions and the effects of actual gun ownership rates. Controlled comparisons with direct survey data on gun ownership, however, indicated that the actual impact could be even more extreme than the proxy measures indicated.[53]

---

[48] Gius, "The Effect of Gun Ownership Rates," 1689.
[49] Gius, "The Effect of Gun Ownership Rates," 1689.
[50] Arthur L. Kellerman, Frederick P. Rivara, Norman B. Rushforth, Joyce G. Banton, Donald T. Reay, Jerry T. Francisco, Ana B. Locci, Janice Prodzinski, Bela B. Hackman, and Grant Somes, "Gun Ownership as a Risk Factor for Homicide in the Home," *New England Journal of Medicine* 329, no. 15 (October 7, 1993): 1087. The difference was due primarily "to a substantially greater risk of homicide at the hands of a family member or intimate acquaintance" (1090).
[51] Gius, "The Effect of Gun Ownership Rates," 1690.
[52] Michael Siegel, Craig S. Ross, and Charles King III, "The Relationship between Gun Ownership and Firearm Homicide Rates in the United States, 1981–2010," *American Journal of Public Health* 103, no. 11 (November 2013): 2098, quote at 2102.
[53] Siegel, Ross, and King, "Relationship," 2103.

Other earlier studies found even stronger correlations between gun ownership and homicide rates, and one study of county-level data even addressed the question of causation by ruling out the possibility that gun ownership increased as a result of higher homicide rates.[54]

More recently, an additional study has added nuance to these correlations, suggesting that the links between gun ownership and homicide rates are particular to certain types of murders. By separating murders by victims' relationships to their killers, a team of researchers found that a state's gun ownership rates had a direct correlation with murders committed by family members or an intimate partner but not "nondomestic homicides."[55] As with the 2014 study, this link was substantial, as "states with the highest firearm ownership had a 64.6% higher incidence rate of domestic firearm homicide relative to states with lower firearm ownership rates."[56] This study suggests that the frequently observed relationship between gun ownership rates and homicide rates is an artifact of the increase in domestic violence deaths that translates into an aggregate increase in the overall murder rate, although the study's lead author also acknowledged that this does not rule out a link between gun availability more generally (rather than gun ownership) and nondomestic homicides.[57] Even if the correlation is exclusively restricted to domestic homicides, though, this still represents a significant way in which firearm availability impacts the distribution of lethal violence, making the links between gun ownership and homicide rates morally consequential. This is particularly true given the magnitude of the impact identified in cases of domestic homicide and the structural factors involved in domestic violence victimization rates described above. An intervention that could significantly reduce domestic violence deaths is therefore an opportunity Catholics ought to pursue eagerly as a result of their commitment to solidarity in the face of structural sin.

---

[54] Siegel, Ross, and King specifically compare their results with Matthew Miller, Deborah Azrael, and David Hemenway, "Rates of Household Firearm Ownership and Homicide across US Regions and States, 1988–1997," *American Journal of Public Health* 92, no. 12 (2002): 1988–1993. For the causality study, see Anthony Hoskin, "Household Gun Prevalence and Rates of Violent Crime: A Test of Competing Gun Theories," *Criminal Justice Studies* 24, no. 1 (2011): 125–136. In their own study, Siegel, Ross, and King suggest reverse causality is unlikely based on their dataset but also admit that they could not determine causation ("Relationship," 2103).

[55] Aaron J. Kivisto, Lauren A. Magee, Peter L. Phalen, and Bradley R. Ray, "Firearm Ownership and Domestic Versus Nondomestic Homicide in the US," *American Journal of Preventative Medicine* 57, no. 3 (September 2019): 313.

[56] Kivisto, Magee, Phalen, and Ray, "Firearm Ownership," 319.

[57] Aaron Kivisto quoted in Sarah Mervosh, "Gun Ownership Rates Tied to Domestic Homicides, but Not Other Killings, Study Finds," *New York Times*, July 22, 2019, www.nytimes.com/2019/07/22/us/gun-ownership-violence-statistics.html.

Beyond murders, the availability of firearms has also been shown to affect the distribution of other types of lethal violence within the United States, just as it does internationally. Suicide rates, for example, are connected to gun ownership rates even more strongly than homicide rates. A 2002 study expanding upon research linking the availability of a gun in the home with elevated suicide risks found significant correlations between household gun ownership rates at the state and regional level and the suicide rate.[58] A later study by the same authors and an additional collaborator found a similar relationship, estimating that a 10 percentage point decrease in gun ownership at the regional level would translate into a 2.5 percent reduction in total suicides via a 4.2 percent reduction in firearm suicides.[59] Subsequent studies have confirmed the same type of correlation, repeatedly demonstrating in cross-sectional comparisons with diverse controlled variables that firearm availability has a direct statistical relationship with suicide rates.[60]

Overall, these data reveal that firearm availability has a measurable impact on the distribution of lethal violence when suicide is the cause of death. Nevertheless, the particular features of the correlation raise further questions. Specifically, the fact that gun ownership rates have stronger effects on firearm suicides than on overall suicides raises the possibility that a reduction in firearm prevalence simply leads people who want to commit suicide to find other means, thereby suggesting that a reduction in gun ownership rates would not have much effect on the actual distribution of lethal violence. Two factors militate against this conclusion, however. First, gun ownership rates still have a statistically significant effect on overall suicide rates, indicating that a

---

[58] Matthew Miller, Deborah Azrael, and David Hemenway, "Household Firearm Ownership and Suicide Rates in the United States," *Epidemiology* 13, no. 5 (September 2002): 521. For one example of the earlier studies on the links between gun ownership and individual suicide rates, see A. L. Kellermann, F. P. Rivara, G. Somes, D. T. Reay, J. Francisco, J. G. Banton, J. Prodzinski, C. Fligner, and B. B. Hackman, "Suicide in the Home in Relation to Gun Ownership," *New England Journal of Medicine* 327, no. 7 (August 13, 1992): 467–472.

[59] Matthew Miller, Deborah Azrael, David Hemenway, and Steven J. Lippmann, "The Association between Changes in Household Firearm Ownership and Rates of Suicide in the United States, 1981–2002," *Injury Prevention* 12, no. 3 (June 2006): 180.

[60] Augustine J. Kposowa, "Association of Suicide Rates, Gun Ownership, Conservatism, and Individual Suicide Risk," *Social Psychiatry and Psychiatric Epidemiology* 48, no. 9 (2013): 1437–1474; Matthew Miller, Catherine Barber, Richard A. White, and Deborah Azrael, "Firearms and Suicide in the United States: Is Risk Independent of Underlying Suicidal Behavior?," *American Journal of Epidemiology* 178, no. 6 (September 15, 2013): 948–951; Augustine J. Kposowa, David Hamilton, and Katy Wang, "Impact of Firearm Availability and Gun Regulations on State Suicide Rates," *Suicide and Life-Threatening Behavior* 46, no. 6 (December 20116): 688–689.

reduction in firearm availability can reduce this form of lethal violence, likely because "substitution appears to be incomplete" for those who do not have access to a firearm but would consider suicide by other means.[61] Second, the aforementioned fact that guns are the most lethal suicide method means that even if substitution were to occur 100 percent of the time, fewer firearms would still mean fewer deaths.[62] Policies reducing firearm availability can thus serve as an act of care for those whose battles with despair and mental illness make suicide seem like the only choice, representing another way Catholics can answer the call to love their neighbor.

Finally, unintentional deaths are also affected by firearm availability. A 2001 study evaluating data on unintentional deaths from 1979 to 1997 found that "a disproportionately high number [of victims of accidental firearm deaths] died in states where guns were more prevalent," resulting in "a robust, positive, and statistically significant association ... between gun availability in a given state and that state's level of unintentional firearm deaths."[63] The authors found a statistically significant correlation even when controlling for other variables, like poverty or urban density, that would seem to affect firearm deaths and determined that the risk of unintentional firearm death was 10 times greater in the states with the highest level of firearm availability than it was in states with the lowest prevalence of guns.[64] A subsequent review of variations in state-level firearm death rates likewise determined that firearm availability had a direct correlation with unintentional firearm deaths, but only at a level "approaching significance."[65] As these authors note, however, this is still an important correlation to consider in the evaluation of gun policies, particularly because firearm availability has a clear effect on homicides and suicides and has a dramatic effect on unintentional gun

---

[61] Miller, Azrael, and Hemenway, "Household Firearm Ownership," 523.

[62] For more on the lethality of different suicide methods and the ways this variation impacts the relationship between firearm availability and the overall suicide rate, see Miller, Barber, White, and Azrael, "Firearms and Suicide," 951–952.

[63] Matthew Miller, Deborah Azrael, and David Hemenway, "Firearm Availability and Unintentional Firearm Deaths," *Accident Analysis and Prevention* 33, no. 4 (July 2001): 479.

[64] Miller, Azrael, and Hemenway, "Firearm Availbility," 480. These results align with studies showing that household gun ownership increases an individual's risk of unintentional firearm death. Douglas J. Wiebe, "Firearms in US Homes as a Risk Factor for Unintentional Gunshot Fatality," *Accident Analysis and Prevention* 35, no. 5 (September 2003): 711–716.

[65] James H. Price, Amy J. Thompson, and Joseph A. Dake, "Factors Associated with State Variations in Homicide, Suicide, and Unintentional Firearm Deaths," *Journal of Community Health* 29, no. 4 (August 2004): 281; see also 277, 280.

deaths when focusing on childhood victims.[66] Given that children are the demographic group with the highest risk of accidental firearm death, it is not hard to imagine how a reduction in firearm availability could translate into a reduction in unintentional deaths for those most vulnerable to these tragic accidents.[67]

Across these international and domestic studies, then, a consistent pattern comes into view: firearm availability has a consequential relationship with gun deaths. As Catholics consider how they wish to respond to the epidemic of gun violence in the United States, with all the entanglements in structural sin that this current state of affairs entails, they can begin to build a productive, prudential response on the basis of these empirical insights. More precisely, they can use this information to better judge potential public policy solutions, aiming to identify the legal changes that would affect firearm availability in the most effective ways. Of course, as this effort unfolds, epistemic humility will be an essential virtue.[68] After all, few of the studies were able to determine causality because of the nature of the available datasets, although—again—some did suggest a causal link and those that could address reverse causality all ruled out the possibility that higher rates of gun deaths lead to a greater prevalence of firearms. In light of the earlier comments about certainty and empirical data, these links form a sufficient basis for policy considerations, particularly given the moral obligation Catholics have to challenge the status quo on gun violence. The final part of this article uses these empirical trends to establish some concrete policies that would affect firearm availability in ways most likely to yield the reduction in gun deaths that Catholic theological commitments demand.

CONCRETE POLICY PROPOSALS: COUNTERACTING THE STATUS QUO MOST EFFECTIVELY

On an intuitive level, the most obvious way to apply the links between firearm availability and firearm mortality in order to reduce gun deaths would seem to be through laws restricting firearm ownership. The shift from this empirical relationship to public policy is not quite so straightforward, however. Although there is some

---

[66] Price, Thompson, and Dake, "Factors Associated with State Variations," 280, 281. For the impact of firearm availability on unintentional firearm deaths among children, Price, Thompson, and Dake point to Matthew Miller, Deborah Azrael, and David Hemenway, "Firearm Availability and Unintentional Firearm Deaths, Suicide, and Homicide among 5–14 Year Olds," *Journal of Trauma*, 52, no. 2 (2002): 267–275.

[67] Fowler, Dahlberg, Haileyesus, Guiterrez, and Bacon, "Childhood Firearm Injuries," 8.

[68] On the value and function of epistemic humility, see Lisa A. Fullam, *The Virtue of Humility: A Thomistic Apologetic* (New York: Edwin Mellen, 2009), esp. 135–173.

evidence that stricter gun control laws in the aggregate can in fact yield the sorts of reductions in gun deaths Catholics should prioritize, there are a wide array of gun control policies and not all of them have the same effect.[69] If the goal is to reduce the number of gun deaths, particularly for those geographic areas and demographic groups most at risk, a multipronged approach will be necessary. Specifically, Catholics interested in counteracting the status quo on gun violence will need to pursue changes in policies affecting gun sales and storage in order to address the damaging link between gun availability and gun deaths. They will also need to resist efforts to loosen existing gun laws, for these changes tend to have the most negative effects on gun deaths.

To begin, one of the most popular gun control proposals at the moment—universal background checks—can play an important role in efforts to challenge the distribution of lethal firearm violence.[70] A comprehensive review of multiple studies examining background check laws found that mandatory background checks reduced firearm homicides, in some cases by as much as 40 percent. One study included in the review evaluated the opposite effect, where a strict background check law (enforced via a requirement to procure a permit in order to purchase a gun) was repealed, and identified a 29 percent increase in the statewide firearm-homicide rate.[71] Laws ensuring that gun sales only occur alongside a background check therefore represent an important policy tool to counteract the unjust distribution of deaths by firearm homicide, which disproportionately affect communities of color, by reducing not only the overall availability of firearms but also the ease with which someone can access them. A simple background check law will not be a panacea, however, because the effectiveness of these laws depends on the strength and comprehensiveness of the lists used in the background check itself. For example, when the background check process includes consulting a list of restraining

---

[69] Julian Santaella-Tenorio, Magdalena Cerdá, Andrés Villaveces, and Sandra Galea, "What Do We Know about the Association between Firearm Legislation and Firearm-Related Injuries?," *Epidemiological Review* 38, no. 1 (January 2016): 152; Elinore J. Kaufman, Christopher N. Morrison, Charles C. Branas, and Douglas J. Wiebe, "State Firearm Laws and Interstate Firearm Deaths from Homicide and Suicide in the United States," *JAMA Internal Medicine* 178, no. 5 (May 2018): 692–700.

[70] On popular support for expanding background checks across the political spectrum, see "Amid a Series of Mass Shootings."

[71] Lois K. Lee, Eric W. Fleegler, Caitlin Farrell, Elorm Avakame, Saranya Srinivasan, David Hemenway, and Michael C. Monuteaux, "Firearm Laws and Firearm Homicides: A Systematic Review," *JAMA Internal Medicine* 177, no. 1 (January 2017): 116. For the repeal study, see Daniel Webster, Cassandra Kercher Crifasi, and Jon S. Vernick, "Effects of the Repeal of Missouri's Handgun Purchaser Licensing Law on Homicides," *Journal of Urban Health* 91, no 2 (April 2014): 293–302. The reported increase of 29.4 percent was reduced to 23 percent when controlling for other variables.

orders and not just criminal convictions, gun deaths from intimate partner violence decrease.[72] In light of this evidence, Catholics can confidently pursue a reduction in firearm access through the implementation of strict background checks for all gun sales in order to challenge the disproportionate burden of lethal firearm violence on women and communities of color.

Second, Catholics must also consider additional gun control policies to address the strikingly high rates of suicide in the United States, as well as the risks of accidental deaths afflicting children especially. Although background check laws are effective at reducing homicides, they so far appear to have no substantive effect on suicides, although if they eventually did reduce the number of guns in circulation and not just the speed at which guns are acquired, background check laws would have a sizeable impact on suicides as well.[73] Given that many suicides, particularly firearm suicides, are impulsive, some have suggested that a waiting period to purchase guns could be an effective remedy that would reduce suicides by allowing one's initial suicidal impulses enough time to dissipate.[74] While these laws can be effective in some circumstances, most firearm suicides involve guns purchased years in advance, so "it is more important for suicide prevention to restrict access to already owned guns by depressed suicidal persons than it is to prevent them from purchasing a gun."[75] This can be achieved by the so-called red flag laws that allow law enforcement to confiscate firearms from certain at-risk individuals. These laws introduce a useful law enforcement tool, but they must be implemented carefully to ensure they do not create the sort of stigmatization of mental illness making treatment less likely.[76]

The best resource to limit access in a manner that can prevent suicides, then, is to enforce safe storage practices, a strategy that will also have the greatest impact on accidental gun deaths. A number of laws target safe gun storage by requiring guns to be stored unloaded and unlocked or in locked containers, and a review of multiple studies on these requirements has found a decrease in suicides and accidental deaths, particularly among children, and has established the strongest

---

[72] Santaella-Tenorio, Cerdá, Villaveces, and Galea, "What Do We Know?," 147–148.
[73] David Hamilton and Augustine J. Kposowa, "Firearms and Violent Death in the United States: Gun Ownership, Gun Control, and Mortality Rates in 16 States, 2005–2009," *British Journal of Education, Society, and Behavioral Science* 7, no. 2 (2015): 94; J. John Mann and Christina A. Michel, "Prevention of Firearm Suicide in the United States: What Works and What is Possible," *American Journal of Psychiatry* 173, no. 10 (October 2016): 971, see also 975.
[74] Kposowa, Hamilton, and Wang, "Impact of Firearm Availability," 694.
[75] Mann and Michel, "Prevention of Firearm Suicide," 973.
[76] Mann and Michel, "Prevention of Firearm Suicide," 973.

decreases in states with the harshest penalties for violations.[77] These safe storage laws, coupled with clear education about the requirements, can significantly help address the role of firearms in suicide and accidental death. The effectiveness of these strategies will still hinge on compliance. To address this challenge, personalization technologies, like fingerprint locks, can ensure that guns are not accidentally or intentionally discharged by someone other than the permitted owner, removing a significant number of suicides and accidental deaths.[78] Together, these access laws can lower suicide rates and lead to fewer accidental deaths, serving as an appropriate Catholic response to the ways these types of lethal gun violence disproportionately affect two marginalized groups. If fingerprint locks are readily and cheaply available as a retrofit option, perhaps as part of a public health initiative, the impact of this particular policy could be dramatic.

Finally, beyond thinking about the pursuit of new laws that can reduce the number of gun deaths and thereby address the maldistribution of firearm lethal violence, Catholics must also consider the ways proposals to loosen gun restrictions can affect this structural problem. After all, some have championed easier access to guns as a response to concerns about firearm violence, usually employing the premise that gun possession can have a deterrent effect on would-be gun criminals.[79] Overall, the empirical evidence indicates that loosening restrictions on gun ownership and gun access does not lead to a reduction in gun deaths, a result consistent with the link between firearm availability and firearm mortality.[80] When these legal expansions take the form of "stand your ground laws," which make it easier for someone to avoid legal liability if they can assert that they killed a person in a broadly defined notion of "self-defense," the effects are even more pronounced, yielding a dramatic increase in homicide rates overall and firearm homicide rates in particular.[81]

---

[77] Santaella-Tenorio, Cerdá, Villaveces, and Galea, "What Do We Know?," 149.

[78] Mann and Michel, "Prevention of Firearm Suicide," 976–977. These technologies could also help address the fact that safe storage laws on their own do not affect gun homicide rates (Lee, Fleegler, Farrell, Avakame, Srinivasan, Hemenway, and Monuteaux, "Firearm Laws and Firearm Homicides," 116–117).

[79] Notably, legal changes making gun access easier were the most common state-level response to the 2012 elementary school massacre in Newtown, Connecticut. See Steven P. Lanza, "The Effect of Firearm Restrictions on Gun-Related Homicides across US States," *Applied Economics Letters* 21, no. 13 (2014): 902.

[80] Lanza, "Effect of Firearm Restrictions," 904–905; see also Webster, Crifasi, and Vernick, "Effects of the Repeal."

[81] David K. Humphreys, Antonio Gasparrini, and Douglas J. Wiebe, "Evaluating the Impact of Florida's 'Stand Your Ground' Self-Defense Law on Homicide and Suicide by Firearm: An Interrupted Time Series Study," *JAMA Internal Medicine* 177, no. 1 (2017): 44–50. Santaella-Tenorio, Cerdá, Villaveces, and Galea, "What Do We

Given both of these implications, and in light of the ways Catholics should respond to the well-established empirical connection between firearm availability and gun deaths, Catholics ought to take an active role in resisting changes that would loosen gun laws. While this is an important contribution to the public policy debate about gun control, it is especially incumbent in the case of stand your ground laws, which go beyond their general effects on homicide rates to reinforce distrust between white individuals and people of color and endanger young black and brown men in particular.[82] Out of both a genuine commitment to solidarity in the face of structural sin and a deep and abiding commitment to the inherent, equal dignity of each human person made in the image and likeness of God, Catholics must reject this pursuit of a false sense of security and instead enter into debates about gun control policy with an eye toward reducing the prevalence of and access to firearms. The common good demands nothing less.

Naturally, there will likely be resistance to these concrete proposals, even among faithful Catholics. After all, some of these links between gun laws and reduced gun deaths are not 100 percent certain, and questions of causality remain. Given the broader public discourse about guns, meanwhile, some will likely balk at the idea that there should be additional legal restrictions on firearm ownership because they view this as infringing on the rights of gun owners. However predictable, neither of these concerns provides a sufficient objection to halt Catholic support for the policy proposals just discussed. First, the identified impacts of these particular gun laws on gun deaths are all more likely than not, and most have likely impacts at significant levels. According to the interpretations of certainty described above, this is more than enough evidence for a prudential judgment, for as Thomas Aquinas explains, when "experience reduces the infinity of [possible outcomes] to a certain finite number which occur as a general rule ... the knowledge of these suffices for human prudence" (ST II-II q. 47, a. 3, ad 2). Because the beneficial correlations of background checks and safe storage laws and the harmful correlations of looser restrictions on gun deaths have all been established by data indicating they occur as a general rule, Catholics ought not insist on an even higher degree of certainty for their prudential judgments about advocating for the first two policies and against the last, particularly given the stakes involved. Rather than demonstrating prudence, a refusal to act in this case would indicate a

---

Know?," 152, although these authors did report one outlier study finding a decrease after the introduction of a stand your ground type law (146).

[82] For more on the ways stand your ground laws reflect a broader culture eroding the equal dignity of all regardless of race, see Brown Douglas, *Stand Your Ground: Black Bodies and the Justice of God*.

callous, even if unintentional, disregard for the human lives lost under the status quo. Instead, Catholics can, and as a matter of prudence should, use the current empirical insights to pursue these policy changes as an extension of their theological commitments to solidarity and neighborly love.

Second, although the question of rights may be attractive in the current political context, from a Catholic perspective, its appeal is deceptive because it relies on a reductionistic view. Much of the contemporary discourse on gun laws revolves around appeals to the "right ... to keep and bear Arms" described in the US Constitution's Second Amendment. Some gun rights advocates read this language in absolutist terms, but Catholics are called to approach this and other rights claims from a more nuanced perspective. This right is a legal one, not a natural one, and therefore like all laws it must be ordered to the common good if it is to have any true authority (ST I-II q. 96, a. 4). The common good must account for "the good of all and of each individual" (see again *Sollicitudo Rei Socialis*, no. 38), which means that the legal right to bear arms cannot trump the natural right to life that the empirical evidence indicates is at risk from an absolutist application. Moreover, the Catholic social teaching understanding that rights always entail responsibilities (*Compendium*, no. 156) further rebuts an absolutist interpretation. In fact, this presupposition suggests that those committed to a right to keep and bear firearms must consider their responsibilities to ensure that this right is not exercised in ways that undermine the common good. The current empirical data on the links between gun ownership and gun deaths indicate, unfortunately, that this right is often exercised in just such a fashion. Pursuing universal background checks, ensuring safe storage, and resisting a dramatic loosening of firearm restrictions all represent a reasonable form of responsibility accompanying any right to bear arms. Even if one still imagines that this involves a conflict of competing rights, the Catholic commitment to the common good puts this competition in perspective, because one's right to a *sense* of safety (the chief rationale gun owners cite for acquiring guns) is not a justification to overrule another's right to be safe (what lax gun laws require those disproportionately burdened with gun deaths to sacrifice). Ultimately, Catholics have significant reasons to promote the policies outlined here, and little reason to oppose them, based on both the current empirical data and perennial Catholic theological commitments.

CONCLUSION

The main point of this article has been to demonstrate that Catholics can meet the challenges of gun violence in the United States with the kind of prudential judgment their faith requires for engagement in public life. By acknowledging the uneven distribution of firearm lethal violence and its entanglement with structures of sin, Catholics can recognize the need to do something to counteract the status quo. By evaluating empirical data on the links between firearm availability and gun deaths, Catholics can identify a path toward structural reform. Finally, by assessing specific policy proposals in light of an overarching commitment to reduce gun deaths out of a concern for the common good, and with a desire to correct the maldistribution of lethal violence, Catholics can navigate concrete policies and advocate for the most impactful changes. In this way, Catholic convictions can yield a more nuanced approach to the complicated and overly partisan question of how to handle gun violence in the United States, providing resources and rationale for an active form of public engagement on an issue that merges Catholic concerns for life and social justice. Notably, nothing in this evaluation is meant to suggest that these policies are the only ones Catholics should pursue. On the contrary, there is ample evidence that a complete transformation of the current gun violence epidemic will require more than just a few policy changes in isolation.[83] Nevertheless, as an application of Catholicism's constant promotion of the common good and with the insights of empirical data, these policies represent an important minimum that can serve as a springboard for the continual development of a comprehensive response to gun violence. The Catholic defense of life at all its stages demands nothing less.

Conor M. Kelly, PhD, is Associate Professor in the Department of Theology at Marquette University. He is the author of *The Fullness of Free Time: A Theological Account of Leisure and Recreation in the Moral Life* (2020) and *Racism and Structural Sin: Confronting Injustice with the Eyes of Faith* (2023). Forthcoming is a co-edited volume on the moral theology of Pope Francis.

---

[83] Abt, *Bleeding Out*, 140.

Natural Law's Return: Uncovering the Roots of Intractability on Guns as Prelude to New Growth

John E. Carter

GUN VIOLENCE IS A MASSIVE, TRAGIC PROBLEM IN AMERICAN life. Looking only at the worst mass shooting events, those with ten or more fatalities—a threshold higher than that set by many definitions of "mass shooting," which may include those with as few as three or more casualties or fatalities[1]—there have been thirty-three such shootings since 1949: one in the late 1940s, none in the 1950s, one in the 1960s, one in the 1970s, five in the 1980s, three in the 1990s, four in the 2000s, *thirteen* in the 2010s, and five so far in the 2020s.[2] Total gun deaths, including homicides with fewer than ten victims, accidental killings, and suicides, are trending up in

---

[1] See Marisa Booty, Jayne O'Dwyer, Daniel Webster, Alex McCourt, and Cassandra Crifasi, "Describing a 'Mass Shooting': The Role of Databases in Understanding Burden," *Injury Epidemiology* 6, art. no. 47 (2019): doi.org/10.1186/s40621-019-0226-7, discussing the consequences of the lack of agreed definition for "mass shooting" and providing an overview of the methods used and results reached by Everytown for Gun Safety, the Gun Violence Archive, the FBI's Supplementary Homicide Report, and *Mother Jones* in their analyses of shootings for the year 2017.

[2] All but seven of these are listed in "Mass Shootings in the US Fast Facts," *CNN*, May 3, 2020, web.archive.org/web/20200504172259/edition.cnn.com/2019/08/19/us/mass-shootings-fast-facts/index.html. For the other seven, see "A Motive Is Sought in Slaying of 11 in a Family in Ohio," *New York Times*, April 1, 1975, 22; Robert D. McFadden, "10 in Brooklyn are Found Slain inside a House," *New York Times*, April 16, 1984, A1; Bryan Pietsch, Neil Vigdor, and Will Wright, "Gunman Kills 10 in Grocery Store," *New York Times*, March 23, 2021, www.nytimes.com/2021/03/23/us/boulder-colorado-shooting.html; Hayley Smith, Richard Winton, Maura Dolan, and Leila Miller, "Ten Dead, Including Gunman, in San Jose Rail Yard Mass Shooting; Victims Identified," *Los Angeles Times*, May 26, 2021, www.latimes.com/california/story/2021-05-26/police-swarm-active-shooter-incident-in-san-jose; Hurubie Meko and Dan Higgins, "Buffalo Gunman Pleads Guilty in Racist Attack that Left 10 Dead," *New York Times*, November 28, 2022, www.nytimes.com/2022/11/28/nyregion/buffalo-shooting-guilty-plea.html; María Méndez, "Uvalde School Shooting: What We Know One Year Later," *Texas Tribune*, May 24, 2023, www.texastribune.org/2023/05/24/uvalde-school-shooting-what-to-know; Summer Lin, "Monterey Park Gunman Sent Manifesto to Law Enforcement, Sheriff Says," *Los Angeles Times*, July 21, 2023, www.latimes.com/california/story/2023-07-21/monterey-park-gunman-sent-manifesto-before-mass-shooting-sheriff-says.

recent years—48,830 in 2021—though the per capita level is lower than the record level reached in 1974,[3] raising the macabre question of what an "acceptable" level of gun deaths might look like.

Yet over the last forty years, legal issues pertaining to gun control and gun rights have become among the most intractable in American society. In 1991, Warren Burger, former chief justice of the United States (1969–1986), famously declared that promoting belief in an individual right to bear arms under the Second Amendment was a "fraud" perpetrated on the American public.[4] In 2008, a very differently constituted Supreme Court than the one Burger had led established as binding precedent the reading Burger had denounced as fraudulent, in the case *District of Columbia v. Heller*. Relatedly, the politics of guns has been similarly tumultuous, with the National Rifle Association on one side and billionaire and former New York City mayor Michael Bloomberg (whose "super PAC" Everytown for Gun Safety often targets NRA-supported candidates) on the other being particular figures of scorn and opprobrium, depending on one's respective political sympathies.[5]

Intractability has moreover become a signal characteristic of many issues in American life. Alasdair MacIntyre has argued that intractability in moral discourse is the result of incommensurability between liberalism and communitarian moral traditions. More recently, Cathleen Kaveny has argued instead that intractability in US contexts is a consequence of Americans' eschewing practical moral deliberation in favor of the more polemical prophetic indictment, the latter being a form of "moral chemotherapy" with the potential to kill the patient if used indiscriminately.[6]

While overarching accounts like these are important, I would suggest that at the same time, each issue is intractable for its own sets of reasons. Intractability is never the result of just one or even two factors but rather accounted for by a set of reasons, a perfect storm of weaknesses and gaps in the ability of a society to conduct moral

---

[3] John Gramlich, "What the Data Says about Gun Deaths in the US," *Pew Research Center*, April 26, 2023, www.pewresearch.org/short-reads/2023/04/26/what-the-data-says-about-gun-deaths-in-the-u-s/.

[4] Warren Burger, interview with Charlayne Hunter-Gault, *MacNeil/Lehrer NewsHour*, December 16, 1991, YouTube, youtu.be/Eya_k4P-iEo.

[5] Chris Cillizza and Aaron Blake, "Michael Bloomberg's One-Man Crusade for Gun Control," *Washington Post*, December 18, 2012, www.washingtonpost.com/news/the-fix/wp/2012/12/18/michael-bloomberg-the-public-face-of-gun-control-2; Reid J. Epstein, "Bloomberg's Gun Control Group Pours $15 Million into Races in 8 States," *New York Times*, July 23, 2020, www.nytimes.com/2020/07/23/us/politics/bloomberg-guns.html.

[6] See Cathleen Kaveny, *Prophecy without Contempt: Religious Discourse in the Public Square* (Cambridge, MA: Harvard University Press, 2016), 15–45, where Kaveny engages MacIntyre directly.

deliberation. Accordingly, in this essay I will unwind some of the history around guns in the US, with a focus on the legal issues precisely because, as Kaveny argues, the law is one of the most important areas of practical moral deliberation.[7] In this case especially a focus on legal issues is important, as the breakdown in moral reasoning around gun rights and gun control is the single most visible symptom of a shift in legal discourse away from natural-law and common-law reasoning and towards naked positivism. This has resulted in a parsing of the language of the Second Amendment which places far greater weight on the latter's wording than it can reasonably support.

The right to self-defense was originally supported by natural law, and the Second Amendment "right of the people to keep and bear Arms" was both intrinsically bound up with and logically distinct from this natural-law right. By the early twentieth century, natural law was no longer recognized as a valid source for understanding the law. Legal realism and positivism became the dominant modes of legal theory and interpretation, so there was a need to find the natural right in the written language of the Constitution if it was to be cognizable at all. This was achieved to some degree in the *Heller* decision, which is a poor fit—like having to wear two left, wrong-sized shoes.

The *Heller* Court achieved this "forced fit" by arguing that the popularly understood meaning of the Constitution at the time of its adoption—including associated natural rights—is an important source for understanding what the Constitution should mean today. Essentially, this was a way to bootstrap a natural-law understanding of the individual right to self-defense into the positive right guaranteed by the Second Amendment. The problem is that this approach necessarily is an anachronistic enterprise, since it relates only to a snapshot of natural law from the time of the Constitution's adoption and not a meaningful engagement with the natural-law tradition as such.

Could the intractability around gun issues be remedied by renewed engagement between the legal tradition and contemporary natural-law discourse? The answer is unclear. Any problem, however, is made easier to solve by careful analysis of the specific nature of the impasse and the factors that led to distension of the deliberative process in the first place. I would add that before meaningful engagement can occur, both sides need a better understanding of the issues at play. Such are the goals of this essay.

In the first section, I will discuss the history of natural law in US legal tradition, including a discussion of Andrew Forsyth's recent

---

[7] Kaveny, *Prophecy without Contempt*, 422.

book *Common Law and Natural Law in America: From the Puritans to the Legal Realists*. As Forsyth persuasively argues, the relationship between natural and common law is more interwoven than generally recognized. In the second section I will summarize the recent history of gun politics. In the third, I will discuss a few of the most relevant cases pertaining to the Second Amendment, including the *Heller* decision, in the context of recent shifts in constitutional theory. In a brief concluding section, I will offer an overview of the current, recently invigorated state of natural-law discourse and describe what a renewed engagement between that discourse and the legal tradition might look like.

I do *not* describe what some *détente* between the warring parties might look like. It is likely that no side will ever convince the other of its moral rightness. The place of guns in American life has been contested throughout this country's history and will continue to be so, long into the foreseeable future. It need not, however, remain a defining fault line in the political landscape and, more to the point, the grim statistics of gun deaths must not continue unabated.

THE INTERTWINED HISTORIES OF COMMON AND NATURAL LAW

Law in the United States generally follows the forms of reason of the common law, taken to mean that all law is understood according to binding judicial case opinions known as case law. Originally, the term "common law" described the law "common" to all of England, as opposed to local custom. Over time the phrase came to distinguish the "common law" legal systems of England and its colonial progeny (including the US and forty-nine of fifty US states) from the "civil law" system used in those Continental nations such as France and Spain descended from the Roman law tradition and their colonial progeny (including the US state of Louisiana). These civil law systems traditionally have given little weight to interpretative judicial opinions and look to the legal codes anew when applying them. Moreover, the nature of judicial inquiry in civil law jurisdictions is often administrative or investigatory rather than conducted by an impartial arbiter within a co-equal branch of government distinct from the executive and legislative. The phrase "civil law" itself is derived from the Roman *ius civile*, which referred in the Roman legal system to the positive national laws of a state, contrasted to the *ius gentium* (law of all nations) and the *ius naturale* (natural law).[8]

Within the current US legal system, there is a continuum between areas of law mostly dominated by codes, such as criminal law, and areas where the controlling law consists almost entirely of case law,

---

[8] Daniel R. Coquillette, *The Anglo-American Legal Heritage: Introductory Materials*, second ed. (Durham, NC: Carolina Academic Press, 2004), 7–8.

such as torts (the area of law that includes private causes of action such as negligence), with contract law somewhere in the middle. Criminal law used to be closer to contract law and torts, but this changed with the promulgation of the Model Penal Code, published in 1962 by the American Law Institute as an advisory document for states.[9] The MPC served as a template for many states to systematize their criminal codes, an opportunity to reform or reject doctrines which existed in case law alone. The trend towards codification and standardization extended to procedural areas as well. For example, the Federal Rules of Evidence were adopted in 1975, replacing a motley set of common-law rules which had governed the topic. Even after this wave of codification, however, the role of the common-law judge remained unchallenged, with judicial precedent still maintaining an important, often dispositive role.[10] While the role of the judge remained unchallenged, the theoretical basis for the role, as well as the judge's proper function, increasingly came into question.

Under the traditional "declaratory theory" of common law, judges never make law, they merely announce what the law has always been.[11] This understanding was originally based (at least in part) in natural law, where common law functioned as human law had for Aquinas—that is, as conclusions from and specifications of natural law.[12] With the rise of codification in the twentieth century, there was the potential for fundamental mismatch between statutes and regulations increasingly understood as positive law and the natural-law-based practices and reasoning of common law. One can shift emphasis to the natural-law basis for the legislature to *make* the law or for the authority of nation-state-based legal systems more broadly (as Jean Porter does in her book *Ministers of the Law: A Natural Law Theory of Legal Authority*), but that is not a small shift.[13]

The potential mismatch never quite came to pass, however, due to the erosion of any role the natural law might play, a shift that occurred

---

[9] Paul H. Robinson and Markus D. Dubber, "The American Model Penal Code: A Brief Overview," *New Criminal Law Review* 10, no. 3 (Summer 2007): 324.

[10] Anders Walker, "The New Common Law: Courts, Culture, and the Localization of the Model Penal Code," *Hastings Law Journal* 62, no. 6 (July 2011): 1634–1635. See also Mark D. Rosen, "What Has Happened to the Common Law? Recent American Codifications, and Their Impact on Judicial Practice and the Law's Subsequent Development," *Wisconsin Law Review* 1994, no. 5 (1994): 1119–1286.

[11] Allan Beever, "The Declaratory Theory of Law," *Oxford Journal of Legal Studies* 33, no. 3 (2013): 425–426.

[12] Also operative here were custom and (often legendary) claims about the now-lost written laws of the Anglo-Saxons. See generally Candace Barrington and Sebastian Sobecki, eds., *Cambridge Companion to Medieval English Law and Literature* (Cambridge: Cambridge University Press, 2019), 1–80.

[13] Jean Porter, *Ministers of the Law: A Natural Law Theory of Legal Authority* (Grand Rapids, MI: Eerdmans, 2010).

during the early decades of the twentieth century.[14] While this decline in a natural-law basis for common law and the rise of codification several decades later were not directly related, it seems fair to say that the former cleared the way for the latter, and conversely that the latter trend solidified the former.

By the postwar period, to some extent it was *all* positive law, at least insofar as all law, whether statutory or case law, had been severed from its natural-law roots. For some commentators, the longstanding, historical role that common-law judges had played as a check on legislative and executive power was now its own argument for the continuation of the practice.[15] In a democracy, however, with its rhetorical commitments to majoritarian rule, that was (and is) a difficult argument to make.

The problem became manifest as a result of a series of progressive decisions by the Warren Court perceived by some as lacking popular assent. In the absence of natural law as a basis for the judge's authority or as a distinct source of law for common-law reasoning, a backlash against these decisions occurred, and a theory of constitutional "originalism," with its focus on the "original intent" of the Constitution, soon came to prominence. The *judges* might no longer have authority as instruments of natural law, but at least the US Constitution, the *writing* they were charged with interpreting (and which in a positivist sense gave them their power under Article III), might. For conservatives, originalism solved the problem of a judge's authority, left murky in the aftermath of natural law's demise, but it did so as a one-way ratchet with regard to outcomes, since it precluded the progressive interpretations of the Constitution that had been a hallmark of the Warren era.

This demise notwithstanding, Andrew Forsyth has recently attempted to restore an understanding of the role of natural law in US legal history with his book *Common Law and Natural Law in America: From the Puritans to the Legal Realists*, which examines selected periods in US history from the colonial era to the early decades of the twentieth century and the subsequent rise of the legal realists. Forsyth describes the role natural law had in the Puritans' approach to the legal system as well as for the early colleges they founded.[16] He states, "Such a [natural-law] vision [of society] simply

---

[14] See especially Oliver Wendell Holmes, "Natural Law," *Harvard Law Review* 32, no. 1 (November 1918): 40–44.

[15] David A. Strauss, *The Living Constitution* (New York: Oxford University Press, 2010), 37–38.

[16] The natural law of the Puritans had marked differences from the Catholic natural-law tradition. Due to their Calvinist theology, the Puritans understood natural law as (one might say) composed in a minor but sonorous key. For an early analysis, see John

formed the background assumptions of the age: rationality and morality go together, they thought, and human laws accordingly derive their authority from their correspondence with the moral order."[17] As insightful as nearly all of Forsyth's book is, his chapter on William Blackstone is most relevant to the discussion here.

William Blackstone (1723–1780), the first Oxford professor of common law, is most well known in the United States for his *Commentaries on the Laws of England*, published from 1765 to 1769 and based on lectures he delivered at Oxford. The *Commentaries* are Blackstone's four-volume compendium of English common law, but the impact of the Blackstone *Commentaries* far exceeds this brief description. By way of comparison, the best parallel in the history of moral theology, both in scope and impact, might be Peter Lombard's *Sentences*, also in four volumes.

As Forsyth explains, Blackstone weaves natural law into his description of English common law in a variety of ways. At the general level, Blackstone affirms that "knowledge of ... principles [of good and evil] is available through the exercise of right reason," even though, following Locke, "human reason is sufficiently weakened that it needs the support of the revealed law of Scripture."[18] This is very close to the classic definition of synderesis, the "understanding of principles" (ST I q. 79, a. 12) of good and evil that "survived even the Fall"[19] and makes the application of right reason to understand natural law possible.[20] Similarly, human law is only right or wrong based on its consonance with natural law, at least where natural law is not silent.[21] Natural law also provides Blackstone with the organizational structure of common law. Forsyth states, "With Blackstone's eighteenth-century adoption and adaptation of natural-law concepts, he transformed a list of writs into a system of concepts and categories."[22] But natural law not only supplies first principles and organizing structures to common law generally, it also

---

D. Eusden, "Natural Law and Covenant Theology in New England, 1620–1670," *Natural Law Forum* 5 (1960): 1–30.

[17] Andrew Forsyth, *Common Law and Natural Law in America: From the Puritans to the Legal Realists* (New York: Cambridge University Press, 2019), 23.

[18] Forsyth, *Common Law and Natural Law in America*, 51, 52.

[19] Kenneth R. Himes, OFM, "The Formation of Conscience: The Sin of Sloth and the Significance of Spirituality," in *Spirituality and Moral Theology: Essays from a Pastoral Perspective*, ed. James Keating (New York: Paulist, 2000), 60.

[20] For Aquinas, "All other precepts of the natural law are based upon ... [what is known through synderesis, to do good and avoid evil]: so that whatever the practical reason naturally apprehends as man's good (or evil) belongs to the precepts of the natural law as something to be done or avoided" (ST I-II q. 94, a. 2). "Wherefore we judge naturally both by our reason and by 'synderesis'" (ST I q. 79, a. 12, ad 3).

[21] Forsyth, *Common Law and Natural Law in America*, 55–56.

[22] Forsyth, *Common Law and Natural Law in America*, 57.

undergirds, explains, and justifies specific laws or defenses. ... [For example,] in volume three [published in 1768], concerning private wrongs, Blackstone suggests that the best justification of self-defense is the prompting of nature. Self-defense, indeed, is "justly called the primary law of nature," he says, because of its direct relationship to the human drive to survival.[23]

Blackstone's opponents, both contemporary and modern, accuse him of invoking natural law to bolster his defense of the status quo.[24] These opponents omit, argues Forsyth, the occasions when Blackstone invokes natural law to critique specific existing laws, particularly the disproportionate and arbitrary use of capital punishment.[25] As Forsyth states, "Blackstone recognizes ... that human positive law stands in tension with natural law."[26] He concludes:

> [For Blackstone], in matters of legal determination, human law is in conversation with natural law. And this conversation, he suggests, is not one in which natural law necessarily has the final word. One result is that natural law may explain and stabilize human laws while simultaneously rendering them contingent and revisable. Given the realities of sin, says Blackstone, human reason must be suitably modest in its claims to track natural law's revelation of God's reason and will.[27]

Ultimately, Blackstone's success in weaving natural and common law together may have had a paradoxical effect, in that by tying the two together so well, he muddied the distinction between them and made possible the eclipsing of natural law by common law in the work of his successors. Forsyth states, "Believing natural law to structure the law of England, and to serve, with divine law, as one of its foundations, Blackstone devotes little time to distinguishing natural law from English common law. In his treatment of laws, penalties, and procedures, natural law and common law are combined or separated depending on immediate context."[28] After years of updates and competitors, written by Joseph Story and others, "The *Commentaries* slipped from the prescriptive to the historical: a book consulted for what the law *is* became a record of what the law once *was*."[29] As we

---

[23] Forsyth, *Common Law and Natural Law in America*, 58.
[24] See most notably Duncan Kennedy, "The Structure of Blackstone's *Commentaries*," *Buffalo Law Review* 28, no. 2 (Spring 1979): 205–382.
[25] Forsyth, *Common Law and Natural Law in America*, 59.
[26] Forsyth, *Common Law and Natural Law in America*, 61.
[27] Forsyth, *Common Law and Natural Law in America*, 69.
[28] Forsyth, *Common Law and Natural Law in America*, 60.
[29] Forsyth, *Common Law and Natural Law in America*, 68.

will see, this would have special relevance in debates about the Second Amendment.

GUN POLITICS

As has been well documented, while the National Rifle Association has roots going back to the nineteenth century, a major turning point in its recent history occurred in 1977, when conservative gun activists led by Harlon Carter and Neal Knox staged a takeover of NRA leadership at the annual meeting, known as the Cincinnati Revolt, named after the city where the meeting was held. With the federal Omnibus Crime Control and Safe Streets Act and the Gun Control Act of 1968 passed in the aftermath of a wave of political assassinations and the perception of growing urban crime, gun advocates were on the defensive. Prior to 1977, the NRA had adamantly opposed gun control legislation,[30] but for its conservative members, it was not adamant enough. As one of the activists explained the perception motivating the "revolt," "Before Cincinnati, you had a bunch of people who wanted to turn the NRA into a sports publishing organization and get rid of guns."[31] In the words of legal scholar Reva B. Siegel:

> What the insurgents wanted was freedom for the ILA [the Institute for Legislative Action, the NRA's lobbying arm created two years prior] to defend "the political, civil, and inalienable rights of the American people to keep and bear arms as a common law and Constitutional right both of the individual citizen and of the collective militia." Thereafter, *American Rifleman* ran an article reporting on the difference between a "collective" right and an "individual" right interpretation of the Second Amendment, and insisting that reports of Supreme Court precedents to the contrary were mistaken: the collective right view could not be historically or legally substantiated.[32]

---

[30] See James E. Serven, ed., *Americans and Their Guns: The National Rifle Association Story through Nearly a Century of Service to the Nation*, compiled by James B. Trefethen (Harrisburg, PA: Stackpole, 1967), 290–302.

[31] Joel Achenbach, Scott Higham, and Sari Horwitz, "How NRA's True Believers Converted a Marksmanship Group into a Mighty Gun Lobby," *Washington Post*, January 12, 2013, www.washingtonpost.com/politics/how-nras-true-believers-converted-a-marksmanship-group-into-a-mighty-gun-lobby/2013/01/12/51c62288-59b9-11e2-88d0-c4cf65c3ad15_story.html. See also Andrew C. McKevitt, *Gun Country: Gun Capitalism, Culture, and Control in Cold War America* (Chapel Hill: University of North Carolina Press, forthcoming).

[32] Reva B. Siegel, "Dead or Alive: Originalism as Popular Constitutionalism in Heller," in *The Second Amendment on Trial: Critical Essays on* District of Columbia v. Heller," ed. Saul Cornell and Nathan Kozuskanich (Amherst: University of Massachusetts Press, 2013), 95, citing Joseph P. Tartaro, *Revolt at Cincinnati* (Buffalo, NY: Hawkeye, 1981), 36, and "Institute Reports: The Right to Keep and

It should be kept in mind that this "takeover" or redirection was part of a national mobilization of conservative activism. In 1968, during its annual convention—held the very week Senator Robert Kennedy was assassinated in California—the Southern Baptist Convention passed a resolution commending President Lyndon Johnson for his attempt to "pass laws to bring the insane traffic in guns to a halt."[33] In 1979, it too was subject to a conservative takeover of its leadership, resulting in a radical redirection of that organization continuing to this day. This multifront activism culminated in 1980, when Ronald Reagan, whose 1976 political campaign had been fueled by conservative grievance symbolized by his mocking of an unnamed "welfare queen" in Chicago,[34] was elected president in a landslide vote.[35]

The outsize importance of the NRA's lobbying efforts is often noted.[36] Not only does the NRA publish ratings for members of Congress and other elected officials with regard to their positions on gun control, they also have aggressively gone after scholarship which might reveal their arguments as specious. After historian Saul Cornell published his history on the Second Amendment in 2006 which was critical of an individual right to bear arms,[37] the NRA took the unusual step of paying a gun-rights advocate $15,000 to write a highly critical review of the book, "a truly staggering amount of money when one considers that academic book reviews and articles are typically written without any compensation."[38]

Paying attention only to the NRA's political lobbying and public advocacy campaigns still does not give the whole picture. Two

---

Bear Arms; An Analysis of the Second Amendment," *American Rifleman*, August 1977, 37.

[33] "LBJ Commended in Effort to Get Stronger Gun Control Law," *Biblical Recorder* (NC), June 15, 1968, 9.

[34] "'Welfare Queen' Becomes Issue in Reagan Campaign," *New York Times*, February 15, 1976, 51; Gillian Brockell, "She was Stereotyped as 'The Welfare Queen.' The Truth was More Disturbing, a New Book Says," *Washington Post*, May 21, 2019, www.washingtonpost.com/history/2019/05/21/she-was-stereotyped-welfare-queen-truth-was-more-disturbing-new-book-says.

[35] See Daniel Schlozman, "From the Moral Majority to Karl Rove," in *When Movements Anchor Parties: Electoral Alignments in American History* (Princeton, NJ: Princeton University Press, 2015), 198–222.

[36] See Louis Jacobson, "Counting Up How Much the NRA Spends on Campaigns and Lobbying," *Politifact*, October 11, 2017, www.politifact.com/article/2017/oct/11/counting-up-how-much-nra-spends. See also Frank Smyth, *The NRA: The Unauthorized History* (New York: Flatiron, 2020).

[37] Saul Cornell, *A Well-Regulated Militia: The Founding Fathers and the Origins of Gun Control in America* (New York: Oxford University Press, 2006).

[38] Saul Cornell and Nathan Kozuskanich, "Introduction: The DC Gun Case," in *The Second Amendment on Trial*, 10.

broader developments must also be borne in mind. First, the NRA's rise in political power coincides with the decline of the political parties' institutional importance. Throughout much of US history, the parties played a central role in selecting candidates for the general election. With the rise of party primaries instead of caucuses, the process was significantly democratized, though parties continued to play a large role. In 1976, the Supreme Court case *Buckley v. Valeo* struck down the cap on independent campaign expenditures included in campaign finance reform legislation passed in the wake of Vice President Spiro Agnew's resignation and the wider Nixon-related scandals. The Court's rationale was that in a modern context, money equals speech and therefore held that the limit on independent expenditures violated the First Amendment's free speech protections.[39] Even though donations to political parties for party-building activities and "get the vote out" efforts (known as "soft money") were not affected by the campaign reform legislation (or addressed by the Court), the upshot was that political parties were no longer the exclusive nexus for candidate financing they once were.

In 2002, another wave of campaign finance reform purported to limit "soft money" contributions as well, though the parties and lobbyists eventually found ways around these limitations.[40] Even so, the hampering effect on party fundraising due to this new legislation, though eventually circumvented, likely served to solidify the preexisting trend of outside groups directly financing campaign advertising, and taken together these developments allowed for the supplanting of the political parties' role in selecting candidates for the general election, in favor of an independently funded ad war carried out during primary elections in local television markets and online.[41]

---

[39] See Daniel Liechty, "Campaign Finance Reform," in *Culture Wars: An Encyclopedia of Issues, Viewpoints, and Voices*, vol. 1, ed. Roger Chapman (Armonk, NY: M. E. Sharpe, 2009), 67–68.

[40] See Andrew Kreighbaum, "Supreme Court Reaffirms Ban on Soft Money, Once a Powerful Factor in Political Campaigns," *OpenSecrets.org*, June 29, 2010, www.opensecrets.org/news/2010/06/supreme-court-re-affirms-ban-on-sof; Carrie Levine, "Soft Money Is Back—And Both Parties Are Cashing In: Critics Deride the Practice as 'Legalized Money Laundering,'" *Politico Magazine*, August 4, 2017, www.politico.com/magazine/story/2017/08/04/ soft-money-is-backand-both-parties-are-cashing-in-215456.

[41] Legally, such expenditures are not supposed to be coordinated with the candidate's campaign committee, but this prohibition is difficult to enforce. See US Federal Election Commission, "Making Independent Expenditures," www.fec.gov/help-candidates-and-committees/making-independent-expenditures; Trevor Potter, "The Failed Promise of Unlimited 'Independent' Spending in Elections," *Human Rights* 45, no. 3 (June 25, 2020): www.americanbar.org/groups/crsj/publications/human_rights_magazine_home/voting-in-2020/the-failed-promise-of-unlimited-independent-spending.

Second, also over this same time period, there has been a shift in political strategy in many general election campaigns. Throughout much of the postwar period, candidates in general elections in the US generally tried to appeal to median voters to win the necessary majority. Because the means for identifying, persuading, and then turning out these voters at the polls were relatively crude, the conventional wisdom was to aim for winning by as big a margin of victory as possible, or at least by a comfortable one. As recently as the 2000 presidential campaign, this was still the dominant strategy. With George W. Bush's reelection campaign in 2004, however, chief campaign strategist Karl Rove took advantage of new comprehensive voter databases enabling analysis of past voting behavior, combined with marketing data about the best ways to persuade voters and then get them to turn out to vote, to make a radical shift from a "median-voter" to a "base-voter" strategy. Moreover, because this data was able to predict behavior with such accuracy, there was no longer a need to build a large coalition. It has long been a truism in politics that a candidate only *needs* fifty percent of the votes plus one to win. With the new targeted voting strategies, this could be done with precision.[42] In this environment, the NRA's ability to generate a highly cohesive group identity,[43] increasingly aligned with the Republican party exclusively,[44] was a perfect fit. The collateral ability of the NRA to funnel donations to various Republican causes[45]—in some cases

---

[42] See "2004: The Base Strategy," www.pbs.org/wgbh/pages/frontline/shows/architect/rove/2004.html, and "How Rove Targeted the Republican Vote," www.pbs.org/wgbh/pages/frontline/shows/architect/rove/metrics.html, interview transcripts from *Frontline*, "Karl Rove—The Architect," written, produced, and directed by Michael Kirk, aired April 12, 2005, on PBS; Todd Purdum, "Karl Rove's Split Personality," *Vanity Fair*, October 30, 2006, www.vanityfair.com/news/2006/12/rove200612.

[43] See Kimberly D. Elsbach and C. B. Bhattacharya, "Defining Who You Are by What You're Not: Organizational Disidentification and the National Rifle Association," *Organization Science* 12, no. 4 (July–August 2001): 393–413; Matthew J. Lacombe, "The Political Weaponization of Gun Owners: The National Rifle Association's Cultivation, Dissemination, and Use of a Group Social Identity," *Journal of Politics* 81, no. 4 (October 2019):1342–1356; Kevin Lewis O'Neill, "Armed Citizens and the Stories They Tell: The National Rifle Association's Achievement of Terror and Masculinity," *Men and Masculinities* 9, no. 4 (April 2007): 457–475.

[44] See Amber Phillips, "The NRA-ification of the Republican Party," *Washington Post*, August 14, 2015, www.washingtonpost.com/news/the-fix/wp/2015/08/14/the-nra-ification-of-the-republican-party; and Karen Pinchin, "With NRA under Investigation, Former Fundraiser Says Gun Group Is Republican 'Through and Through,'" *Frontline*, March 24, 2020, www.pbs.org/wgbh/frontline/article/aaron-davis-nra-lapierre-trump-republican-investigation-guns.

[45] See Alex Isenstadt, "NRA Meltdown Has Trump Campaign Sweating," *Politico*, July 3, 2019, www.politico.com/story/2019/07/03/nra-guns-trump-campaign-1395970; Luke Johnson, "NRA's 2016 Donation to Trump's Campaign Pays Off," *Fortune*, August 21, 2019, fortune.com/2019/08/21/how-much-did-nra-contribute-trump-campaign.

allegedly including funds from foreign sources[46]—in the context of the various limitations placed on campaign fundraising mentioned above only tightened the relationship further.

Stepping back for a moment, we can see the detrimental effect this fragmentation of the electorate into minute segments—each given a narrowly tailored message designed to generate political campaign donations and voter turnout—would have on all political discourse, not just discourse around guns. More specifically, we might say that it both takes advantage of and exacerbates the breakdown of "Cold War liberalism"[47] as a unifying Rawlsian public reason. In the aftermath, "neutral" public reason seems to be a dog's breakfast of legal and constitutional textual analysis, scientific research (which finds itself increasingly politicized, whether in the context of climate change or public health), economic growth measured in capitalist metrics ("jobs!" referring to quantity not quality, and worker productivity not satisfaction), and an individualistic, blandly spiritual-but-not-religious right to happiness, played out in a field of Machiavellian power politics—which the recent infatuation with game theory has encouraged—fueled in many cases by ideology serving only as opportunistic means for personal ambition. Everything else, under the guise of libertarianism, is relegated to private morality.

Notice that I included legal and constitutional textual analysis in this list as one of the few areas still putatively broadly accessible as a form of public reason in the US. In the absence of a broader, socially, culturally, philosophically, and theologically "thicker" public reason (of the type a retrieved natural-law tradition might provide), it is unclear how long the US can abide by a constitutional process where the literal interpretation of *any* bare text is the only recourse for resolving some of the most complicated political issues, such as those involving guns. As I have explained in this section, the problem is not only legal. Rather, a variety of political factors have conspired to place more pressure on the legal system and its modes of reasoning than they

---

[46] See Chris Smith, "'Coincidence Number 395': The NRA Spent $30 Million To Elect Trump. Was It Russian Money?," *Vanity Fair*, June 21, 2018, www.vanityfair.com/news/2018/06/the-nra-spent-dollar30-million-to-elect-trump-was-it-russian-money; "Timeline of Russian Plot to Infiltrate NRA and GOP," *CBS News*, September 10, 2018, www.cbsnews.com/news/time line-of-russian-plot-to-infiltrate-nra-and-gop; Mark Maremont and Julie Bykowicz, "NRA's Ties to Russian Nationals Alleged in New Report," *Wall Street Journal*, September 27, 2019, www.wsj.com/articles/nras-ties-to-russian-nationals-detailed-in-new-report-11569593888; Heather Cox Richardson, "The NRA within the Sights," *BillMoyers.com*, August 7, 2020, billmoyers.com/story/the-nra-within-the-sights.

[47] On Cold War liberalism, see Jan-Werner Müller, "Calming the Ideological Storms? Reflections on Cold War Liberalism," in *Ideological Storms: Intellectuals, Dictators, and the Totalitarian Temptation*, ed. Vladimir Tismaneanu and Bogdan C. Iacob (New York: Central European University Press, 2019): 465–485.

may be able to bear—at least that is a question to keep in mind for the succeeding sections of this essay.

HELLER AND ITS PROGENY IN THE CONTEXT OF CONSTITUTIONAL LITIGATION AND THEORY

As described above, originalism arose in the 1970s as a reaction to the perception that judges lacked a proper basis—implicitly in natural law, though it was not framed this way—for the power they were able to wield, and specifically to the relative indifference to the written Constitution shown in some "decisions of the Warren and early Burger Courts, which by the standards of the time, aggressively protected the rights of racial and religious minorities, women, and criminal defendants."[48] For the supporters of these decisions and the civil rights advances they represented, originalism represented an attack on these advances; for the decisions' critics, originalism was "predominantly a theory of judicial restraint."[49] Over this same period, the opposite of originalism came to be known as "living constitutionalism," the idea that the constitution is a living document that should be interpreted differently in different times.[50]

It is widely observed that until *Heller* in 2008, the Supreme Court had never ruled on the issue of whether the Constitution guarantees a collective right to bear arms or an individual one, and there was a paucity of opinions by lower courts on this issue as well. In 1994, constitutional scholar William Van Alstyne attributed this dearth of relevant case law to the absence of substantial effort to regulate personal gun ownership and use until the twentieth century,[51] though the subsequent work of Saul Cornell and other historians belies this assertion.[52] Again, though, there were broader trends at work.

For one thing, the rise in popularity of suing for money damages for a violation of one's constitutional rights seems likely to have contributed to perceiving one's rights under the constitution as primarily *individual*. Major turning points here were *Monroe v. Pape* (1961) and *Monell v. Department of Social Services of the City of New*

---

[48] Andrew Coan, "Living Constitutional Theory," *Duke Law Journal Online* 66 (June 2017): 101, scholarship.law.duke.edu/dlj_online/26/.
[49] Coan, "Living Constitutional Theory," 101.
[50] See Lawrence Solum, "Legal Theory Lexicon: Living Constitutionalism," *Legal Theory Blog*, November 25, 2018, lsolum.typepad.com/legaltheory/ 2018/11/legal-theory-lexicon-living-constitutionalism.html.
[51] William Van Alstyne, "The Second Amendment and the Personal Right to Arms," *Duke Law Journal* 43, no. 6 (April 1994): 1240.
[52] See Kevin M. Sweeney, "Firearms, Militias, and the Second Amendment," in *The Second Amendment on Trial*, 310–382.

York (1978),[53] offering new interpretations of 42 U.S.C. § 1983, the Reconstruction-era statute which allowed an individual cause of action for the violation of certain constitutional rights. While actions for injunctive relief (such as *Heller*) could be brought before that—and in the area of the Second Amendment, they were—the rise of individual actions for damages would at least partially explain why belief in an *individual* right to bear arms became prominent in the national consciousness and why litigation over this issue became more common after this development. As constitutional scholar Walter Dellinger wrote during this era in a related context, "Once it is admitted that the Constitution may be used as a sword in litigation, the issues raised, unsurprisingly, extend far beyond the specific questions litigated."[54] This increasing focus on individual rights coincided with the rise in US contexts of what might be termed the "opt-out conscience," the notion that an individual should be exempted from a generally applicable rule based on the demands of conscience; obviously if one can claim the protection of a constitutional provision for a right to opt-out (in this case, from gun control provisions), all the better.[55]

Moreover, *because* so many constitutional issues are now litigated as arising under § 1983, the courts have adopted certain rules for dealing with such claims which tend to carry over to constitutional theory more generally. For example, when a constitutional violation is alleged in a § 1983 case, "the first step ... is to identify the specific constitutional right allegedly infringed."[56] There *is* a way to allege a violation of a right *not* specifically enumerated in the Constitution, the "substantive due process claim," a claim pertaining to rights "so rooted in the traditions and conscience of our people as to be ranked as fundamental."[57] As such, their denial is deemed to constitute a potential violation of the Due Process Clause "regardless of the fairness of the procedures used" to do so.[58] Because of the courts' strong preference to avoid substantive due process claims or identify fundamental rights where there already is a constitutional provision that seems to pertain, the courts will almost always decide the case

---

[53] Monroe v. Pape, 365 US 167 (1961), and Monell v. Department of Social Services of the City of New York, 436 US 658 (1978).

[54] Walter E. Dellinger, "Of Rights and Remedies: The Constitution as a Sword," *Harvard Law Review* 85, no. 8 (June 1972): 1564. Decades later, Dellinger was the lawyer who argued *Heller* on behalf of the District of Columbia in the Supreme Court.

[55] See James Keenan, SJ, "Redeeming Conscience," *Theological Studies* 76, no. 1 (2015): 134–135.

[56] Albright v. Oliver, 510 US 266, 271 (1994). Internal citations and quotation marks in case quotations are omitted throughout.

[57] *Albright*, 282.

[58] Daniels v. Williams, 474 US 327, 331 (1986).

under the apparently applicable provision. As the Supreme Court stated in *Albright v. Oliver* (1994), "Where a particular Amendment provides an explicit textual source of constitutional protection against a particular sort of government behavior, that Amendment, not the more generalized notion of 'substantive due process,' must be the guide for analyzing these claims."[59] The *Albright* Court justified its extreme reluctance to rely on Fourteenth Amendment substantive due process doctrine by referring to the "scarce and open-ended guideposts" associated with substantive due process analysis.[60]

This at least helps explain why cases—such as *Heller*—involving an *individual's* right to carry a gun are framed and funneled through the Second Amendment (instead of some generalized natural- or common-law right), despite the Amendment's seeming inappositeness to such cases based on its language associating the right to bear arms with "a well-regulated militia." Cornell has pointed out that confusion over whether the Second Amendment protects the right to bear arms solely in the context of a militia formed for the "public defense" versus "the individual right to bear a gun in self-defense" is not *completely* novel and has roots dating to the Jacksonian era.[61] The Court's overwhelming preference for deciding cases based on explicit rights rather than implicit ones seems to have made a Second Amendment framing for cases alleging an individual right all but certain. Ironically, the fact that there was wide historical consensus in the twentieth century that the Second Amendment had been rendered anachronistic by the "replace[ment] [of] the Founding era's universal militia with the modern National Guard," thereby restricting the Amendment's applicability to "participants in legally sanctioned military organizations,"[62] only heightened the availability of the Amendment for use as a vehicle for individual gun rights, insofar as the Amendment had been vacated of its original meaning and thus there was no competing contemporaneous use of it in a different context which might make its reinterpretation more difficult.

A last background factor for consideration here is the slow evolution of the "selective incorporation doctrine," the principle that many (though not all) of the rights contained in the Bill of Rights, which on their own terms apply only to the federal government, were made applicable to the states via the Fourteenth Amendment, adopted in 1868 as part of Reconstruction. While Cornell's historical research has highlighted the high degree of weapons regulation which appertained to militia participation during the Revolutionary period,

---

[59] *Albright*, 273.
[60] *Albright*, 275. See more recently NASA v. Nelson, 562 US 134, 147, n. 10 (2011).
[61] Cornell, *A Well-Regulated Militia*, 4.
[62] Cornell, *A Well-Regulated Militia*, 6.

laws forbidding the carrying of handguns and other concealed weapons—that is, laws of the type most objected to by gun-rights activists—were largely a nineteenth-century initiative in state legislatures, and therefore a matter whose limits were a matter of state constitutional interpretation.[63] It was only in the twentieth century, in the context of a broader shift to federal regulation in many areas of American life, that *this* type of gun regulation was taken up at the national level,[64] and thus it took some time for the issue to be presented as one for the federal courts. Since it is easier for the Court to apply a reading of the Second Amendment that includes an individual right to bear arms to the states via the Fourteenth Amendment when it has already found such a right to exist in the first place, there was no rule to even apply to the states (that is, restricting a state or local government from regulating firearms) until the new rule was devised with regard to the federal government itself.

With this context as background, on its face *District of Columbia v. Heller* is a straightforwardly originalist decision. In the opinion, written by Justice Scalia, the Court first parsed the structure of the Second Amendment, deciding that the Amendment is "naturally divided into two parts: its prefatory clause and its operative clause" and that the prefatory clause serves only to clarify situations not resolvable by the operative clause.[65] The remainder of the opinion decides the case by applying the operative clause alone, essentially rendering the prefatory clause "a well regulated militia, being necessary to the security of a free State" a nullity. The Court analyzed the language of the operative clause in its historical context, especially the phrases "the people" and "keep and bear arms"[66]—including an analysis of the Amendment's reception history[67]—to determine whether these indicate an individual or collective right. Finding that they support an individual right and that no precedent of the Court precludes such a reading,[68] the Court then determined the individual right to exist and struck down the general prohibition on possession of handguns at issue in the case.[69] In doing so, however, the Court specified that the Second Amendment right to bear arms only applied

---

[63] Cornell, *A Well-Regulated Militia*, 4–5.
[64] The National Firearms Act was enacted in 1934, which Cornell calls "the first comprehensive federal firearms law" (*A Well-Regulated Militia*, 200). Nonetheless, even today the majority of firearms restrictions are matters of state and local law.
[65] District of Columbia v. Heller, 554 US 570, 577 (2008).
[66] *Heller*, 579–595.
[67] *Heller*, 605–619.
[68] *Heller*, 619–626.
[69] The challenged weapons regulation was enacted by the local government of the District of Columbia. Because DC is under direct federal jurisdiction (and not part of any state), the incorporation doctrine was not at issue.

originally to those weapons "in common use at the time" and did not include "dangerous and unusual weapons"[70] and that the Court would apply the Amendment similarly today—notwithstanding that such a reading would preclude allowing the type of weapons necessary to modern military applications. The Court stated, "Indeed, it may be true that no amount of small arms could be useful against modern-day bombers and tanks. But the fact that modern developments have limited the degree of fit between the prefatory clause and the protected right cannot change our interpretation of the right."[71]

Straightforward enough, right? The problem is, the *Heller* opinion is both bad history and bad constitutional theory. The opinion is bad history because, as a threshold matter, the framing of the question as one of individual versus collective rights is anachronistic. As Cornell has stated, "The original understanding of the Second Amendment was neither an individual right of self-defense nor a collective right of the states, but rather a civic right that guaranteed that citizens would be able to keep and bear those arms needed to meet their legal obligation to participate in a well-regulated militia."[72] Stated differently, we might say that the Second Amendment right to bear arms was a civic imperative that vested as an individual right, indivisible from one other. That this imperative was understood in the broader context of a natural-law or common-law right to individual self-defense is uncontested, as Cornell and Kozuskanich admit: "There is little disagreement among scholars that an individual right of self-defense was well understood to be protected under common law."[73] But that is not the same as saying that the individual right to keep and bear arms for self-defense, severed from the civic imperative, was protected activity under the Second Amendment as it was originally understood.

More generally, an originalist understanding of the Bill of Rights might not require the individual right of self-defense to be found in the words of the Second Amendment itself to be valid—nor would such a right necessarily be vitiated by the Amendment's repeal. On this point, it is helpful to note James Madison's perspective on the Bill of Rights and his initial reluctance to write it for fear that to enumerate a few rights would be interpreted as excluding those not listed—the legal canon of construction here is *expressio unius est exclusio alterius*—hence the explicit statement in the Ninth Amendment that the people retain all rights not otherwise mentioned. Madison was persuaded to write the Bill of Rights in order to obtain assent to ratification of the

---

[70] *Heller*, 627.
[71] *Heller*, 627–628.
[72] Cornell, *A Well-Regulated Militia*, 2.
[73] Cornell and Kozuskanich, "Introduction: The DC Gun Case," 11.

Constitution by certain holdouts who insisted on its inclusion, though he did come around to agreeing first on the bill's utility and later on its importance. Like nearly everyone in his day, Madison still held to a robust notion of natural rights, and the question of whether the failure to list a natural-law right in the Bill of Rights might mean it did not enjoy legal protection was an open (or at least disputed) one in early Supreme Court jurisprudence if not for Madison himself.[74]

Alternatively, an originalist reading might compare the language of the Second Amendment to the language of similar provisions in state constitutions which explicitly protected the right to bear arms as related to *both* an individual right to self-defense *and* the civic imperative to participate in a militia,[75] and thereby find, precisely under the legal canon cited above, that the Second Amendment does not protect an individual right to bear arms as part of a right to self-defense because it only mentions one of these bases and not the other. Instead, Scalia takes the different tack of arguing that the Constitution and Bill of Rights should be read as codifying those preexisting rights associated with the enumerated rights, so that the individual right to self-defense, merely by virtue of its general recognition when the Second Amendment was drafted and ratified, is included in the purview of the Second Amendment's protection of the right to bear arms in association with the necessity of a well-regulated militia.[76]

There are several problems with Scalia's approach. The first is that Scalia claims more objectivity (and therefore determinative value) for his history than it merits. As noted above, there has been an overall breakdown in public political discourse across many important issues in American life. To make a putatively "objective" reading of history

---

[74] See James Madison to Thomas Jefferson, New York, October 17, 1788, in *The Mind of the Founder: Sources of the Political Thought of James Madison*, ed. Marvin Meyers, rev. ed. (Hanover, NH: Brandeis University Press/University Press of New England, 1981), 156–157; Ralph Ketcham, *James Madison: A Biography* (Charlottesville: University Press of Virginia, 1990), 290–292, 293–296. On the natural law and early Supreme Court jurisprudence, see H. Jefferson Powell, "Calder v. Bull," in *The Oxford Guide to United States Supreme Court Decisions*, ed. Kermit L. Hall and James W. Ely, Jr., 2nd ed. (New York: Oxford University Press, 2009): www.oxfordreference.com/view/10.1093/acref/9780195379396.001.0001/acref-9780195379396-e-75; Douglas S. Mock, "Natural Law in American Jurisprudence: *Calder v. Bull* and *Corfield v. Coryell* and Their Progeny" (PhD diss., Boston University, 2017), ProQuest Dissertations & Theses.

[75] *Heller*, 584–585. See Saul Cornell, "The Changing Meaning of the Right to Keep and Bear Arms: 1688–1788; Neglected Common Law Contexts of the Second Amendment Debate," in *Guns in Law*, ed. Austin Sarat, Lawrence Douglas, and Martha Merrill Umphrey (Amherst: University of Massachusetts Press, 2019), 33–34.

[76] See Nelson Lund, "The Second Amendment, *Heller*, and Originalist Jurisprudence," in *The Second Amendment on Trial*, 155–158, discussing Scalia's approach to preexisting rights. See also Cornell, "The Changing Meaning of the Right to Keep and Bear Arms: 1688–1788," 21.

dispositive in the recognition of natural rights in the absence of functioning public reason is to make a situation where the NRA pays someone $15,000 to write a negative review of Cornell's work inevitable and the urge to commit eisegesis in reading the historical record inescapable.[77] Conversely, in raising historical speculation to determining significance, moral theology and philosophy have been excluded from what might be an extraordinarily valuable role in debating the parameters of what is at root a natural-law right.

Two years later, in *McDonald v. City of Chicago*, the Court was asked to extend *Heller* to the states via the incorporation doctrine (described above), which the Court did, in an opinion written by Justice Alito rather than Scalia.[78] In doing so, the Court recapitulated the history of the Court's application of the Bill of Rights to the states and noted that, while at a previous point in its jurisprudence it had considered the rights set forth in the Bill of Rights under the general analysis of substantive due process claims and fundamental rights, this approach had been replaced by a more mechanical application of the Bill of Rights to the states via the incorporation doctrine, coinciding with a general disfavoring of (if not outright hostility towards) the recognition of non-enumerated fundamental rights.[79] Accordingly, the Court did not consider the issue as arising under a natural-law, common-law, or substantive-due-process-type "fundamental" right to self-defense, only the right's centrality to the Second Amendment, as the *Heller* Court had held.

This disclaimer notwithstanding, Alito nonetheless framed the question as "whether the right to keep and bear arms is fundamental to our scheme of ordered liberty ... or ... deeply rooted in this Nation's history and tradition," language highly similar to that used in cases decided under substantive due process analysis.[80] Likewise, parts of his discussion could be described as "popular constitutionalism," the theory that the Constitution means what it is popularly understood to mean, as when he states:

> Self-defense is a basic right, recognized by many legal systems from ancient times to the present day, and in *Heller,* we held that individual self-defense is the *central component* of the Second Amendment right. ... Explaining that the need for defense of self, family, and property is most acute in the home, we found that this right applies to handguns because they are the most preferred firearm in the nation to "keep"

---

[77] See Cass Sunstein, "Second Amendment Minimalism: *Heller* as *Griswold*," in *The Second Amendment on Trial*, 262–263.

[78] McDonald v. City of Chicago, 561 US 742 (2010). Alito's opinion was not a majority opinion in its entirety; portions had the support of only four justices not five.

[79] *McDonald*, 759–766.

[80] *McDonald*, 767.

and use for protection of one's home and family. ...Thus, we concluded, citizens must be permitted to use handguns for the core lawful purpose of self-defense.[81]

While Alito does not address the natural-law right directly, this language certainly is more compatible with natural-law reasoning than Scalia's narrow (and politically biased) historical analysis—and therefore more amenable to engagement by moral theologians and philosophers in natural-law discussions.

Perhaps more interesting is the recent Seventh Circuit case *Kanter v. Barr*, in which a person challenged the lifetime prohibition of his ability to possess a firearm, as required by a state statute based on his conviction of a non-violent felony. The question was whether a state statute could permissibly subject *all* felons to a blanket lifetime firearm ban, with the ability to have possession rights restored upon executive pardon or expungement of record, or whether the statute's application should be restricted to only those convicted of *violent* felonies, based on *Heller*. The majority held that the statute as written was permissible. In dissent, however, was then-Circuit Judge (now Supreme Court Justice) Amy Coney Barrett, who wrote a lengthy opinion explaining her views. Barrett explained that precisely because the individual right to bear arms, "intimately connected with the natural right of self-defense,"[82] was not tied to a civic right (as Justice Stevens had argued in his *Heller* dissent that it was, drawing on Cornell), there was no basis for presumptively imposing what was essentially a "virtue" test on gun ownership. Barrett specified that it *was* permissible to impose virtue tests on the right to vote and the right to serve on a jury, because it had been historically permissible to do so and because these rights *were* tied to a civic right.[83]

Here, a natural-law analysis would seem to be highly relevant. Obviously a person does not lose the right to defend themselves in a physical conflict no matter how vicious they might be or what they had been convicted of. Tying the natural right to self-defense to the right to possess a handgun, as the Court did in *Heller*, confuses the issue, and Barrett takes advantage of this confusion to argue that the right to possess a handgun is more fundamental than the right to participate in self-government through voting. To put the matter more directly, we might say that the right to self-defense and the right to participate in collective self-government through voting are both properly understood as natural rights, while the right to bear arms, by

---

[81] *McDonald*, 767–768. See also Siegel, "Dead or Alive," 81–89, which understands *Heller* as adopting an originalist variant of popular constitutionalism.
[82] Kanter v. Barr, 919 F.3d 437, 464 (7th Cir. 2019) (Barrett, dissenting).
[83] *Kanter*, 462–464 (Barrett, dissenting).

itself, is not. By following the reasoning of *Heller* tying the positive right to bear arms with the natural right to self-defense, Barrett is able to argue that legislative attempts to deny a person the right to purchase and carry a handgun face a higher hurdle than denying a person the right to vote.

One might think, based on originalism's dominance, that courts are not likely to return to explicit engagement with natural law anytime soon, beyond the piecemeal, anachronistic question of what natural law rights were implicitly assumed as part of the explicit guarantees of the Constitution. As illustrated by the Supreme Court's opinion in *Obergefell v. Hodges* recognizing a fundamental right to marriage, including for same-sex couples, that return may already be upon us. In fact, Justice Kennedy's majority opinion in *Obergefell* is remarkable precisely for its natural-law-style discussion of the history of marriage.[84] More intriguingly, Kennedy describes the Court's role in terms starkly different from that described by Scalia in *Heller*. As Kennedy states:

> The identification and protection of fundamental rights is an enduring part of the judicial duty to interpret the Constitution. That responsibility ... has not been reduced to any formula. Rather, it requires courts to exercise reasoned judgment in identifying interests of the person so fundamental that the State must accord them its respect. That process is guided by many of the same considerations relevant to analysis of other constitutional provisions that set forth broad principles rather than specific requirements. History and tradition guide and discipline this inquiry but do not set its outer boundaries. That method respects our history and learns from it without allowing the past alone to rule the present.[85]

In any event, moral theologians and philosophers need not wait for such explicit engagement to analyze legal issues in terms of natural law, where the issue is already rooted in such a history, as the right to defense most certainly is.

Lastly, the issue has taken on added urgency with the development of a new theory of constitutional interpretation known as "common-good constitutionalism," developed by Harvard Law professor Adrian Vermeule. This theory is based on two principles: that "government [should] help direct persons, associations, and society generally toward the common good, and that strong rule in the interest of attaining the common good is entirely legitimate."[86] To that end,

---

[84] Obergefell v. Hodges, 576 US 644, 656–676 (2015).
[85] *Obergefell*, 663–664.
[86] Adrian Vermeule, "Beyond Originalism," *The Atlantic*, March 31, 2020, www.theatlantic.com/ideas/archive/2020/03/common-good-constitutionalism/609037.

common-good constitutionalism rejects any pretense of originalism, or even of liberalism, in favor of an emphasis on the natural-law basis for "the right, duty, and authority of the ruling power, whatever form that power might take in a particular jurisdiction, to act through and by means of law, that is, by means of rational ordinances for the common good."[87] As Vermeule states, the "main aim" of common-good constitutionalism "is certainly not to maximize individual autonomy or to minimize the abuse of power (an incoherent goal in any event), but instead to ensure that the ruler has the power needed to rule well."[88]

Vermeule's understanding of the "common good" is striking for the absence of meaningful individual participation in collective self-government in its conception, and his theory of "common-good constitutionalism" has unsurprisingly elicited a flurry of critical responses from a variety of quarters and may elicit more study over the years to come. While a meaningful engagement with Vermeule's proposal is not possible in the current essay, even this brief mention is enough to highlight that originalism is beginning to show its limitations, and some type of return to natural law seems likely to play a role in the next chapter of constitutional theory. I would suggest that moral theologians and philosophers have an interest in (and should be prepared for) this debate.

NATURAL LAW RETURNED

As readers of this journal are well aware, natural law has had a comeback of late in moral theology, and not merely as a result of the "new natural law" approach of Germain Grisez and John Finnis. Church historian Mark Massa, SJ, has highlighted, for example, the "robust realism" of Jean Porter's work on natural law, as well as Lisa Sowle Cahill's natural-law-based approach to feminist global ethics.[89] Theological ethicist Stephen Pope has illustrated the ways in which a natural-law approach might be adapted to the scientific understanding of human evolution.[90] Other groundbreaking work by Cristina L. H.

---

[87] Adrian Vermeule, "Common-Good Constitutionalism: A Model Opinion," *Ius & Iustitium*, June 17, 2020, iusetiustitium.com/common-good-constitutionalism-a-model-opinion.

[88] Vermeule, "Beyond Originalism."

[89] Mark S. Massa, SJ, *The Structure of Theological Revolutions: How the Fight Over Birth Control Transformed American Catholicism* (New York: Oxford University Press, 2018), 128–175.

[90] Stephen J. Pope, *Human Evolution and Christian Ethics* (New York: Cambridge University Press, 2007), 268–296. Pope has also written an excellent summary of the history of natural law, "Natural Law and Christian Ethics," in *Cambridge Companion to Christian Ethics*, 2nd ed., ed. Robin Gill (Cambridge: Cambridge University Press, 2012), 67–86.

Traina, Vincent W. Lloyd, and Craig A. Ford, Jr., has insisted that natural-law ethics can and must be informed by the human bodies, lived experiences, and distinct traditions of those who historically have not been considered when the prevailing norms were made unless it was to ensure their exclusion.[91] Adding to this rich conversation from a different direction is theological ethicist Kevin Jung and his work on "commonsense morality," which retrieves an intuitionist account of moral realism, persuasively defending against those who would discount the entire enterprise as too historically and sociologically contingent to have much value.[92]

Taken as a whole, one sees that far from natural law merely being a primitive stage in the development of law, from which first common law and then positivism could develop, it rather is a rich tradition in its own right that has continued to grow and develop in robust and innovative fashion. One also senses what is lost when the legal tradition values only a Revolutionary-era conception of natural law, literally and figuratively "antebellum," without taking account of its potential as a source of contemporary moral and legal reflection. It bears adding that natural law is also not without its own rigor—it hardly is an "anything goes" bastion of moral relativism—as it consists of an identifiable tradition of moral theory, with its own standards and sources at least as clear as the history in which originalists like Scalia claim to find refuge. And it is one which, even in its contemporary form, is compatible with the methods of common-law reasoning still used in US jurisprudence, given its roots and history.

More importantly, natural law provides an arena for engagement, beyond the narrow echo chambers and politicized, walled-off media environments in which our culture wars are fought, and offers the potential to reconnect legal discourse with a rich tradition of moral reflection, without the intellectual dishonesty of anachronistically asking, to paraphrase a hackneyed catchphrase, "What Would Blackstone Do?" Rather, were constitutional jurisprudence to reengage with natural law, it would manifest a return to the *method* of

---

[91] See Cristina L. H. Traina, *Feminist Ethics and Natural Law: The End of Anathemas* (Washington, DC: Georgetown University Press, 1999); Vincent W. Lloyd, *Black Natural Law* (New York: Oxford University Press, 2016); Craig A. Ford, Jr., "Transgender Bodies, Catholic Schools, and a Queer Natural Law Theology of Exploration," *Journal of Moral Theology* 7, no. 1 (January 2018): 70–98.

[92] Kevin Jung, *Christian Ethics and Commonsense Morality: An Intuitionist Account* (New York: Routledge, 2015). See also Kevin Jung, "Models of Moral Realism in Christian Ethics," *Harvard Theological Review* 108, no. 4 (October 2015): 485–507; Kevin Jung, "Christian Morality: An Intuitionist Account," *Heythrop Journal* 53, no. 4 (July 2012): 560–573.

Blackstone and Madison, and not merely impose mechanically their worldview.[93]

John E. Carter is Visiting Assistant Professor of Law at the Wake Forest University School of Law and in the Program for Leadership and Character and Visiting Assistant Professor of Religion, Law, and Public Life at the Wake Forest University School of Divinity. He holds a PhD in theological ethics from Boston College and a JD from Duke University.

---

[93] Sincere thanks to H. Jefferson Powell for his invaluable feedback on an early draft of this essay. Remaining errors of any sort are my own.

Concealed Carry, Agency, and Attention in a Technocratic Context

Luis G. Vera

CONVERSATIONS ABOUT FIREARMS AS TECHNOLOGIES TEND to follow a certain script: attention to the prevalence and costs of gun violence inspires proposals for more stringent gun regulation. Gun rights supporters respond that (a) the problem lies not in guns themselves but the will of individuals who use them for either good or bad purposes: "Guns don't kill people, people kill people." Gun regulation proponents typically reply that the presence of a gun exerts a distinct and significant influence on people's behavior. One version of this move draws attention to (b) the gun's structure as a portable weapon designed to tear flesh at a distance by concentrating explosive and accurately-directed force onto a small projectile. The other version focuses instead on (c) how practices in which guns are used and legitimized mediate broader sociocultural problems (e.g., white supremacy, toxic masculinity, or militarized citizenship).

This "default script" rehearses three important positions on the agency and moral valance of any technology. (a) *Instrumentalism* views technologies as compliant expansions of preexisting human capacities, as morally neutral means that serve ends posited by users, and hence as extensions rather than interruptions or deflections of each user's purposes and moral habits. (b) *Technological determinism* insists that a tool's form can influence our actions, habits, moral vision, and purposes despite our initial intentions and even without our conscious awareness. Finally, (c) *cultural materialism* looks behind the tool's form to social and cultural dynamics framing that tool's design, normative uses, marketing, demand, and competitive advantage, such that the tool's influence on users is primarily a function of how it embodies, benefits from, or helps sustain those broader dynamics.[1] Given how often and readily gun debates trace these main positions, it is not surprising that references to these

---

[1] Here I follow James F. Caccamo's analysis in "What's in a Tech? Factors in Evaluating the Morality of Our Information and Communication Practices," *Journal of Moral Theology* 4, no. 1 (2015): 151–180.

debates are ubiquitous in technology critics' attempts to help others think more deeply about technologies more broadly.

Much can and remains to be achieved within this default script. For example, while social scientists have explored a fair range of possibilities from a cultural materialist perspective, they have only recently pursued robust determinist analyses by focusing sustained attention on how and why guns themselves exert a distinct influence upon the actions, emotions, or symbolism that form part of gun-related practices.[2] The default script, however, does not tell us the whole story about guns as technologies. This article seeks to move beyond this script and identify some productive routes forward. I shall do so by interpreting gun use via what has become a central point of departure for Catholic reflection on technology: Pope Francis's *Laudato Si'*. Francis's critique of what he calls the "technocratic paradigm" identifies the importance of reading everyday technologies not only in terms of their structure or how they fit into broader sociocultural dynamics (e.g., capitalism), but also in terms of how modern technoscience operates as a general and sufficiently coherent sociocultural force in its own right, deeply influencing the design and use of everyday technologies as well as other dynamics cultural materialists habitually discern as orienting frameworks for such production and use.[3]

Given its growing prominence in the United States, I will focus our attention on concealed-carry defensive gun use within the culture of armed citizenship. I will explore how concealed carry embodies a search for *skilled agency* and *attention to the world*—two important tasks a robust response to the technocratic paradigm requires. On both counts, concealed carry's resistance to that paradigm is meaningful and deserves fuller attention. But closer reflection, informed by sociologically-informed technology criticism that resonates with *Laudato Si'*, reveals that concealed carry as generally performed today does not deal successfully with these two challenges. In fact, precisely where concealed carry appears to promise gun owners real resistance

---

[2] For a key step in this direction, see Jonathan Obert, Andrew Poe, and Austin Sarat, eds., *The Lives of Guns* (New York: Oxford University Press, 2018).

[3] Cultural materialism's central insight is to expose how specific technological innovations (and their uses) are embedded in broader sociocultural patterns. Thus, while it can and often does analyze specific tools in terms of broader patterns not directly related to technology, it is also in principle open to treating modern technoscience itself as its own background dynamic. As Caccamo points out, authors such as Jacques Ellul and Langdon Winner have offered a version of such an approach by framing various innovations within specifically technocratic sociocultural dynamics ("What's in a Tech?," 159). Literature on guns, however, tends to focus only on *other* sociocultural factors (race, class, and gender) rather than reading gun use within the broader story of modern technology.

to the technocratic paradigm, it ends up largely playing into that paradigm's hand. Concealed carry's pursuit of skilled agency undercuts the sociocultural conditions needed for such agency by expressing this aspiration in terms of unsituated independent choice. Meanwhile, the practice of situational awareness through which concealed carry affirms attention to the world is focused on the anticipation of an event one cannot regularly practice. This leaves such attention wide open to undisciplined uses of memory and imagination, and these in turn prevent true attention to the world. Concealed carry is thus locked in a cycle of failed resistance to technocratic society.

"Gun Instrumentalism": Myth or Theory?

Before turning to Francis, let me begin by explaining how the gun debate itself calls for his general critique of the technocratic paradigm. Consider a puzzle that has emerged in my conversations with students, friends, and family members about the ethics of gun use. In these contexts, gun rights advocates seem easily convinced that the presence or absence of a gun can exert a morally relevant difference in how a heated and potentially violent conflict is likely to arise, proceed, and conclude. These interlocutors also admit with surprising readiness that good gun use relies heavily upon an embodied and storied formation supported by specific cultural ecologies requiring care and attention by many people. None of this guarantees that the conversation will lead these interlocutors to acknowledge the full range of concerns commonly raised about guns and defensive violence. For one thing, more "intimate" forms of violent conflict resolution have their own morally complicated cultural locations and histories.[4] On the other hand, recognitions that responsible gun use depends on specific formative frameworks can also replicate problematic assumptions about race or gender.[5] Still, these responses display an important gap between language and life. While centered in the rhetoric of instrumentalism, these gun rights supporters' experience of gun use— and their attempts to make sense of that experience—slips readily into determinist and cultural materialist analyses.

---

[4] See, e.g., Mika LaVaque-Manty, "Dueling for Equality: Masculine Honor and the Modern Politics of Dignity," *Political Theory* 34, no. 6 (2006): 715–740.

[5] Charles Fruehling Springwood, "Gun Concealment, Display, and Other Magical Habits of the Body," *Critique of Anthropology* 34, no. 4 (2014): 467; Jennifer Carlson, *Citizen-Protectors: The Everyday Politics of Guns in an Age of Decline* (New York: Oxford University Press, 2015); Angela Stroud, *Good Guys with Guns: The Appeal and Consequences of Concealed Carry* (Chapel Hill: The University of North Carolina Press, 2015).

Similar slippage appears in ethnographic accounts of gun users.[6] One particularly prominent and telling example is the "Rifleman's Creed," which has been part of basic training for the United States Marine Corps since 1942:

> This is my rifle. There are many like it, but this one is mine.
> My rifle is my best friend. It is my life. I must master it as I must master my life.
> My rifle, without me, is useless. Without my rifle, I am useless. I must fire my rifle true. I must shoot straighter than my enemy who is trying to kill me. I must shoot him before he shoots me. I will...
> My rifle and myself know that what counts in this war is not the rounds we fire, the noise of our burst, nor the smoke we make. We know that it is the hits that count. We will hit...
> My rifle is human, even as I, because it is my life. Thus, I will learn it as a brother. I will learn its weaknesses, its strength, its parts, its accessories, its sights and its barrel. I will ever guard it against the ravages of weather and damage as I will ever guard my legs, my arms, my eyes and my heart against damage. I will keep my rifle clean and ready. We will become part of each other. We will...
> Before God, I swear this creed. My rifle and myself are the defenders of my country. We are the masters of our enemy. We are the saviors of my life.
> So be it, until victory is America's and there is no enemy, but peace![7]

Here we see a clear affirmation not only of the importance of formative "use practices" that fully appropriate the rifle into one's agency, but also of how each Marine is simultaneously conformed to the rifle's structure and its corresponding "affordances" (the applications a tool suggests and the ends it opens up to the user's moral vision). Marine and rifle "become part of each other." The rifle "is human, even as I, because it is my life." Neither guns nor people kill on their own. It is the marine-rifle temporary cyborg that defends country, masters enemies, and saves life. It would be hard to outdo the Rifleman's Creed as a popular translation of Bruno Latour's anti-instrumentalist account of gun use: "You are different with a gun in your hand; the gun is different with you holding it. You are another subject because you hold the gun; the gun is another object because it has entered into a relationship with you. The gun is no longer the gun-

---

[6] See especially Springwood, "Gun Concealment"; Patrick Blanchfield, "Prosthetic Gods: On the Semiotic and Affective Landscape of Firearms in American Politics," in *Gun Studies: Interdisciplinary Approaches to Politics, Policy, and Practice*, ed. Jennifer Carlson, Kristin A. Goss, and Harel Shapira (New York: Routledge, 2019), 196–210.

[7] "Marine's Rifle Creed," Marine Corps University, www.usmcu.edu/Research/Marine-Corps-History-Division/Frequently-Requested-Topics/Marines-Rifle-Creed/.

in-the-armory or the gun-in-the-drawer or the gun-in-the-pocket, but the gun-in-your-hand, aimed at someone who is screaming."[8]

How do we make sense of this frequent disconnect between the instrumentalist rhetoric often invoked by gun rights supporters and their lived (and sometimes reflective) acknowledgement that the ethics of guns (as technologies) must be considerably more complex? One could simply interpret "gun instrumentalism" less as a theory about guns as technologies than as a myth that shores up individual freedom while concealing both the gun's agency and the user's transformation. On this view, the slippage between rhetoric and reflective experience results from that myth's inherent instability. By insisting that guns are "merely" self-defense tools, the myth remains charged with a reminder that to carry a gun is to hold "the power to decide life and death."[9]

While fruitful, this interpretation runs against two limitations that can, ironically, reinforce the inconsistent deployment of gun instrumentalism. First, it only partly explains why the myth gets traction in the first place. One reason would be the NRA's catechetical activities and how these fit within US political traditions that encourage users to see guns as a smooth means for securing individual freedom against state and individual threats—especially in a context of increasingly tenuous power in politics, economics, and culture.[10] What remains unclear, however, is how and why people come to see their moral agency vis-à-vis *guns themselves* as a given rather than as an arduous and uncertain achievement. Here the NRA's catechetical activities offer us very little explanation, since they in fact insist upon a strong normative ideal of gun ownership that requires a robust personal investment in technical and especially moral training.[11]

A more promising explanation of how this myth gets traction opens up when we consider a second limitation: The myth isolates guns as the only tools under critical scrutiny even though (i) they are part of the broader story about modern technology and (ii) instrumentalism can operate as a myth with regard to *any* device. Isolating guns in this

---

[8] Bruno Latour, "On Technical Mediation—Philosophy, Sociology, Genealogy," *Common Knowledge* 3, no. 2 (1994): 33.

[9] Jonathan Obert, Andrew Poe, and Austin Sarat, "The Lives of Guns: An Introduction," in *The Lives of Guns* (New York: Oxford University Press, 2019), 5–6.

[10] See Elizabeth Anker, "Mobile Sovereigns: Agency Panic and the Feeling of Gun Ownership," in *The Lives of Guns*, 21–42, and Firmin DeBrabander, *Do Guns Make Us Free? Democracy and the Armed Society* (New Haven, CT: Yale University Press, 2015). Both studies profitably confront gun violence as a political and not simply technical problem. However, they overcorrect by attending to technology and its bearing on agency only as a medium for other sociocultural forces.

[11] Carlson, *Citizen-Protectors*, 58–84.

way is convenient for *both* sides of the current gun debate. On the one hand, gun-use cultures often express critical stances before *other* modern technologies. Selective deployment of instrumentalism shields gun use from such scrutiny, but also inhibits the clarity, depth, and coherence that would result from a more integrated response to technology. On the other hand, by denouncing the myth of instrumentalism strictly in its application to guns, critics can isolate "naïve gun owners" as a discrete problem while using similarly instrumentalist discourse to support other expressions of a technocratic posture before the world. For example, gun critics often reduce the question to a technical issue adequately interpreted through criminological and public health statistics and sufficiently addressed by implementing a properly tuned regulatory apparatus. In fact, simply engaging in debate or activism about guns can entangle us in the complications of technocratic society. Who, among us, while deeply concerned about social media's threats to democracy, has not set these worries aside and claimed easy agency over such technologies when the issues at stake in a click bait story seemed too important for fussing about the medium's structural complications? Unless our critique of instrumentalism is comprehensive, we risk the incoherence of critiquing gun rights supporters for their instrumentalism while we continue to think as instrumentalists on other fronts.

Inconsistent deployment or critiques of instrumentalism must be recognized as a common discursive pitfall in the work of confronting modern technology.[12] The standard script for the gun debate, however, treats instrumentalism as a theory about technology that one may or may not adopt, rather than as a myth or discursive pitfall *all* sides of the gun debate must learn to overcome. That standard script thus fails to address why this myth has gained a foothold in the language and imagination of gun rights supporters even against their own reflective experience. It also obstructs the development of a more integrated and coherent confrontation with both guns and modern technology across all its various forms. Hence, reflection on guns must be rooted more fully within a critique of modern technology as a general sociocultural dynamic in its own right. Fortunately, Pope Francis's *Laudato Si'* offers moral theologians ample starting points for that task.

---

[12] In addition to shielding the speaker from similar criticism, such selectivity can reasonably be considered a symptom of living in a society whose technocratic character confronts us as a *general* problem. In this case, selective critiques of instrumentalism also appeal because of the exhaustion and despair we feel before such a trenchant and variegated problem, our yearning for concrete acts of resistance, and craving for good conscience (and a sense of given rather than tenuous agency) when it comes to the *other* faces of the problem we have chosen not to confront.

LAUDATO SI' AND THE TECHNOCRATIC PARADIGM

Theologians and others have rightly focused on how *Laudato Si'* interprets the *content* of the technocratic paradigm. Less attention has fallen on the *form* of its critique. For Francis, however, the problem of technology is not simply a matter of subjecting our tools to the right ends, identifying morally relevant trends in how certain devices are structured, or remembering the victims at the underside of modern progress. The challenge is to systemically confront a deep-seated, metastasized, and often unobserved posture for confronting the world and perceiving the nature and "place of human beings and of human action in the world."[13] Accordingly, that posture shapes our encounters with technology at every level of human activity:

> It can be said that many problems of today's world stem from the tendency, certainly not always conscious, to make the method and aims of science and technology an epistemological paradigm which shapes the lives of individuals and the workings of society. The effects of imposing this model on reality as a whole, human and social, are seen in the deterioration of the environment, but this is just one sign of the reductionism which affects every aspect of human and social life.[14]

Under this paradigm, "technological products ... create a framework" that conditions not only our uses of such products but our entire "lifestyles and social possibilities" in service to "the interests of certain powerful groups" (no. 107) and ultimately to modern technology's "ironclad logic" oriented to power as its own end (no. 108). The paradigm both sets the terms for and is mediated by (i) the mutually supporting processes of technological design, production, marketing, and use, along with (ii) how those processes fit into and shape our lives and communities. This, of course, is perfectly consistent with Francis's repeated insistence that "everything is interconnected" and especially his efforts towards a fully integral ecological ethic (nos. 137–162).

The logic and content of the technocratic paradigm trades on an important dichotomy. It "exalts the concept of a subject who, using logical and rational procedures, progressively approaches and gains control over an external object." That object—a particular thing, or the world itself—is construed as lacking intrinsic meaning or structure except as raw material to be processed and used in service to whatever

---

[13] Pope Francis, *Laudato Si'*, no. 107. Here Francis locates the problem in "a way of understanding human life and activity." As the document proceeds it becomes clear that Francis is more concerned with our operative moral vision than with our explicit theories about ourselves, the world, or technology (nos. 106 and 109).

[14] Francis, *Laudato Si'*, no. 107, with emendations to the Vatican's English translation.

ends people happen to impose on it. We find ourselves "in the presence of something formless, completely open to manipulation." Outside of this "one-dimensional" posture, interventions in nature could mean "being in tune with and respecting the possibilities offered by the things themselves." Within such a posture, however, "we are the ones to lay our hands on things, attempting to extract everything possible from them while frequently ignoring or forgetting the reality in front of us" (no. 106).

Three implications relevant to our discussion follow from this. First, by imposing a single mode of knowledge upon all reality—the scientific method's "technique of possession, mastery, and transformation" (no. 106) and "the specialization which belongs to technology"—the technocratic paradigm marginalizes contemplative and integrative forms of knowledge. This matters to Francis for many reasons, not least being the threat it poses to ecological thinking—that is, thinking that can confront contemporary problems in their full complexity and grasp the relation of parts within the cosmic whole (no. 110).[15]

Second, since people are here construed in terms of unhindered volition while nature is an "insensate order" of raw material (no. 115), there is nothing intrinsic to the world that coincides with the human person. Such a world is alien and external to us. Our relationship to it becomes fundamentally conflictual (no. 106). The world cannot inform or delimit our ends except through its own temporary and technologically surmountable intransigence (nos. 115–116). Thus, the cosmos becomes "a 'space' into which objects can be thrown with complete indifference." Since freedom and power are no longer intrinsically ordered to reality's meaningful goodness, their "only norms are taken from alleged necessity, from either utility or security" (nos. 115, 105). This amounts to handing freedom over to "the blind forces of the unconscious, of immediate needs, of self-interest, and of violence" (no. 105).

Third, with human personhood identified with freedom so construed, the foregoing posture before the world bleeds over into our regard for our neighbors and bodies, especially when these prove "troublesome and inconvenient" for our independence, utility, and security (nos. 115–123). Yet insofar as we are also the objects of such power (and lack compelling grounds for limiting it), we also come to experience this condition as a kind of slavery: "We stand naked and exposed in the face of our ever-increasing power, lacking the

---

[15] This may help further explain how we come to apply instrumentalism to guns in an isolated way. Pervasive patterns of technocratic thinking themselves discourage us from fully "ecological" confrontations with both the various tools at our disposal and the discursive frameworks we bring to those tools.

wherewithal to control it" (no. 105). Notably for our discussion, one of Francis's first examples of this tendency is nuclear warheads and the "increasingly deadly arsenal of weapons available for modern warfare" (no. 104).

How does US gun use relate to these dynamics of the technocratic paradigm? The answer is not simple. As we shall see, there are clear and important ways in which the diversity of US gun cultures embody that paradigm. But they also involve significant forms of friction against it. For example, the historical (and still prevalent) use of guns as hunting tools imposes power upon creatures and construes them as objects of lethal violence. It also frequently involves practices of silent, patient, and participative attention to the natural world (often in concert with "meat eating regimes" more conducive to an integrative perception of the food on one's plate). Similarly, as influencer videos on YouTube illustrate, gun ownership often overlaps with "off the grid" lifestyles and corresponding forms of resistance to mainstream contemporary life that converge with Francis's critique of technocracy. Unfortunately, the paucity of sociological and anthropological attention to these aspects of US gun use makes it difficult to more fully assess them.[16]

Yet these sectors do not represent the main (and swelling) center of gravity for US gun use. Summarizing quantitative and qualitative studies of recent US trends, the sociologist David Yamane speaks of a shift in emphasis "from recreational shooting to armed self-defense." The latter, which he calls "Gun Culture 2.0," is less intimately bound up with activities like hunting and focuses on exercising fully one's right to carry firearms as part of an ethic of "armed citizenship" aimed at protecting oneself and others against violent threats in a world viewed as profoundly unsafe. This cultural shift is both reflected in and facilitated by the liberalization of concealed carry laws[17] and, more recently, the enactment of Stand Your Ground laws (which extend the "no duty to retreat" principle from inside one's home to public spaces).[18] This kind of gun use deserves our primary attention

---

[16] See David Yamane's review, "The Sociology of US Gun Use," *Sociology Compass* 11, no. 7 (2017), 1–10, especially at 3–4, doi.org/10.1111/soc4.12497. Stroud offers a promising move in this direction, but only in terms of disaster preparation (*Good Guys with Guns*, 128–132). Anthropological attention to off-the-grid living has not yet attended to how gun use intersects with these practices. See, e.g., Phillip Vannini and Jonathan Taggart, *Off the Grid: Reassembling Domestic Life* (New York: Routledge, 2015).

[17] Yamane, "The Sociology of US Gun Use," 5–6. For even more recent data that supports this trend, see Pew Research Center, "America's Complex Relationship with Guns: An In-Depth Look at the Attitudes and Experiences of US Adults," June 22, 2017, www.pewsocialtrends.org/2017/06/22/americas-complex-relationship-with-guns/.

[18] See Carlson, *Citizen-Protectors*, 4–7.

and has received more attention by social scientists. Let us now turn our attention to how gun use within "Gun Culture 2.0" construes personal agency and the world in ways consistent with Francis's description of the technocratic paradigm.

GUNS, AGENCY, AND MEANINGFUL RESPONSIBILITY

The question of technology is often one about agency. The complex interactions between human and device agency must be carefully accounted for. Moreover, the way in which human agency is both construed and cultivated in the face of outside forces stands regularly in need of careful critique. In what sense, then, does US concealed carry overlap with or resist the technocratic paradigm's specific construal of human agency? An important degree of overlap is easily discernible: the user is equipped with an immense amount of power which remains unknown to the world, is not shareable with others, and can be activated swiftly and directed indiscriminately from a distance to "stop" another person. Insofar as users have a specific kind of person in mind, the world disclosed by defensive gun carry is not simply, as Francis says, "a 'space' into which objects can be thrown with complete indifference." Yet the intended targets are people who pose violent and unjust threats to the freedom and security of the user and those the user hopes to protect. Such potential aggressors are regularly depicted as thoroughly and irredeemably "bad guys" (or "monsters," as the NRA's Wayne LaPierre likes to say) who cannot be reasoned with and whom "good guys" can only neutralize through violence.[19] Thus the discourse justifying potential gun violence posits a fundamental and irreconcilable conflict that can only be addressed by force. There is a meaningful sense, then, in which we are faced with the kind of subject Francis sees as the product of a technocratic society—that is, one who obtains freedom and security, vis-à-vis essentially alien objects that exercise no moral claims upon us, through the skillful deployment of exquisitely engineered force.

Social scientists have shown, however, that the discourses by which gun users interpret their pursuit of agency through concealed carry often exceed the narrative of "defense of oneself and loved ones from violent crime." Sometimes this lack of fit emerges in practice—as, e.g., when a user habitually carries his gun into the bathroom in case he needs it to repel criminals, while regularly leaving his teenage daughters alone and unarmed at home.[20] Other user narratives clearly link defensive gun carry to an identity as a responsible adult or to a vague but deeply felt sense of political and economic disenfranchise-

---

[19] DeBrabander, *Do Guns Make Us Free?*, 32–34; Stroud, *Good Guys with Guns*, 83–135, 155.
[20] Springwood, "Gun Concealment," 460.

ment.[21] Especially relevant for our purposes is the work of Jennifer Carlson, whose interviews with users in the Detroit metropolitan area reveal a consistent turn to concealed carry as an act of citizenship (and thus an exercise of duties to oneself and others rather than simply the claiming of a right) through which users strive to negotiate real and perceived insecurities stemming from postindustrial socioeconomic decline (e.g., precarious employment, police inefficacy in the face of rising crime, reduced access to other social services, deteriorating social capital, and a resulting alienation from one's community and state). For male users, what Carlson dubs the "citizen-protector" model also offers a means of reclaiming their dignity, relevance, and authority as moral and responsible adults now that their traditional role as breadwinners is increasingly beyond their reach.[22]

Defensive gun use, then, is a site in which many users seek not only security against irrational and irredeemable criminals, but also an ideal of personal responsibility considered crucial for the pursuit of a meaningful life. However, this ideal is often asserted in the face of real problems that can be easily identified as indirect effects of the technocratic paradigm. This turn to concealed carry as an assertion of meaningful responsibility has a deeper and more direct connection to technocracy. Guns call forward the user's skilled agency. And a persistent, direct outcome of technocratic social arrangements is to render skilled agency increasingly out of reach. Understanding why this is so helps us understand how defensive gun use offers an opportunity to resist technocratic imperatives that is *both* meaningful *and* ultimately ineffective against (and symptomatic of) our broader predicament.

Francis signaled how the technocratic paradigm yields a frequent experience of compromised agency: we turn to technical power to exercise unhindered individual will over a world construed as raw material devoid of intrinsic meaningful structure—and yet as objects in that world we also experience ourselves as "naked" when others

---

[21] Anker, "Mobile Sovereigns."
[22] Carlson, *Citizen-Protectors*. See also Stroud, *Good Guys with Guns*. It is along these lines that many cultural materialist interpretations of US gun use get some of their best traction. For quite often the armed protector, unjust aggressor, and those in need of protection—or, in users' common parlance, the sheepdog, the wolf, and the sheep—are portrayed in ways that reflect and reproduce destructive gender, race, and class dynamics. The analysis developed in this article is meant to complement rather than supplant accounts of gun use that highlight those dynamics. That said, I am certainly arguing that race/class/gender analyses are not enough. An anti-technocratic analysis is also necessary if we seek an adequate account of why gun owners see themselves as lacking agency, why they regard concealed carry as an opportune means for cultivating and expressing responsibility, and why their construal of this search for responsibility is ultimately self-defeating.

wield that same power against us without acknowledging our own intrinsic meaningful structure. Documenting and interpreting some such pattern as it compounds across the landscape of modern life is well trod ground for technology critics. A relatively visible and alarming example of this pattern is what Shoshana Zuboff calls "surveillance capitalism": the pervasive and fundamental structuring of digital apps, hardware, and infrastructure over the last two decades in service to the monetization of user information. Almost any instance of digital media use has become a "raw material supply operation" that extracts user behavior data in ways that aggressively bypass and erode our cultural and legal privacy protections. That data is processed through (and helps optimize) machine learning algorithms that predict and influence people's behavior so as to link individuals to consumer goods more effectively. Thus, digital media use also becomes an arena for the deployment of prediction and influence instruments, usually without users' knowledge, genuine consent, or ability to exercise any form of meaningful resistance. This logic in turn shapes other businesses and their respective slices of everyday life. Landlords and employers can "optimize" their choices of applicants by purchasing predictions about them. Insurance companies can calculate risk more directly and then discipline users in real time by indexing their behavior to reward point systems, rate changes, or fines.[23]

Zuboff helps us appreciate how this logic—whereby technical knowledge that purports to give us mastery over a pliable world comes to objectify us as docile raw material—confronts us across a wide spectrum of daily activities. Yet examples such as these can also mask how modern technology's agency-corroding influence across daily life has a much longer history and proceeds in ways often far less aggressive and deliberate than those orchestrated by firms like Google or Facebook. Still, her distinction between the Internet's "public-facing text" (the content and services users enjoy) and its "shadow text" (the story told about us but not for us through the vast accumulation and processing of user data)[24] links up with a broader body of literature that surmounts the limitations inherent in these examples by tracing a pervasive pattern in which the compromise of user agency is tied up with a persistent separation between the goods a tool offers users and how that tool actually operates.

Albert Borgmann, for example, interprets modern technology in terms of the slow and often inconspicuous ascendancy of a "device paradigm." Devices make "commodities" (goods provided easily,

---

[23] Shoshana Zuboff, *The Age of Surveillance Capitalism: The Fight for a Human Future at the New Frontier of Power* (New York: Public Affairs, 2019).
[24] Zuboff, *The Age of Surveillance Capitalism*, 183–187.

safely, and with minimal temporal and spatial restrictions) available to users through "machinery" that is concealed, increasingly impossible for users to understand or tinker with, and only extrinsically instrumental to the commodity's desirability. The commodity is easily available precisely because the machinery hides from view (and thus from practical reason) whatever is burdensome, risky, or otherwise demanding in the procurement of the goods sought. But those burdensome aspects are precisely the ones that call forward personal skill as well as a more fully attentive, receptive, and mutually-attuned engagement with our natural and social environments. For example, central heating makes warmth easily, safely, instantaneously, and ubiquitously available within a home without need for the discipline, skill, and attention to social and natural ecologies involved in procuring wood and tending a hearth. Fast food similarly offers a maximally available commodity, but precisely for that reason fails to call forward our skillful and patient attention to the food served, the world gathered through that food, and those with whom we share a meal.[25] One could provide similar accounts of weather forecasts, music recordings, automatic car transmissions, supermarkets, many of the pills we take, and (more recently) Google Maps or the Instant Pot. Considered individually, some of these tradeoffs may at times be prudent judgments in service to a comprehensively good life. But as exhibiting a recurring pattern deeply intertwined with our consumer economy, those tradeoffs compound to reduce skilled agency and its deep entanglement in the world.

Two further aspects of Borgmann's work are especially pertinent to our discussion. First, by discerning the "device paradigm" in objects that no longer stand out to us as alarming innovations, he invites us to appreciate the paradigm's longstanding, taken-for-granted centrality in the basic structure of modern life. Second, while he devotes a fair amount of attention to how political, economic, and cultural factors interact with technological development, Borgmann provides a compelling account of how modern life's corrosion of meaningful agency occurs in our relationship to our tools and not only, as the NRA would have us believe, in our relationships with other people.

This pattern is a key dynamic of the sociocultural landscape where the drama of US gun use continues to play out, particularly defensive gun carry. One point of convergence is in the intense focus on the production of handguns, holsters, purses, and clothing that maximize comfort, safety, inconspicuousness, and a quick, smooth draw when

---

[25] Albert Borgmann, *Technology and the Character of Contemporary Life: A Philosophical Inquiry* (Chicago: The University of Chicago Press, 1984), 40–78 and 196–210.

duty calls. Many Americans otherwise interested in concealed carry opt not to carry a gun because it is not comfortable to do so.[26] The aim is for concealed handguns to become like other wearable technologies such as fitness trackers and smart watches, following the device paradigm's search for commodiously available goods provided through properly concealed machinery. But this convergence between Fitbits and concealed handguns is importantly incomplete; for multiple reasons, guns are not the sort of object you forget that you are carrying. The ideal of armed citizenship encourages constant vigilance against potential threats. Further vigilance is necessary to avoid carrying into a gun-free zone or accidentally showing one's gun, which can cause awkward or dangerous social situations (and may also break local laws regarding improper exhibition or "brandishing"). Unlike other wearables, handguns loaded with hollow-point bullets (the standard choice for self-defense) are designed to immobilize bodies by tearing large holes into them and sending pressure waves that can cause severe organ damage. Even the gun's material design has a way of keeping it in the user's awareness even if it aims for concealment from the world.[27] Hence, fully realizing concealed carry requires relearning how to physically carry one's body through the full course of daily life. Tasks as simple as going to a public restroom require extensive tactical reasoning about—in this case, which stall to occupy and how to pull down one's pants without ceasing to have the gun in control, concealed from people in adjacent stalls, and ready-to-hand should defensive action be required.[28]

Guns, moreover, do not simply command attention. They call forward skillful engagement. As Timothy Luke explains, "Shooters must learn to take guns in hand, manipulate their actions, work with varied ammunition on the range, and fire in different conditions. …To know a gun will fire, remain ready for use, and hit where aimed in shooting is an elaborate set of complex skills that requires practice and focus."[29] Shooting, in turn, tends to be nested inside a wider web of practices "with their own different demands and complicated challenges," e.g., "gunsmithing, weapon cleaning, ammunition loading, bullet casting, weapon maintenance, target placement," and gun modification. In Borgmann's terms, users here are remarkably engaged with the machinery and not just with the commodity. Each of

---

[26] David Yamane, "The First Rule of Gunfighting is Have a Gun: Technologies of Concealed Carry in Gun Culture 2.0," in *The Lives of Guns*, 167–193.
[27] Dan Baum, "Happiness Is a Worn Gun: My Concealed Weapon and Me," *Harper's*, August 2010, 33.
[28] Harel Shapira, "How to Use the Bathroom with a Gun and Other Techniques of the Armed Body," in *The Lives of Guns*, 194–206.
[29] Timothy W. Luke, "Counting Up AR-15s: The Subject of Assault Rifles and the Assault Rifle as Subject," in *The Lives of Guns*, 83.

these practices make up "regimes of discipline that constitute multiple layers of gun control." Within the orbit of the central internal good of shooting well, such practices call forward mindfulness, responsibility, and fully engaged action that integrates a broad range of bodily and psychic capacities.[30] In light of Borgmann's insistence that agency-building practices must draw us into attentive and receptive engagement with our environments, it is also worth noting that, though shooting well may not be the most world-disclosing practice, it can at least meet this condition modestly. Shooters must attend closely and repeatedly to their bodily posture and stamina, environmental factors bearing on the bullet's trajectory, the gun being fired, and the target being fired at. While this is a far cry from the world-gathering potential of a festive meal, and while the act of shooting can also be an intoxicating exercise of power, it nevertheless requires from the practitioner a real degree of respect for and collaboration with a world that does not *simply* obey one's will.

As a search for skilled agency, then, gun use might seem appealing as a form of resistance to the technocratic paradigm. Unfortunately, this resistance runs into serious problems that, as with the myth of instrumentalism, stem from limitations in the moral language gun users often adopt to understand and justify concealed carry. Carlson and others have discerned a neoliberal ethos behind defensive gun carry's search for meaningful responsibility (along with its disdain for reliance on police protection or its individualist understanding of crime and social decline). According to this critique, the ethic of armed citizenship renounces state-provided security (and other social services) to opt instead for privatized security and citizenship through the cultivation of a responsible subject whose "participation in the market," as Carlson puts it, "surpasses her relationship to the state … in defining her rights, duties, and obligations as a citizen."[31] But Carlson acknowledges that concealed carry is different from, say, private police or home alarm systems since only the former requires "the cultivation of particular manual skills and mental capacities." Concealed-carry security is performed and not just purchased.[32] More important than a shift from the state to the market as reference point for responsible citizenship, then, is gun users' frequent defense of personal responsibility and skilled agency through a discourse focused

---

[30] Luke, "Counting Up AR-15s," 84–85. Simply loading a handgun involves rarely used finger muscles with increasing force as the magazine fills up. Even experienced users may wind up with bruised and swollen hands after loading and firing a high number of rounds (Shapira, "How to Use the Bathroom with a Gun," 197–199).
[31] Carlson, *Citizen-Protectors*, 68. See also Anker, "Mobile Sovereigns," 24–36; Stroud, *Good Guys with Guns*, 114–132 and 154.
[32] Carlson, *Citizen-Protectors*, 68–69.

stringently on individual independence from the conditions that situate action (state support being but one example of such conditions).

Meaningful personal responsibility expressed in skilled agency, however, does not require and is very poorly served by this individualist discourse—especially in a technocratic society. This point has been developed particularly well by Matthew Crawford, another technology critic who emphasizes how the growing gap between commodities and machinery depletes our skills.[33] One might think appeals to skilled agency should aim to shore up a muscular individual who can stand up against the "choice architectures" that herd our attention to consumer experiences while our inner resources shrivel as their operations are outsourced onto our devices. But that, argues Crawford, would actually play directly into the problem. For it would put forward a self who can act well in *any* human ecology—regardless of access to friendships, shared attention to a complex world, cultural scaffolds that orient practical reasoning, objects to which our skills are fruitfully attuned, and the necessarily contingent and particular habits through which we are equipped for such attunement. Skilled agency is and must be situated, and a self who can be situated is one delimited through attunement to specific ecologies. Unsituated selves are, by contrast, fragile—that is, easily frustrated by deep conflicts between will and world because they are not yet equipped for responsive, adaptive, and joyful interaction with the world in its specificity. Such fragility, along with pliability to attention engineering, is the ultimate outcome of the "modern identification of freedom with choice" enshrined in our modern liberal political traditions. Such choice, Crawford writes,

> is understood as a pure flashing forth of the unconditioned will. ... Thus understood, choice serves as the central totem of consumer capitalism, and those who present choices to us appear as handmaidens to our own freedom. When the choosing will is hermetically sealed off from the fuzzy, hard-to-master contingencies of the empirical world, it becomes more "free" in a sense: free for the kind of neurotic dissociation from reality that opens the door wide for others to leap in on our behalf, and present options that are available to us without the world-disclosing effort of skillful engagement. For [an unsituated self], choosing (from a menu of ready-made solutions) replaces doing, and it follows that such a person should be more pliable to the choice architectures presented to us in mass culture.[34]

Thus, for example, slot machine gambling has long been justified and defended from regulation by its industry's ability to construe

---

[33] Matthew B. Crawford, *The World beyond Your Head: On Becoming an Individual in an Age of Distraction* (New York: Farrar, Straus, and Giroux, 2015), 23–78.
[34] Crawford, *The World beyond Your Head*, 76.

gambling addiction as rooted in weakness of will, morally bad choices, or—more recently—specific individuals' blameless and preexisting predilections that compromise resistance to internal impulses. In this way, the public is distracted "from the fact that conditioning gamblers to play 'to extinction' is the design script that animates every aspect of the gambling experience, from the interior design of casinos to the minutiae of the machines' displays to the carefully calibrated frequency of wins."[35] In reality, addiction results from interactions between normal human psychology and the carefully engineered gambling experience: "repetition coupled with random reinforcement issues in addiction."[36] The machinery, then, is built upon a keen recognition of humans as situated agents. But liberal political economy hamstrings efforts at taking collective responsibility for these ecologies. We have built an economic system upon the assumption of an individually self-responsible "autonomous subject capable of acting in his own self-interest" independently of situating conditions. We therefore lack the ability to name encroachments upon our agency by commercial interests that actively engineer our situating conditions. Thus, we continue rehashing the association of heteronomy with state regulation when the most important and insidious forms of coercion come from elsewhere.[37]

Accordingly, Crawford concurs with critics of neoliberalism when they note that deregulation of the economy tends to "ratchet up the burden of *self*-regulation," which in turn amplifies existing inequalities. Self-discipline accumulates with capital within families, and not everyone has the financial means to offshore some of the self-regulation burden to accountants and SAT-prep companies.[38] But putting the problem simply as a standoff between private responsibility and state involvement also misconstrues, Crawford argues, how situated action grounds skilled agency. For various reasons, the twentieth century also saw the dismantling of broader cultural scaffolds that, though far from perfect, were coherent and robust enough to support individual people and households in their attentional and self-regulatory burdens. "The disciplinary functions of culture have in fact not been dissolved so much as privatized. They are located less in a shared order of meaning such as Protestant thrift, parental authority, or injunctions against gluttony, and more in the

---

[35] Crawford, *The World beyond Your Head*, 106. Here he draws heavily on Natasha Dow Schüll, *Addiction by Design: Machine Gambling in Las Vegas* (Princeton, NJ: Princeton University Press, 2012).
[36] Crawford, *The World beyond Your Head*, 107.
[37] *Crawford, The World beyond Your Head*, 107–112. Zuboff, we should note, makes a very similar case regarding surveillance capitalism.
[38] *Crawford, The World beyond Your Head*, 41–42.

professional nagging services provided by financial planners, tutors, and personal trainers."[39] But shareable public cultural ecologies are crucial for sustaining the coherent situatedness of skilled action. They also sustain fully political confrontations about the goods served by various features of shared environments. Such confrontations are our only real alternative to the anonymous nudging of attention engineers.[40] Hence, the central problem of skilled agency is not primarily that of strengthening individual self-responsibility but rather one of articulating and cultivating the full range of human ecologies needed for skilled agency to thrive.

Critics of armed citizenship as neoliberal self-responsibility have shown that gun owners regularly make use of language similar to that by which casinos defend their business model. This helps further explain gun instrumentalism's coexistence with a strong emphasis on proper formation. Instrumentalist rhetoric resonates easily with our prevailing view of freedom as unsituated choice, while an emphasis on individual self-regulation makes it both possible and imperative to affirm the need for rigorous personal formation while disavowing any institutional support or regulation.[41] But gun owners' interest in responsible agency, as well as their experience of shooting well as a craft calling forward such agency, is neither properly explained nor served well through individualizing models of personal responsibility. To best articulate why skilled agency is a pressing issue in our time, to make the best out of practices where we rightly intuit that we are beginning to cultivate what a technocratic society corrodes, and to foster such agency across our daily life with enough consistency as to build a serious and resilient alternative—in each case we must recognize skilled humans as situated beings, who are properly attuned to, reliant upon, and creatively interacting with specific social, technological, and natural ecologies. Such a reorientation would require real work. It would also do far better justice to and render more fruitful some of the most central and defensible concerns driving the culture of armed citizenship.

SITUATIONAL AWARENESS AND ATTENTION TO THE REAL WORLD

Have we thereby endorsed defensive-carry gun culture as essentially on the right track and needing only the above adjustments? Not quite. Recall how, in arguing that guns elicit skilled agency, Timothy Luke had to put forward "shooting well" as the central internal good around which other ancillary practices (e.g., weapon maintenance and modification) closely orbit. Recall also how

---

[39] Crawford, *The World beyond Your Head*, 43.
[40] Crawford, *The World beyond Your Head*, 41–44, 127–160, and 181–193.
[41] I am grateful to Paul Scherz for this point.

Borgmann and Crawford stressed that skilled agency depends fundamentally upon practices and things that reveal the world to and equip us for fully human action within that world. Shooting well may be a modestly world-disclosing activity, and concealed carriers certainly practice shooting their guns. But shooting well is not the center of gravity for armed citizenship. The goal is effective armed defense against an assailant. But with a few exceptions (e.g., fighting as an infantry soldier) such an act is not the sort of thing people can actually practice. For the overwhelming majority of armed citizens, defensive gun use is an object of endless preparation exercised under safe (and therefore radically different) conditions. While many armed citizens spend a fair bit of time doing bodily drills or working through imagined scenarios on a weekly or even daily basis, what engages their daily attention more than anything else (and has the best chance of counting as a practice with internal goods) is active vigilance against such unhoped-for events—what they call "situational awareness." All of this has important implications with regard to the quality of armed citizens' attention to the world. Rather than opening users to the real world, concealed carry produces the subjective experience we normally associate with world-disclosing practices while instead setting users' imaginations loose into largely fantastical accounts of their social environments.

It would be difficult to overstate the importance of situational awareness as a core imperative orienting and integrating the daily actions, conversations, instruction, and regular bodily as well as spiritual exercises that make up the culture of armed citizenship. At a basic level, situational awareness has to do with incorporating into one's daily life, to the fullest possible extent, a habit of attentive vigilance against potential threats. Such vigilance is mapped into schemas of highly embodied awareness intended to track one's current situation and trigger appropriate responses. The default setting for an armed citizen is "condition yellow," a state of relaxed alertness that habitually scans for potential threats in one's environment. Condition orange begins with the identification of a specific potential threat (someone acting suspiciously) and involves keeping one's eye on this person and coming up with a tactical plan for taking evasive or (if necessary) defensive action if the threat is actualized. Should that happen, one enters condition red and enacts the self-defense plan. To observe condition yellow is also to distinguish oneself from the sheep who remain in condition white—that is, lack of awareness of one's surroundings and failure to remain alert for potential threats.[42] It also involves a disposition to inhabit spaces in particular ways (e.g., taking

---

[42] Jon Anderson, "Gun Owners, Ethics, and the Problem of Evil," *HAU: Journal of Ethnographic Theory* 7, no. 3 (2017): 43; Baum, "Happiness is a Worn Gun," 32–33.

restaurant seats against walls and with a clear view of the entrance).[43] More generally, situational awareness helps coordinate ethical claims constitutive of armed citizenship (obliviousness and victimhood are bad; willingness to violently defend is good), the bodily experience of carrying and shooting a gun, and important mental practices (e.g., reflecting on what kinds of violence one is prepared to exercise and why).[44] Thus, for instance, gun owners might report feeling calmer, safer, and less aggressive when carrying, not just because they can defend themselves but also because the gun elicits greater attentiveness to one's surrounding or responsibility for staying out of petty arguments.[45]

Given our widespread difficulties with media representations that inhibit robustly attentive engagements with the world, ought we not celebrate the embodied attentiveness of condition yellow that is part of concealed-carry gun culture? Not if the picture of the world such attention yields is generally inaccurate in its content and skewed in its affective dispositions. Although gun violence is a serious problem in this country, the rate of violent crime (including gun homicide) has continued to drop dramatically since the early 1990s due to a range of factors among which the influence of armed civilians has yet to be demonstrated.[46] Moreover, the risk of victimization varies widely by age, income, race, and geography. In general, the risk is higher for people who are young (16–34), urban, black, and poor.[47] The data we have on concealed carry permits shows that white men are overwhelmingly more likely to submit an application and receive approval.[48] The great majority of armed citizens already live in relative safety from gun violence. Some might recognize this fact and respond that carrying is still reasonable because the consequences of being unprepared are simply too high.[49] Nevertheless, the world as disclosed

---

[43] Carlson, *Citizen-Protectors*, 80.
[44] Anderson, "Gun Owners, Ethics, and the Problem of Evil," 44; Carlson, *Citizen-Protectors*, 73–80.
[45] Baum, "Happiness is a Worn Gun," 33–34; Carlson, *Citizen-Protectors*, 76–77.
[46] See Stroud for a good summary of this and relevant sources (*Good Guys with Guns*, 7–8).
[47] For a recent discussion of risk ratios based on the National Crime Victimization Survey, see Heather Warnken and Janet L. Lauritsen, "Who Experiences Violent Victimization and Who Accesses Services? Findings from the National Crime Victimization Survey for Expanding Our Reach," Center for Victim Research, April 2019, navaa.org/wp-content/uploads/2021/02/CVR-Article_Who-Experiences-Violent-Victimization-and-Who-Accesses-Services-1.pdf.
[48] Harel Shapira, Katherine Jensen, and Ken-Hou Lin, "Trends and Patterns of Concealed Handgun License Applications: A Multistate Analysis," *Social Currents* 5, no. 1 (2018): 3–14. The trend is similar for gun ownership (Pew Research Center, "America's Complex Relationship with Guns").
[49] DeBrabander, *Do Guns Make Us Free?*, 13; Stroud, *Good Guys with Guns*, 2.

to them by the practice of armed citizenship is one in which they and their loved ones are profoundly vulnerable and where potential threats can be lurking in every corner. Stroud compellingly explains how her interlocutors' stories of perceived threat consistently lack evidence that the suspect was in fact dangerous or acted in a threatening manner. They also lack evidence of a disciplined commitment to remembering these events with accuracy and precision or to recalibrating one's situational awareness accordingly. Some carriers are set off by everyday loud noises or seeing someone with a handheld barcode scanner at Walmart. One respondent reinterprets (and profoundly regrets) his life before becoming a concealed carrier as foolishly vulnerable despite the fact that he and his family suffered no victimizations during that time. Another one compares her responsivity to her surroundings as what is experienced by "someone who's been raped or attacked."[50]

Moral theologians can identify a number of reasons why this way of reading one's environment is problematic even if it does not lead directly to more gun violence. Here, however, I will focus on how such a practice of committed attention to one's surroundings can become so disconnected from reality. The way in which cultural forces like racism can set the content of such attention is certainly relevant—a number of Stroud's interlocutors indicate no other reason for feeling threatened than the fact that the other person was black.[51] A whole cocktail of other forces is also surely involved: neoliberal interpretations of poverty, media depictions of fictional gun violence, news coverage of crime, NRA fearmongering, our relatively abstract relationship to real violence,[52] or the way in which many gun owners reduce immensely complex social and cultural problems that are truly hurting them into a more cognitively manageable standoff between good and bad guys.[53] But how can a practice so centered on paying attention nevertheless be so incapable of offering resistance or correction to these cultural pressures?

This inability to offer resistance is baked into the practice of armed citizenship and hidden from view by the subjective experience of focused attention that situational awareness elicits. Carlson explains how the unpredictability and slim likelihood of actual defensive gun use sets off defensive training from other gun practices and, we should add, practices such as driving a car that require us to negotiate a meaningful degree of lethal risk:

---

[50] Stroud, *Good Guys with Guns*, 94–111 and 144–150.
[51] Stroud, *Good Guys with Guns*, 94–104.
[52] DeBrabander, *Do Guns Make Us Free?*, 1–50.
[53] Anker, "Mobile Sovereigns."

Concealed Carry, Agency, and Attention 79

> Firearms handling requires a knack for manual dexterity. However, in hunting and target shooting, the shooter receives a clear verification of his or her technical proficiency: Did you hit the game? Is there a hole in the bullseye? For the vast majority of Americans armed for self-defense purposes, there's no verification of their skill readiness. NRA drills do not simulate self-defense encounters, and relatively few gun carriers will ever face an actual criminal encounter to find out whether they have the skills needed to survive. By then, it will be too late to modify their training regimen, anyway.[54]

By contrast with other kinds of shooting, there is no feedback loop here between bodily action and its outcome in the world, and thus also no ongoing informed adjustment *to* the world that can discipline and cultivate perception. This results in a vacuum of concrete engaged experience combined with an insatiable imperative to fill that vacuum and nurture hope that such striving will suffice. As NRA materials for certification courses put it,

> Your plan for responding to a potential threat should … be regularly practiced. … There is nothing—no shooting sport, no motion picture or instruction manual, and no training regimen—that can fully prepare you for the experience of using your defensive firearm against a violent assailant. Nonetheless, those gun owners who avail themselves of every opportunity to prepare mentally and physically for a defensive situation will almost always fare better than those who don't.[55]

While some of this endless training involves repeatedly manipulating one's weapon, a large part of the vacuum is filled with mental exercises like visualizing hypothetical scenarios or imagining a target as an armed assailant. Given that situational awareness already involves proactively imagining potential threats and tactical responses, along with the need to approximate one's training to realistic situations, in a certain sense these visualization exercises themselves become part of the everyday practice of situational awareness. One instructor jokes to Carlson that he does this so habitually that "I've already killed a dozen guys since we've been sitting here."[56] Emotional habits and construals of the armed assailant can also become part of the imaginative training. As another trainer insists, "You want to conquer, destroy. You've got to work on developing this mind-set. Realize the world is a violent place. Understand your opponent, because they are not like you and me.

---

[54] Carlson, *Citizen-Protectors*, 81–82.
[55] NRA, *Guide to the Basics of Personal Protection in the Home* (Fairfax, VA: National Rifle Association of America, 2010), 131, 147 (cited in Carlson, *Citizen-Protectors*, 81).
[56] Carlson, *Citizen-Protectors*, 73–80.

They would cut off your head for your jewelry. ... Visualize. Create movies in your head about you and the bad guy. You have to see yourself winning."[57] Stroud links this blurring between real human ecologies and imaginative training to her interlocutors' difficulty in narrating disciplined stories of actual threatening events ("I was...") without slipping into rehearsals of generic hypothetical situations ("you pull up..."). Thus they tend to "explain any potentially threatening experience as a crime that could have been."[58] Real stories start to operate less as experience that needs to be unpacked, remembered, and applied with care. Instead, they become quick fodder for the imagination in the infinite task of preparing intuitive response scripts for an unforeseeable event. The stakes are high—not only one's own life and that of loved ones, but also one's quality as responsible citizen and protector. One instructor speaks of the death of two students as gun fight "forfeits" because "they chose not to be armed" on "The Big Day."[59] Another instructor is even more explicit: "I feel I have a responsibility, and I believe that in my afterlife I will be judged. Part of the judgment will be: Did this guy look after himself?"[60] And when the bad guys are irrational and fundamentally evil outsiders, justice means winning. It is on these terms that the relevant features of experiences with potentially threatening people are identified, remembered, and repurposed.

Here again we can see concealed carry's entanglement with our technocratic condition. Crawford likens slot machine gambling (by serious players who come to "get in the zone" rather than make money) as lost in a kind of pseudo-autotelic activity. Real autotelic activities "are guided by intimations of something valuable that you are trying to bring more fully into view through your activity." But "with gambling machines, the sense of something real to be apprehended is conjured up by various manipulations of our capacity for detecting patterns, and this probably contributes to their absorbing nature."[61] We get to enjoy a good-enough approximation of *the subjective experience* we would have when pursuing the goods internal to a practice and when growing in agency through that pursuit.[62] This is a tempting apparent solution to the anxiety-inducing

---

[57] Anderson, "Gun Owners, Ethics, and the Problem of Evil," 44.
[58] Stroud, *Good Guys with Guns*, 98.
[59] Tom Givens, "Carry Your Darned Gun!," *Rangemaster Digest* email newsletter, June 3, 2014 (cited in Yamane, "The First Rule of Gunfighting," 169).
[60] Baum, "Happiness is a Worn Gun," 32.
[61] Crawford, *The World beyond Your Head*, 106. He attributes this account of autotelic activities to Talbot Brewer.
[62] Here I rely on Alasdair MacIntyre's account of internal goods in *After Virtue: A Study in Moral Theory*, 3rd ed. (Notre Dame, IN: University of Notre Dame Press, 2007), especially at 181–225.

contradiction of living under the imperative to be unsituated and unhindered choosing selves in a world where genuine agency is increasingly beyond our grasp. "Pseudo-action" appeals to us because, as a kind of space "sealed off from the world, it is experienced as a zone of efficacy and intelligibility."[63] Concealed-carry situational awareness also hunts for the apprehension of something real and is hobbled by a severed loop between action and contingent events in the world. Except that it is now the user, scaffolded by the cultural world shared with fellow armed citizens, who conjures up the phantom of something real. Moreover, instead of staring into a slot machine (or video game, news feed, or string of video recommendations), it is the real world to which the armed citizen is attending. So one can well understand how, under the strain of the tensions inherent in a technocratic society, "condition yellow" looks like a far more engaged and receptive alternative to the more obvious forms of pseudo-action on offer. But it is still a failed attempt to make real forward motion against the challenge that such a society puts before us.

CONCLUSION

We have ventured beyond the default script for reflection on guns qua technologies to catch a better glimpse of this problem from a new vantage point: Pope Francis's critique of the technocratic paradigm as a general sociocultural force in its own right that exercises a detrimental influence across the entire spectrum of modern life. This paradigm trains us to see ourselves fundamentally in terms of unhindered and unsituated volition and to confront nature as an "insensate order" of alien raw material to be coerced through technoscience in service to our utility and security. With Francis's critique in hand, we revisited the culture of armed citizenship in light of two pressing tasks that would be central for any serious challenge to the technocratic paradigm: the cultivation of meaningful skilled agency and of truly world-disclosing practices. On both counts, we found that concealed-carry defensive gun use is caught in a cycle of failed resistance to the technocratic paradigm. The embrace of gun use in the pursuit of meaningful responsibility is chained to a myth of autonomous choice that undercuts the cultural and social conditions necessary for mature skilled agency. Meanwhile, situational awareness in vigilant preparation for an event one cannot repeatedly practice leaves the door wide open to undisciplined imagination in the interpretation of daily experiences and equally undisciplined remembering of those experiences. Since in both cases we do find a meaningful germ of resistance, the growing center of US gun use is

---

[63] Crawford, *The World beyond Your Head*, 93–94.

caught in the technocratic paradigm precisely by appearing to offer an adequate alternative to a life of corroded agency and disconnection from the world. It is also caught in that paradigm because it trains concealed carriers to read unjust assailants as thoroughly evil, irrational "bad guys" to be dominated through highly engineered force.

But can these germs of resistance grow into a genuine alternative? Like the lizard in Lewis's *The Great Divorce*, the myth of autonomous and unsituated choice can be severed from the search for skilled meaningful agency. Though many armed citizens would likely experience this as a profound cultural amputation, the result would make good on the best possible reasons for seeking freedom in a technocratic society.[64] What about situational awareness? In this case the broken feedback loop between bodily action and observable consequences is inherent in the practice itself. The only hope, if there is any, lies in wrapping situational awareness in a web of truly world-disclosing practices that could jointly outrun other sociocultural forces competing to fill the vacuum left open by that broken feedback loop. Concealed carriers' situational awareness simply cannot pull its own weight as a form of attention; it can only have a place in the good life if other practices can stabilize it and give it content. Needless to say, moral theologians have much to contribute here, not least with regard to seeing potential assailants as human beings.

Thus, we return to Francis's call for fully ecological reflection, which in the case of the gun debate would mean leaving behind the myth of gun instrumentalism by integrating questions such as those treated here into a much broader texture of everyday-life confrontations with modern technology. Such a process is difficult for everyone, not just gun owners. Comprehensive reflection upon and active resistance to technology's diverse but compounding effects is exhausting and can elicit fear that other issues we care about will be sidelined. For those of us who have deep objections to how guns are used in the United States, the foregoing discussion should help alleviate that fear. In both of the main questions considered, standard objections to US gun use are not dismissed but simply put in a broader context when gun owners are engaged with regard to how their concerns could be addressed more justly through fully ecological reflection. Properly carried out, such reflection already moves in the direction many critics already hope to go.[65] M

---

[64] C. S. Lewis, *The Great Divorce* (New York: HarperOne, 1973), 106–115.
[65] I am grateful to Michael Grigoni, Barrett Turner, and Joshua Brown for their feedback on this article's argument, as well as to Paul Scherz for his comments on an earlier draft.

Luis G. Vera is Associate Professor and Chair of the Theology Department at Mount St. Mary's University in Emmitsburg, Maryland. A native of Venezuela, Dr. Vera earned his BA from the University of Georgia and an MTS and doctorate from the University of Notre Dame. Dr. Vera's research brings Catholic social teaching and moral theology into engagement with technology ethics and media studies. He is especially interested in the various interactions between our cognitive habits and tool use, as well as how these interactions can best help cultivate virtue, contemplation, and the love of neighbor. He has published or presented on topics such as augmented reality, digital surveillance, artificial intelligence, medieval reading practices, and the role of memory in framing attention and media use. His current project explores the rhetorical patterns that can best serve the fruitful cultivation of memory and judgment in a digital age.

Guns, Construction of Threat, and Lived Ecclesiologies

Katie Day

COMMUNITIES OF FAITH IN THE US CURRENTLY FACE MANY threats—threats to the very existence of religious bodies. The decline in religious participation, noted by researchers and religious leaders alike, is a trend church members experience firsthand, as they see fewer people in the pews with each passing year. Other existential threats lurk as well: a growing economic crisis that exposes just how vulnerable many are to poverty, an undeniably changing climate that brings more extreme weather patterns, contentious political dynamics that divide families and disrupt social cohesion, the exposure of racial injustice which enflames conflict and, of course, a global pandemic that has ravaged through our local communities. These are threats experienced throughout society, as well as by congregations already aware of their own decline.

However, the threat that has particularly galvanized faith communities and shaped their sense of identity—their *lived ecclesiologies*—is violence. In recent years, high-profile shootings in faith communities as people gathered for worship have challenged, if not shattered, a sense of invulnerability. At Mother Emanuel African Methodist Episcopal Church in Charleston, South Carolina, in 2015; First Baptist Church in Sutherland Springs, Texas, in 2017; and the Tree of Life Synagogue in Pittsburgh, Pennsylvania, in 2018—sanctuaries were violated as people of faith were murdered while they prayed. This trend stretches back in time. In 2002, there were shootings at Our Lady of Peace Catholic Church in Lynbrook, New York, and a Benedictine monastery in Conception, Missouri; in 2012, a mass shooting occurred at a Sikh gurdwara in Oak Creek, Wisconsin; and in 2019, two deadly attacks took place in mosques in Christchurch, New Zealand. And there were others in between. No religious tradition or region, it seems, is immune to the threat of gun violence in their sacred spaces. A sense of threat and vulnerability has rippled throughout all religious communities.

Make no mistake: gun violence in houses of worship is still very rare. About 39% of congregations reported experiencing any kind of crime in a single year (2014). These were primarily property crimes, including vandalism and theft. Less than 4% of congregations reported violent crimes with only .44% of responding congregations specifying that they were sites of homicides.[1] Even so, mass shootings in religious spaces have increased. While most were not fatal, in the span of twenty-five years, from 1980 to 2005, there were 139 such shootings—an average of 5.56 per year. In a much shorter period of time—the ten years between 2006 and 2016—there were 147 church shootings at a rate of almost 15 per year, more of which were deadly.[2] With an estimated 350,000+ congregations in the US,[3] gun violence in communities of faith is still a statistical trace element. But it does have a disproportionate impact on the social imaginary. Statistician and essayist Nassim Nicholas Taleb calls such phenomena "Black Swan events."[4] These are seemingly random events, outliers in our experience, but they have an extreme impact on our collective consciousness and push us into constructing explanations.

Religion is in the business of cultivating narratives and making sense of what is going on in the world. Infused with understandings of God as a "rock," "refuge," and "protector," the Abrahamic religions center notions of safety and security in God's relationship to God's people. We gather in "sanctuaries," apart from the noise of the world. The Greek word for church, ἐκκλησία, is a compound word meaning, literally, "called out." In the context of an ecclesiology that emphasizes being set apart and protected, the threats to the social fabric and the planet can seem remote, outside of the sanctuary of faith.

For faith communities, the shock of high-profile shootings in religious contexts has created an acute cognitive dissonance with lived theologies that center an all-powerful deity. Those in the Abrahamic faiths are familiar with the many promises of God's protection in the Psalms: "The Lord will keep you from all evil; he will keep your life" (Psalm 121:7), and "Even though I walk through the valley of the shadow of death, I will fear no evil for thou art with me; thy rod and thy staff comfort me" (Psalm 23:4). How, then, should congregations

---

[1] Christopher Scheitle, "Religious Congregations' Experiences with, Fears of, and Preparations for Crime: Results from a National Survey," *Review of Religious Research* 60, no. 1 (March 2018): 104, journals.sagepub.com/doi/10.1007/s13644-017-0316-3.
[2] "Church Shootings," *Center for Homicide Research*, www.homicidecenter.org/research/church-shootings/; Francie Diep, "Church Shootings are Becoming Much More Common," *Pacific Standard*, November 6, 2017, www.psmag.com/news/church-shootings-are-becoming-much-more-common.
[3] "Fast Facts about American Religion," *Hartford Institute for Religion Research*, www.hirr.hartsem.edu/research/fastfacts/fast_facts.html.
[4] Nassim Nicholas Taleb, *The Black Swan: The Impact of the Highly Improbable* (New York: Random House, 2007).

understand their vulnerability in the face of danger? How might this affect how they see God, as well as themselves in the world?

The challenge confronting lived ecclesiologies has been further complicated by evolving considerations congregations must now address regarding their identity in relation to "the other." All the traditions represented in the grim list of atrocities above teach that "the stranger" and "the alien" should be welcomed. The welcome of the stranger by Mother Emanuel's Bible study hit a nerve with faith communities who understand hospitality as a core value in their mission and identity. This has been new territory for both clergy and lay people alike. Preparing for and responding to the threat of an active shooter is not part of the theological education that forms leaders, nor is it a staple of the theological canon. Violence in the sanctuary is incomprehensible; there exists no language capable of formulating an adequate response. How then might we speak of security in God, and how might we relate this to physical safety?

In this paper, I argue that the manner in which ecclesial communities construct threat—particularly concerning gun violence—exerts a profound influence on their lived ecclesiologies, actively shaping theological self-reflection in real time. After considering the nature of ecclesiology, I will draw on the life and work of German theologian Dietrich Bonhoeffer, who focused deeply on the meaning of the Church in his own violent context of Nazi Germany. As will be seen, the young theologian was writing and teaching whilst he, his students, and his colleagues were in the crosshairs of the Nazis, from 1932 to 1945. The constant threat of violence shaped how Bonhoeffer understood the church in the world. His theological evolution in this circumstance provides insight into the relationship of threat to ecclesiology. After describing some of the specific threats Bonhoeffer encountered, I will show that this led to his understanding of the church that was at once in resistance as well as being radically the "one for others." As communities of faith in the US become conscious of the threat of violence in their contexts, their own ecclesiologies are impacted. I will consider current social research, including my own, that examines how communities are conceptualizing and responding to threat in ways that reflect emerging understandings of themselves. As with the church in Nazi Germany, threat can lead to very different lived ecclesiologies.

WHAT IS ECCLESIOLOGY?

Within systematic theology, ecclesiology is that subdiscipline which reflects on the church itself. Here, theologians engage a number of questions: What, in fact, is the church? What are the marks of the church? That is, what makes the church *the church*? What are its necessary, definitive activities and sacraments? How does it relate to

Christ and salvation? How is the church present in history and society? In what sense is the church holy in relation to sin? Is there an essential and invisible church apart from its institutional manifestations? Can we speak of the unity of the church in the context of such organizational splintering? Theological questions about the church are myriad. Theologians, like the early Bonhoeffer, often write normatively about such questions; that is, in ideal forms of what the church should be.

But finally, ecclesiology is the theological understanding of the church's identity. This identity, however, is not formed within an academic bubble but rather in historical context. The Swiss Catholic theologian Hans Küng frames his work on ecclesiology (called simply *The Church*) in terms of a tension between "essence and form" that allows for changing expressions of the church:

> This constant factor in the history of the Church and of its understanding of itself is only revealed in change; its identity exists only in variability, its continuity only in changing circumstances, its permanence only in varying outward appearances. In short, the "essence" of the Church is not a matter of metaphysical stasis but exists only in constantly changing historical "forms."[5]

Ecclesiology as the identity of the church is a *lived* theological expression constructed from a number of sources, such as tradition and history (which contribute continuity), but also cultural context and experience. This is what Bonhoeffer would call "the concrete." As such, lived ecclesiology changes and adapts through complex social processes which construct and continually reconstruct it.

Lived ecclesiology provides a framework that enables ecclesial communities to locate themselves in their social and historical contexts—who they are in relation to the world. Part of the function of ecclesial identity is to generate and nurture narratives which serve to create social coherence and facilitate meaning-making. A church's sense of its identity, its lived ecclesiology, contributes to the worldview of its members and supplies a lens for meaning-making—so that life, in fact, *makes sense*. In doing so, lived ecclesiologies interpret that which is good and of God, interpret and account for crises, and move the ecclesial community through framing narratives toward the good. The lived ecclesiology of a faith community also provides an understanding of its authority which enables it to differentiate between that which is good, that which threatens it, and how to respond to the perceived threat.

---

[5] Hans Küng, *The Church*, trans. Ray and Rosaleen Ockenden (New York: Sheed & Ward, 1968), 4.

BONHOEFFER AND THE THEOLOGICAL IMPACT OF THREAT

Protestant theologian Dietrich Bonhoeffer was remarkable for many reasons. His decision to join a conspiracy against Hitler and eventual execution just days before the end of World War II are often the first things that come to mind. Also impressive are the volume and quality of the writing he completed during his thirty-nine years, especially considering his voluminous pastoral and ecumenical work, travel, and the Nazi reign of terror from 1933 to 1945. These were not ideal working conditions for a theologian, yet Bonhoeffer was able to write works that have endured even as he was banned from publishing and speaking and then imprisoned for the last two years of his life.[6]

The core questions he wrestled with throughout his work were Christological and ecclesiological: "Who is Jesus Christ for us today?" and "What is the church?" For Bonhoeffer, the two were related and became inseparable as his work developed. His first dissertation, *Sanctorum Communio,* was published in 1927, when he was only twenty-one years old.[7] The formidable Protestant theologian Karl Barth (who would later become a close colleague) called this ecclesiology a "theological miracle."[8] This was followed two years later by a second dissertation, *Act and Being*.[9] The arguments in each are complex and beyond this short treatment to summarize. But they introduce Bonhoeffer's theological approach to understanding Christ and the church as being in dynamic interaction. Both here and throughout his later work, his theology is marked by *sociality*: God, Christ, persons, and church-community cannot be understood apart from their being-in-relationship.[10] His ecclesiology does not present an invisible or abstract understanding of the church, nor a transcendent Christ who is pure being apart from acting. Rather the church, for Bonhoeffer, is how Christ is present and knowable in the world ("in the concrete" was a recurring phrase in his work). Christ is in

---

[6] Ferdinand Schlingensiepen, *Dietrich Bonhoeffer 1906–1945,* trans. Isabel Best (New York: T&T Clark, 2010).

[7] Dietrich Bonhoeffer, *Sanctorum Communio: A Theological Study of the Sociology of the Church,* trans. Reinhold Krauss and Nancy Lukens (Minneapolis, MN: Fortress, 1998).

[8] This is an oft-cited quote by Barth, who was generous in his praise of Bonhoeffer (see *Church Dogmatics* 4.2, 533 and 3.4, 4). This particular quotation is believed to have originated in a private conversation. See Matthew Puffer, "Dietrich Bonhoeffer in the Theology of Karl Barth," Christ College Faculty Publications 52 (2014), n. 33, scholar.valpo.edu/cc_fac_pub/52.

[9] Dietrich Bonhoeffer, *Act and Being: Transcendental Philosophy and Ontology in Systematic Theology*, trans. H. Martin Rumscheidt (Minneapolis, MN: Fortress, 1996).

[10] Clifford Green, "Human Sociality and Christian Community," in *The Cambridge Companion to Dietrich Bonhoeffer,* ed. John W. de Gruchy (Cambridge: Cambridge University Press, 1999), 113–133.

relationship with us, and we are in the church-community with each other in ways at once human and tangible, divine and demonstrable.

As sophisticated as this early ecclesiology of the young theologian was, it came from a rich theological imagination rather than lived experience. Bonhoeffer was not so active in the state-supported Lutheran church growing up. As he matured, his understanding of the church was challenged by experiences that pushed him to refine his ecclesiology. Although the basic concepts presented in *Sanctorum Communio* and *Act and Being* remained defining themes throughout his work—namely, the intimate dynamic of Christ and church in concrete historic context—his ecclesiology changed as it was confronted by the human realities he encountered and the cognitive dissonance it created.

ECCLESIOLOGY AND THREAT

The old community organizing axiom asserts that in order to successfully mobilize people, you need a *villain* and a *victim*. A threat (represented by a villain) must exist to clarify that which is good (represented by an innocent victim) and where the boundaries of the community lie. Bonhoeffer's ecclesiology evolved in relationship to, and was enlivened by, threats encountered by the church to its integrity and existence in the context of Nazism. Despite the well-argued ecclesiology presented in *Sanctorum Communio* and *Act and Being*, Bonhoeffer's tone was decidedly academic; he was in dialogue with philosophy, theology, and the social and psychological theories prevalent in the academy of his day. His early appropriation of the "concrete" notwithstanding, Bonhoeffer's understanding of the church was not drawn from experience. It was only when he came to Union Theological Seminary in New York City in 1930–1931, where he encountered the Abyssinian Baptist Church in Harlem (led by the venerable Adam Clayton Powell, Sr.) that Bonhoeffer's ideas evolved. As he participated in this prominent African American congregation his ecclesiology matured. Here was a congregation threatened by poverty, racism, and violence, yet empowered and joyful in lively worship. Their hope and identity was grounded in their reliance on God. Their "Black Jesus" permeated their sense of identity and agency in the world. The suffering precipitated by external threats animated by white supremacy, from hunger to lynching, did not drain this congregation but defined them as a people of Jesus, who shared in their suffering and gave them life.[11]

Other critical experiences of threat in Bonhoeffer's life contributed to the evolution of his thinking regarding the questions, "Who is Christ

---

[11] Reggie L. Williams, *Bonhoeffer's Black Jesus: Harlem Renaissance Theology and an Ethic of Resistance* (Waco, TX: Baylor University Press, 2014).

for us today?" and "What is the church?" When he returned to Germany in 1931, fascism was on the rise. Shortly after Hitler became Chancellor on January 30, 1933, the totalitarian Nazi regime moved to dominate every aspect of society, including the church.[12] Within the Protestant church, a group called the German Christians developed nazified ecclesiology and theology and sought to infiltrate and dominate churches so that they would align themselves with Nazi ideology. Their efforts generated a backlash within the German Protestant Church, leading to the formation of the Confessing Church, in which the young Bonhoeffer became a central figure. In the spring of 1934, church leaders who opposed the German Christians unanimously approved the Barmen Declaration, a document which became central to the Confessing Church. The Barmen Declaration vehemently and unequivocally denounced the false teachings of the German Christians and asserted the true nature of the church, which owed allegiance only to Jesus Christ, not the *Fuhrer*. The German Christian threat to the very identity and independence of German Protestantism led the Confessing Church movement to establish its boundaries and identity in the Barmen Declaration.[13] Both groups, it should be noted, remained within the German Protestant Church institutionally, but responded to the threat of the state very differently—that is, in terms of compliance or resistance.

In the early years of Nazism, there was an ongoing and contentious battle between the German Christians (who after 1933 held prominent leadership posts in the German Protestant Church) and the Confessing Church. As Nazism tightened its hold on German society, the Confessing Church movement came under growing state pressure. During this period Bonhoeffer became director of one of five underground seminaries of the Confessing Church at Finkenwalde (these seminaries were not recognized by the official Protestant leadership; after 1937 they were banned by the state). Here he was able to move his ecclesiology from the thought experiments of his earlier publications to a social experiment in Christian community: how could "Christ existing as community" be embodied in practice? Ever aware of the looming threats of war and compromise with the German Christian leadership of the church, Finkenwalde was formed as a disciplined community, organized around the daily rhythms of prayer, work, play, and breaking bread, with an intentional balance of solitude and togetherness. Although it drew on monastic models, the purpose of the community was not to be a fortress against the threat of

---

[12] Hitler had signed a Concordat with the Roman Catholic Church on July 20, 1933, ensuring the rights of the Church and its non-engagement with the government.
[13] Victoria J. Barnett, "Transcending Barmen: Confessing in Word and Deed," *Christian Century* 111, no. 16 (May 11, 1994): 495–498.

Nazism that withdrew and isolated itself from the surrounding evil; rather, it sought to prepare seminarians to resist the forces assaulting the church, their country, and those in other countries. Bonhoeffer was intent on forming faithful and courageous Christian pastors who could serve even in the context of Nazism.

The Gestapo closed the seminary in 1937. The following year the Confessing Church unraveled, as half of its clergy took the oath of allegiance to Hitler that Protestant church leadership demanded of all clergy. A number of Bonhoeffer's seminarians were imprisoned during this period for various offenses. In 1939 the vast majority of German clergy and seminarians, including those in the Confessing Church, enlisted to fight in the German army (seeking conscientious objector status was not an option). Of the 181 Finkenwalde students, fifty-two were killed in battle. Bonhoeffer tried to stay in touch with members of the Confessing Church in this diaspora to encourage them in the faith. He also chronicled the experience of Finkenwalde in one of his most beloved books, *Life Together*, a lived ecclesiology.[14]

As any semblance of corporate church-community life became increasingly impossible, and Bonhoeffer's resistance to the morally inverse reality led him into the conspiracy, he did not abandon his core questions. In a letter to his co-conspirators at the end of 1942 he wrote despairingly about what they had lost:

> We have been silent witnesses of evil deeds. We have become cunning and learned the arts of obfuscation and equivocal speech. Experience has rendered us suspicious of human beings, and often we have failed to speak to them a true and open word. Unbearable conflicts have worn us down or even made us cynical. *Are we still of any use?*[15]

Shortly after writing this, he was arrested in April 1943 and spent the next two years in prison. As discouraged as he was, he wrote prolifically in prison, particularly in correspondence with his best friend and muse, Eberhard Bethge. He remained realistic about the threat of destruction of human life, including his, which deepened his questions and reflections about the future of the church, as shall be seen. To him, the church-community, as Christ in the world, does not exist in and for itself, but exists for the other—otherwise it is not the church. Bonhoeffer developed this kenotic view of the church in many of his writings. In fact, while in prison in 1944, he continued to wrestle with the nature and meaning of the church, even as the latter was

---

[14] Dietrich Bonhoeffer, *Life Together*, trans. Daniel W. Bloesch and James H. Burtness (Minneapolis, MN: Fortress, 1996).
[15] Dietrich Bonhoeffer, *"After Ten Years": Dietrich Bonhoeffer and Our Times,* ed. Victoria J. Barnett (Minneapolis, MN: Fortress, 2017), 30.

threatened on all sides by violence, coercion, and complicity. If anything, his realistic assessment of threat sharpened and shaped his ecclesiology. Decades later, in a different time and place, contemporary congregations do not feel threatened by the guns of the state, but by those of individuals who are motivated not by a desire for political dominance, but by various types of hatred—racial, religious, sexual, or social. Still, faith communities must adjust their identities and formulate a response.

THE THREAT OF VIOLENCE AND PRACTICE OF SECURITY

This highly selective look at Dietrich Bonhoeffer's ecclesiology is offered as an invitation to consider the role the sense of threat plays in shaping our own lived ecclesiologies. The ways Christians understand the church impacts their agency in engaging the world. As noted earlier, threat is not the only source of lived ecclesiologies, but it is playing an increasingly definitive role.

Working with fellow sociologist David Yamane, I have spent the last several years (2018–2022; paused in 2020 because of the pandemic and resumed in 2022) studying how congregations have responded to the growing sense of threat posed by gun violence, how congregations are conceptualizing safety and security, and how these factors might be contributing to changes in the lived ecclesiologies of congregations.[16] We have conducted ethnographic research in congregations, participated in national training programs for church security teams, and conducted in-depth interviews with clergy in Texas, Pennsylvania, and North Carolina, representing a diversity of religious traditions, contexts, and racial/ethnic identities.

Our studies have revealed a variety of responses among congregations.[17] Many congregations have increased their security systems, although locking doors during worship has been seen as problematic in light of commitments to hospitality. Some have engaged in active shooter training, although others have felt this heightens anxiety and introduces distrust of newcomers. Many have encouraged members to carry guns to worship, usually "concealed," but in some cases open carry; for other congregations, this is antithetical to their mission of peace. Some have organized "security teams," which can participate in the growing number of trainings for volunteer teams. Others have

---

[16] We are grateful to the Louisville Institute for a Collaborative Inquiry Team Grant for our study, "The Body Armor of Christ: Constructing Safety and Security in Communities of Faith," and our two clergy teammates who assisted in our regional research, Rev. Mark Tyler in Philadelphia, PA, and Rev. Kyle Childress in Nacogdoches, TX.

[17] Katie Day and David Yamane, "Body Armor: Constructing Safety and Security in Communities of Faith," presented at Society for the Scientific Study of Religion, Las Vegas, NV, October 26, 2018.

hired professional security teams. Often these steps were the result of congregational discernment or conflict. The particular strategies adopted were impacted by a number of variables, including the congregation's size and resources, its denomination or tradition (and attachment to it), whether it is independent or part of a connectional system, and its demographic makeup (especially racial and socio-economic), regional location, and cultural context.

These ethnographic findings beg for quantitative data, of which relatively little has been collected. There are few published quantitative studies on security in communities of faith, and the ones that exist do not necessarily pose parallel questions, so comparison and corroboration prove to be difficult. Here, I will primarily draw on three recent studies: a phone survey of 1,000 Protestant clergy and 1,002 Protestant churchgoers conducted in September 2019 by Lifeway Research;[18] a multi religious web and mail survey of 1,380 congregations in the spring of 2015 (Scheitle);[19] and finally the 2020 survey of Faith Communities Today (FACT) that received over 15,000 responses from congregations from eighty denominations and four religious traditions.[20] The FACT study also has responses from before and after the March 13, 2020 pandemic shutdown, which had a dramatic impact on religious communities.

Just prior to the shutdown in March 2020, about five out of ten of FACT respondents reported that they were concerned (somewhat or very) about "personal safety and security when you gather."[21] For megachurches in the sample, there was a marked increase in security measures taken pre- and post-2015. This is not surprising given the recent high-profile church shootings. The terror of these atrocities has impacted communities of faith across theological and geographical spectrums. "Church shootings" has joined our lexicon, along with "school shootings," "mall shootings," and "theater shootings"—shocking because these were violations of spaces the public had considered safe.

Still not all congregations responded in the same way or to the same degree. The FACT study reports that only 16% of congregations

---

[18] Aaron Earls, "Most Churches Plan for Potential Gunman, Divided over Armed Congregants," *Lifeway Research*, January 28, 2020, research.lifeway.com/2020/0128/most-churches-plan-for-potential-gunman-divided-over-armed-congregants/.
[19] Scheitle, "Religious Congregations' Experiences."
[20] "FACT 2020 Survey Results," *Faith Communities Today*, faithcommunitiestoday.org/fact-2020-survey/; see especially "FACT 2020 Common Questionnaire," 7–8, faith communitiestoday.org/wp-content/uploads/2021/10/FACT-2020-Common-Questionnaire-Frequencies.pdf.
[21] This breakdown of the data pre- and post-pandemic shutdown was provided by the Principal Investigator, Scott Thumma, in an email to the author July 31, 2023, and cannot be viewed in the FACT 2020 survey results.

are not at all concerned about safety and security,[22] a proportion also reflected in the Lifeway Research data. These we described as the "do nothing" response. The unimaginable was kept at a distance in the congregational narrative: "It could never happen here." Whether this came out of a belief in the absolute protection of God's people by God, or an exceptionalist rationale that the victims were of a different race, religion, denomination, or from a different region of the country, it served to insulate the congregation from a sense of threat and fear. Hence this group did not take any precautionary measures. For example, one Mainline Protestant minister in Texas reported that his congregation was "completely unaffected" by the horrific shooting in Sutherland Springs, only fifteen months earlier and just four hours away. On the other hand, they did have their historic building evaluated by the Red Cross for tornado-readiness, which was a bigger concern.[23]

Other congregations did take actions in response to a growing concern about safety, but not uniformly so. Scheitle found a correlation between fear levels and experience. That is, those groups more likely to have been victimized by violent crimes, hate crimes (including vandalism), and threats communicated by mail, email, or phone had an understandable fear of future crime. Jews, Muslims, and African American Protestants were much more likely to have been victims of violence, have higher levels of fear than other Christian and nontraditional groups, and take action to prepare against future threats.[24] Interestingly, the "liberal nontraditional" category which included Unitarian Universalists, for example, also reported higher incidents of threats and religious violence. Scheitle suggests that this could be the result of controversial public stands, such as on LGBTQ issues.[25] It should be kept in mind that this research was conducted prior to the high-profile shootings in Charleston and Sutherland Springs, which heightened a sense of vulnerability, especially in Christian communities.

Congregations have taken a range of preventative security measures, from the simplest to the most complex (and expensive) technologies and those involving armed protection. In Scheitle's data, respondents were asked about eighteen possible security measures. More than 40% indicated they took four or more of these measures. Again, percentages were higher for Black Protestants (46%), Muslim (66%), and Jewish (72%) respondents than for Protestants as a whole

---

[22] "FACT 2020 Common Questionnaire," 7.
[23] Interview, Nacogdoches, Texas (2/24/19).
[24] Scheitle, "Religious Congregations' Experiences," 108.
[25] Scheitle, "Religious Congregations' Experiences," 105.

(33%) and the overall sample (40%).[26] And again, this was before the wave of high-profile church shootings that began with Mother Emanuel in June 2015.

As concerns began to rise after Mother Emanuel, local law enforcement began consulting with religious groups in their community. In our research, Yamane and I found that often the first thing law enforcement recommended was to lock the doors of the sanctuary during worship. However, for many congregations this simple action presents a theological challenge to the core value of hospitality. One rabbi described to us the elaborate security system in place in his synagogue. On Shabbat, they allowed themselves to be guided by rabbinic teachings prohibiting any sort of barrier for anyone wanting to come to worship. He concluded, "During the week, we are like Fort Knox. But on Shabbat, we are an open book." A critical point in their religious identity conflicted with the very real sense of threat borne out by experience.

In a Protestant congregation we visited, the suggestion to lock doors during worship had provoked a conflict between members who were parents of young children and the growing number of single (and childfree) adults. After prolonged debate and hurt feelings, the parents prevailed, and the doors were locked. The FACT study found that over 60% of houses of worship are not locked during their sabbath services. For those that are, there has been a shift in the last five years. Only 9% locked their doors prior to 2015; that number has more than tripled by 2020 to accounting for 30%.[27] In taking this seemingly simple step, communities of faith have had to negotiate dimensions of their identity and how they understand themselves within their social contexts. Will they "welcome the stranger" or direct their attention to their own security? Küng's statement that the church's "identity exists only in variability, its continuity only in changing circumstances"[28] resonates.

For those with resources, there exist any number of ways to secure buildings, including alarms, security cameras, and centrally controlled window blinds and locks. Data from Scheitle and FACT show that over a third of houses of worship have installed alarm systems. Again, this number has risen significantly post-2015 according to the FACT study. Scheitle's data show that groups more vulnerable to crime have higher proportion of alarms (African American Protestants: 65%; synagogues: 71%). Prior to 2015, about one in five respondents in Scheitle's study utilized security cameras (23% outside, 19% inside, again with higher rates for Jewish and Muslim communities).[29] This

---

[26] Scheitle, "Religious Congregations' Experiences," 110.
[27] "FACT 2020 Common Questionnaire," 8.
[28] Küng, *The Church*, 4.
[29] Scheitle, "Religious Congregations' Experiences," 110.

aligns with the findings of the FACT study: 13% of all-sized congregations had cameras before 2015. After the media coverage of the massacre at Mother Emanuel in June 2015, 25% more installed security cameras, bringing the total proportion of churches having video surveillance to almost 40%.[30] Increasing security measures is an indicator of a growing sense of threat and concern for safety among people of faith. But here the size of the congregation matters. When broken down by the number of worship attendees, the concern grew with size. Only 44% of small congregations (fewer than 50 attendees) expressed safety concerns but as the number of gathered increased, so did concern for safety and security. Over 67% of largest congregations (with over 1,800 in worship) were worried about safety and concern. They also had more resources for security measures.[31]

Technological security strategies can be incorporated unobtrusively in sacred spaces, invisible to those gathered for worship, and do not therefore challenge ecclesial identification with the value of hospitality. They are precautionary responses, but other strategies draw more on human agency, engaging members at a more conscious level. These include active shooter training, having volunteer or professional security guards, and the introduction of guns into the worship space. The worst-case scenario these strategies anticipate is the possibility of an assailant in the sanctuary. In the Lifeway Research survey, 62% of its responding clergy indicated that they have "an intentional plan for an active shooter situation," which could include any one (or more) of these more agentive strategies.[32] Similarly, 57% of the FACT respondents reported that their congregations did have "training on general safety and security."[33] There are a variety of ways an "intentional plan" or "training" could be understood. It could mean that there is an informational sheet in the hymn rack in each pew (much like the safety sheet on airplanes). Some congregations provide training for ushers to be able to respond in case of an emergency. Some have had law enforcement officers do presentations to the entire congregation, or experiential sessions where congregation members walk through how they might respond in such a situation—how to escape, where to hide, when and how to confront a shooter. However, as the plan and training are implemented, there is increased engagement of congregants with their own vulnerability and confrontation with the possibility that the worship space might not be safe.

---

[30] "FACT 2020 Common Questionnaire," 8.
[31] "FACT 2020 Common Questionnaire," 8.
[32] Earls, "Most Churches Plan for Potential Gunman."
[33] "FACT 2020 Common Questionnaire," 8.

A bigger step is the introduction of armed protection, either by professional guards, volunteer security teams composed of congregation members, or the presence of members carrying their weapons during worship. Many congregations have hired professional security personnel or off-duty police officers—6% according to the FACT study, 16% in the Scheitle study, but 29% in the Lifeway Research data (6% police officers, 23% armed private security).[34] Again, the more vulnerable groups were more likely to turn to security guards—African American, Jewish, and Muslim faith communities (Scheitle). The introduction of armed personnel into the worship space to protect attendees might be unsettling, yet the Lifeway Research survey of congregants found that overwhelmingly *armed* security made them feel safer ("slightly more safe," 35%; "much more safe," 37%). There were demographic differences here with non-white respondents feeling less safe but white evangelicals feeling safer. This reflects findings in a growing body of research which show that white evangelicals are more comfortable with guns than other racial and religious groups, as reflected in higher rates of gun ownership and stronger opposition to gun control policies. There are a variety of correlations with their pro-gun orientation, including region of country, worship attendance, economic distress, and understandings of gender and authoritarianism.[35]

In recent years, there has been a dramatic increase in the number of congregations with volunteer security teams—only 13% had them before 2015 but between 2015 and 2020 the proportion grew to 40%.[36] This trend was no doubt abetted by a proliferation of training programs for church security teams. The Department of Homeland Security, FEMA, and the Department of Justice have developed programs for faith communities in the wake of the Charleston church shooting. In the private sector church security training companies have flourished since 2015. A brief Google search identifies dozens of these organizations, with names such as Sheepdog Church Security, Full Armor Church Safety, Ground Operations Development (G.O.D.), Warrior Poet Society, National Organization for Church Security and Safety Management (NOCSSM), and so on. Through conferences and

---

[34] FACT 2020 Common Questionnaire," 8; Scheitle, "Religious Congregations' Experiences," 110; Earls, "Most Churches Plan for Potential Gunman."

[35] See, for example, Daniel Cox and Robert P. Jones, "Slim Majority of Americans Support Passing Stricter Gun Control Laws," *Public Religion Research Institute*, August 15, 2012, www.prri.org/research/august-2012-prri-rns-survey/; F. Carson Mencken and Paul Froese, "Gun Culture in Action," *Social Problems* 66, no. 1 (February 2019): 3–27, doi.org/10.1093/socpro/spx040; Andrew L. Whitehead and Samuel L. Perry, *Taking America Back for God: Christian Nationalism in the United States* (New York: Oxford University Press, 2020).

[36] "FACT 2020 Common Questionnaire," 8.

courses in which members of church security teams may receive certification, the training aims to "harden" houses of worship, considered "soft" targets. One such conference of the NOCSSM held in 2019 (which Yamane and I attended) typified many of the characteristics of these trainings. Participants were overwhelmingly white men, and many (especially the trainers) came from military and law enforcement backgrounds. This lent a paramilitary feel to the training of congregational security teams: discipline was emphasized, and the language used was militaristic. Meetings are "briefings," information is "intelligence," people are "deployed," and so on. Although preparation is supposedly for all types of threats, including weather events, it was the threat of an active shooter that served as the central focus. Conversations about guns permeated the sidebar conversations at the conference, as weapon training sits at the heart of many of these programs. Since the pandemic, many of the organizations have shifted to selling courses online; a few began advertising in-person conferences in 2021, and by 2023 they were back to in-person training conferences.

Theologically, these organizations reflect evangelical leanings, and "protecting the flock" is framed as a *calling*, with speakers referencing biblical characters and images. In fact, the "shepherd" metaphor is commonly used, including referring to protectors as "sheepdogs" who patrol the fold. The "shepherd knows his flock" and needs to be able to identify those who might threaten it. At NOCSSM, church security teams are taught to pick out suspicious persons, those who "Don't Look Right," or "DLRs." Here a particular ecclesiology is being acted out: one in which a sense of threat is reinforced, which leads to an inward focus. This hermeneutic of suspicion toward strangers cultivates fear. "Security" is the result of human agency, aided by weapons.

Besides the security teams, guns are also present in sanctuaries concealed under the jackets and shirt tails (or in purses) of members. In interviews with people of faith, those who said they bring guns to worship also reported that they are used to carrying them throughout the week for protection. This is not seen as in conflict with but rather as an extension of one's personal faith. For example, one lay leader in a large affluent church told me: "God has given me life and he means for me to protect it." His sense of responsibility extended to his family and congregation. When asked if he thought others carried in his church, he said, "God, I hope so!" It is hard to know how many people are "packing in the pews." Most of the clergy Yamane and I spoke with were ambivalent and did not want to know who was carrying. There were of course exceptions: some clergy encourage their members to carry guns as part of their security effort. Robert Jeffress, pastor of First Baptist Church in Dallas, has said the presence of guns in the congregation makes him feel safer. "I'd say a quarter to a half of our members are concealed carry. They have guns, and I don't think there's anything wrong with that."[37] Later, in reference to the possibility of an armed assailant in his church, Jeffress added, "if somebody tries that in our church, they may get one shot off or two shots off, but that's it, and that's the last thing they'll ever do in this life."[38] Still, there is very little quantitative data on carrying in church.

However, if the Lifeway Research data are accurate, Rev. Jeffress is not far off the mark. In their survey, 45% of clergy reported that their security measures included having armed congregation members.[39] There were differences by theological tradition, region, and gender: carrying in the pews was more prevalent among evangelical respondents and in the South and West; male clergy were much more likely to report carrying in worship (50%) compared to female clergy (19%).[40] These trends are reflected in patterns of gun ownership in society at large. We know that men own guns at a higher rate than women, whites more than people of color, Northeasterners have the lowest rate of gun ownership, and evangelicals own guns at a higher rate than Mainline Protestants or Catholics (especially Latino Catholics).[41] In fact, white evangelical gun owners are more likely to carry their guns with them (65%) than gun owners in general (57%).[42] Again, since personal protection is the most cited motivation for owning guns, with two-thirds of gun owners reporting this,[43] this raises the question of who is seen as a threat. Ironically, the populations most vulnerable to violence and having an understandable cause for fear—people of color, women, Jews, Muslims—are the least

---

[37] Charles Marsh, "The NRA's Assault on Christian Faith and Practice," *Religion and Politics,* January 3, 2018, religionandpolitics.org/2018/01/03/the-nras-assault-on-christian-faith-and-practice/.

[38] Marsh, "The NRA's Assault on Christian Faith and Practice."

[39] Lifeway Research, "Pastors' Views on Church Security: Survey of American Protestant Pastors," September 2019, research.lifeway.com/wp-content/uploads/2020/01/Report-Pastors-Security-Sept-2019.pdf.

[40] Lifeway Research, "Pastors' Views on Church Security."

[41] Kim Parker, Juliana Horowitz, Ruth Igielnik, J. Baxter Oliphant, and Anna Brown, "America's Complex Relationship with Guns: An In-Depth Look at the Attitudes and Experiences of US Adults," Pew Research Center, June 22, 2017, pewresearch.org/social-trends/2017/06/22/americas-complex-relationship-with-guns/; Cox and Jones, "Slim Majority of Americans Support Passing Stricter Gun Control Laws."

[42] Kate Shellnut, "Packing in the Pews: The Connection between God and Guns," *Christianity Today,* November 8, 2017, www.christianitytoday.com/news/2017/november/god-gun-control-white-evangelicals-texas-church-shooting.html.

[43] Pew Research Center, "America's Complex Relationship with Guns."

likely to own guns and the most likely to support stronger control on gun ownership.[44]

There are also communities of faith which have neither been unresponsive to the threat of violence, nor turned to some manner of armed security, but have exercised agency in enacting policies in prohibiting guns on their premises. According to the Lifeway Research data, just over one quarter of all congregations (27%) and half of African American congregations reported that they had a no-firearms policy.[45] This did not preclude them, of course, from implementing security measures that would deter violent threats (such as locking doors, installing alarms and security cameras, etc.). For these congregations, guns were simply incompatible with worship. Often there was support for this stance from their denominations and traditional teachings. One Mainline Protestant denomination, the Presbyterian Church (USA), issued attractive posters stating, "No Guns in God's House," displayed at the discretion of individual congregations. Catholic leaders, such as the bishops of the Diocese of Dallas and dioceses of Georgia, implemented such a prohibitive policy locally. In 2019 the Church of Latter-Day Saints issued a policy forbidding carrying weapons onto church property, except for law-enforcement officers. In Texas, however, the burden is put on congregations in countering state law, which permits licensed concealed carry owners to bring weapons into houses of worship. Congregations must post two large signs at each entrance stating that neither concealed nor open carry of guns is allowed in the building. In the context of a strong gun culture such as Texas, for a church to be a gun-free zone is, indeed, a counter-cultural act.

LIVED ECCLESIOLOGIES OF FORTRESS AND HOSPITALITY

The various ways faith communities have understood that which threatens them and how they have responded to such threats has not occurred in a vacuum. Both *threat* and *security* are social constructions in a continual process of being constructed, reinforced, challenged, and reconstructed. They emerge out of lived ecclesiologies—understandings of who we are as a people of faith, where we are located, and how we engage our social context ("the world"). This is at the heart of religious identity which draws on many sources; from history, tradition, and theology, as well as the built environment, experience, and broader social phenomena. Finally, ecclesiology is performed. For example, whether we think of our faith community as "the salt of the earth" or "the city on the hill" will lead

---

[44] Pew Research Center, "America's Complex Relationship with Guns"; Research findings by Ryan Burge, twitter.com/ryanburge/status/1530276523416100866.
[45] Earls, "Most Churches Plan for Potential Gunman."

to different moral orientations and organizational trajectories. For analytical purposes, I would like to turn to two distinct lived ecclesiological models—fortress versus hospitality—recognizing that in human society there are never pure types, and that variations exist within social groups as well as between them. Still, typological models can provide a framework for analyzing lived theological dynamics.

As we have explored, recent high-profile shootings in houses of worship have contributed to how ecclesial communities construct threat. While there have been perceptions of threat in the wider culture fueling fear of the other, this heightened sense of fear has centered on communities of faith—the fear that armed strangers threaten their very existence. In response, congregations have been encouraged by law enforcement and the growing church security training industry to "harden" themselves—that is, fortify themselves against vulnerability.

In his book *Following Jesus in a Culture of Fear*, theologian Scott Bader-Saye argues that fear becomes a moral issue when we allow our sense of threat to shape moral action. This produces alternative "virtues," such as suspicion and pre-emption ("do unto others before they do unto you").[46] This can be seen in congregations in which the avoidance of risk becomes the highest moral good. Whether through self-identified individual "sheepdogs" or armed security teams that verge on the paramilitary, the stated priority is to protect oneself, family, and community of faith. This is seen as a role of sacrificial faithfulness, and occasionally heroism. Stephen Willeford lived across the street from First Baptist Church in Sutherland Springs. On the November morning in 2017 when a gunman entered the sanctuary and murdered twenty-six people and injured twenty others, Willeford confronted the shooter as he went to his car, armed with his own AR-15 semi-automatic rifle. He wounded him, then gave chase until the shooter ran off the road and ended his life. Willeford has been publicly praised as a hero by state and local officials, the media, and the NRA. Heroes symbolize the highest virtues of a social group, and their veneration contributes to the collective narrative of such groups—or for purposes of this argument, their lived ecclesiology.

In "protecting the flock," the boundaries of the community are necessarily defined and limited: who is in and who is out? As NRA leader Wayne LaPierre famously said after the 2012 massacre at Sandy Hook Elementary School in Newtown, CT, "The only way to stop a bad guy with a gun is a good guy with a gun."[47] This phrase is frequently heard in security trainings for faith-based groups. It reflects

---

[46] Scott Bader-Saye, *Following Jesus in a Culture of Fear* (Grand Rapids, MI: Brazos, 2007), 33.
[47] "NRA: Good Guys with Guns Stop Bad Guys with Guns," *BBC*, December 12, 2012, www.bbc.com/news/av/world-us-canada-20817967.

two important values. First, the solution to gun violence is more guns; guns will address our fears even though guns are the source of the threat. The escalation of gun ownership in this country—an arms race, to be sure—has put us far ahead of any other developing country in terms of the number of guns in civilian hands. This flies in the face of reason, however. If guns made us safer, we would be the safest country on earth. Instead, we also lead in the number and rate of gun deaths—in 2021, there were over 48,000 firearm-caused deaths in the US, the greatest proportion of which were firearm-caused suicides.[48] Still, the Lifeway Research study found in their 2019 online survey of Christian laypeople that a majority (73%) reported that seeing uniformed police officers or security guards made them feel "more safe." This was especially true for whites, evangelicals, and those in the south.[49]

The second value is reflected in the clear delineation of "good" and "bad" guys. There is an assumption that those armed in churches are "the good guys." In religious traditions that confess the universality of human moral failing (sinfulness), the uncritical assignment of good to armed protectors remains uninterrogated. This also serves to harden the boundaries with strangers and outsiders, cultivating suspicion as reflected in the code "DLR" (Don't Look Right). While this serves to reinforce the "bonding" social capital within a community of faith, it deteriorates the "bridging" social capital and trust essential to the functioning of society.[50]

In the lived ecclesiology of "fortress," threat is constructed; social walls are built and protected. In this ecclesiology, one's community is privileged over those outside the literal and figurative walls. The focus of concern is the potential danger to one's tribe, not to those who might be at risk or suffering outside one's walls. Bader-Saye summarizes Aquinas's analysis of how fear undermines social solidarity: "When we fear excessively, we live in a mode of reacting to and plotting against evil, rather than actively seeing and doing what is good and right. Excessive fear causes our scope of vision to narrow, when what is needed is for it to be enlarged."[51] To be concerned with one's own safety and that of one's family and congregation is not wrong, but when that concern is narrowly focused, it changes us. Hospitality is

---

[48] John Gramlich, "What the Data Says about Gun Deaths in the US," Pew Research Center, April 26, 2023, www.pewresearch.org/short-reads/2023/04/26/what-the-data-says-about-gun-deaths-in-the-u-s/; Gun Violence Archive, www.gunviolencearchive.org/.
[49] Lifeway Research, "Protestant Churchgoer Views on Church Security: Representative Survey of American Protestant Churchgoers," September 2019, research.lifeway.com/wp-content/uploads/2020/01/Churchgoers-Security-Sept-2019.pdf.
[50] Robert Putnam, *Bowling Alone: The Collapse and Revival of American Community* (New York: Simon and Schuster, 2001).
[51] Bader-Saye, *Following Jesus in a Culture of Fear*, 56.

undermined when the stranger is suspected rather than welcomed. Seeing guns in the sanctuary, knowing that one's pewmates are armed reinforce the operative construction of threat and effect a lived theological understanding of security. Security becomes equated with safety, of which God is not the author; rather, safety is the result of human agency.

Recently, this fortress ecclesiology has responded to unexpected factors. In the early count of FACT's 2020 survey (those who responded before the pandemic shutdown in March of that year), almost 30% of congregations reported that they were concerned about "personal safety and security when you gather." This dropped to 19% later in the year as congregations worshipped remotely.[52] Suddenly, with the pandemic, the threat to congregations was not an active shooter but an invisible virus. After coming back to worship in person, one church member explained why church security was not as big a concern as it had been before the pandemic shutdown: "It sort of fell off our radar. We were more afraid of a virus than a bad guy."[53]

There is a need to materialize a threat, to make the threat tangible.[54] In *The Courage to Be* Paul Tillich argued that humans live with an anxiety about our very existence—an anxiety that renders us helpless because we cannot really contemplate non-existence. We therefore strive to convert this amorphous anxiety into *fear*, whose object can be engaged and overcome.[55] In the same way, "security" seems vague and unknowable, so we move toward *safety* as a more concretized response. During the pandemic the numbers of gun sales spiked—first in March, as anxiety about the unknown became fixated on fears of scarcity, and again in June, as Black Lives Matter marches filled city streets with those protesting the deaths of George Floyd, Breonna Taylor, and others. Both months broke previous monthly records of gun sales.[56] Anxiety focused on fears that could be encountered.

---

[52] "FACT 2020 Common Questionnaire," 7. This breakdown of the data pre- and post-pandemic shutdown was provided by the Principal Investigator, Scott Thumma, in an email to the author on July 31, 2023.

[53] Focus group, congregation in Nacogdoches, TX (4/30/22).

[54] There is a vast literature on fear and its relationship to perceived threat, a survey of which is beyond the scope of this article. It becomes particularly relevant in the field of advertising, for example, as advertisers often tap into anxieties and identify a particular threat and therefore a product that can neutralize the threat. For example, undifferentiated female body anxiety which can be focused on a tangible threat such as offensive body odor or body fat by an advertiser, who has just the product to address that threat.

[55] Paul Tillich, *The Courage to Be* (New Haven, CT: Yale University Press, 1952), chapter 2.

[56] Daniel Nass, "Gun Background Checks Surged to New High in June," *The Trace*, July 1, 2020, www.thetrace.org/2020/07/gun-background-checks-june-record/.

Protestors personified threat, and a majority of gun sales during this period were by first time gun owners.

Now that communities of faith are returning to their sacred spaces to worship, will the fortress ecclesiology be tempered, or will it again focus on potential threats of violence to congregations? With new guns now in circulation, will congregations turn more to armed security strategies? As ecclesiologies interact with a variety of forces in their construction and reconstruction, what changes will emerge? Is it possible that the pandemic will leave us more aware of our vulnerability, more compassionate to those who are suffering, more willing to be open to strangers in our midst?

As the threats under Nazism continued to be horrifically realized—both threats to Jews, Roma, LGBTQ people, the differently-abled, and those who dared to resist, on the one hand, and threats to human rights and values that had made life meaningful—Bonhoeffer continued to contemplate the meaning of the church during his waning days in prison. He described what he called the world "come of age," by which he meant that there had been a turn in society toward science and the logics of the Enlightenment. "Human beings have learned to manage all important issues by themselves, without recourse to the 'working hypothesis: God.'"[57] Religion was no longer needed to make sense of the cosmos, law, or ethics; the role and act of faith had changed. Society had become "religionless." For Bonhoeffer, the church had become a hollow institution weak in its stance against tyranny and even complicit with evil in the interest of its survival. At this point, Bonhoeffer could very well have become a mystic, trying to escape the crumbling of church and society, or bitterly abandoned the idea of church altogether.

Instead, he took up the question of ecclesiology with renewed energy. What is the church in the context of this worldliness? What might a worldly, "religionless Christianity" look like? Unfortunately, he was not able to develop this idea, or if he did in his remaining months in prison, the writings did not survive. In the end, for Bonhoeffer, when all was stripped away, at the core of his theology and ecclesiology was Christ. His ecclesiology, which he had begun to address as a twenty-one-year-old academic in *Sanctorum Communio*, continued to be highly interactive with his Christology as he moved from the abstract to the concrete, in engaging the harsh realities of his time and place. In his posthumously published *Ethics*, he wrote:

---

[57] Dietrich Bonhoeffer, "To Eberhard Bethge, Tegel, June 8 and 9, 1944," in *Letters and Papers from Prison*, trans. Isabel Best, Lisa E. Dahill, Reinhard Krauss, and Nancy Lukens (Minneapolis, MN: Augsburg Fortress, 2010), 425–426.

Jesus was not the individual who sought to achieve some personal perfection, but only lived as one who in himself has taken on and bears the selves of all human beings. His entire living, acting, and suffering was vicarious representative action (*Stellvertretung*). All that human beings were supposed to live, do, and suffer was fulfilled in him.[58]

The same *Stellvertretung*—vicarious representative action—becomes the basis of ethics for the individual Christian as well as the church-community. Even as he had seen the moral decay of the institutional churches in Germany, Bonhoeffer believed Christ continued to be present as the church in ways that transcended structures. In fact, as he had presented in earlier lectures on Christology, Christ is the church:

> I can never think of Jesus Christ in his being-in-himself, but only in his relatedness to me. This in turn means that I can think of Christ only in existential relationship to him and, at the same time, only within the church-community. Christ is not in-himself and also in the church-community, but the Christ who is the only Christ is the one present in the church-community *pro-me*. ... That means he *is* the church-community. He is no longer acting *for* it, on its behalf, but rather *as* it, in his going to the cross, dying, and taking the sins of the church-community upon himself.[59]

In his dark context, existentially aware of threats all around, Bonhoeffer here makes a bold statement about the church: the church is Christ in the world, a lived, even living ecclesiology. If this is true, how do we recognize this? His answer: we must look at reality "from below, from the perspective of the outcasts, the suspects, the maltreated, the powerless, the oppressed and reviled, in short from the perspective of the suffering."[60] In July 1944, he wrote of this perspective to his friend Bethge: "This is what I call this-worldliness: living fully in the midst of life's tasks, questions, successes and failures, experiences, and perplexities—then one takes seriously no longer one's own sufferings but rather the suffering of God in the world. ... This is how one becomes a human being, a Christian."[61] Just as Christ was essentially "the one for others," so too must the church be. In an incomplete outline of a book he hoped to write, he had handwritten an idea he wanted to develop: "The church is church *only*

---

[58] Dietrich Bonhoeffer, *Ethics*, trans. Reinhard Krauss, Charles C. West, and Douglas W. Scott (Minneapolis, MN: Fortress, 1995), 258.
[59] Dietrich Bonhoeffer, "Lectures on Christology," in *The Bonhoeffer Reader*, ed. Clifford J. Green and Michael P. DeJonge (Minneapolis, MN: Fortress, 2013), 274–275.
[60] Bonhoeffer, "After Ten Years," 30.
[61] Bonhoeffer, *Letters and Papers from Prison,* 486.

when it is there for others ..."⁶² It is clear from earlier writings that to be "the one for others" meant far more than just doing charitable acts; rather, it requires radical solidarity with those who are suffering. This was an indictment of much of what he saw of the church. It also represented a stunning hope in Christ's presence in the world.

Bonhoeffer did not live to complete his ecclesiology, but even in its early form, it is antithetical to a lived ecclesiology of fortress. Indeed, even the Confessing Church in its slogan, "Let the church be the church," was a call to separate from a troubled context and withdraw into a fortress of its own making. Bonhoeffer's theology of the church was indeed one shaped by threat—but for Bonhoeffer, the threat was not to bodily existence nor institutional survival. The greatest threat was to the integrity of the church itself. Its purity does not depend on profiling people who "Don't Look Right," but on concrete action in welcome, service, companionship, and presence, especially with those who are suffering. His is an ecclesiology of hospitality that does not privilege one's community, but others. As such, it upholds a hospitality that is not without risk. To press further, in a lived ecclesiology of hospitality, security is uncoupled from physical safety and takes on a deeper meaning, rooted in the community of Christ. A community's identity is not established by exclusion but inclusion. Boundaries are porous and newcomers represent a source of vitality.

Still, decisions about security in the context of an intentional examination of a congregation's identity—who we are and want to be—are not easy ones. Rev. Kyle Childress, pastor of Austin Heights Baptist Church in Nacogdoches, Texas, has led a series of congregational conversations about security over the past several years. In deeply red East Texas, Childress and his congregation find themselves immersed in gun culture, and the massacre of fellow Texas Baptists in Sutherland Springs has intensified their deliberations. Childress writes about a pivotal moment in one church discussion about the risks of hospitality:

> A longtime member stood up and reminded us that the heart of the issue was baptism. "When we are lowered into the waters, the pastor says, 'Buried with Christ in baptism,'" he said. "In other words, our lives are not our own. And when we come up from the waters, the words said are, 'Raised to walk in newness of life.' This is no guarantee of a risk-free life. It's a guarantee that we are not alone when we walk the way of resurrection."⁶³

---

⁶² Bonhoeffer, *Letters and Papers from Prison,* 503.
⁶³ Kyle Childress, "A Texas Church's Real Talk about Guns," *Christian Century,* January 3, 2018, www.christiancentury.org/article/first-person/texas-churchs-real-talk-about-guns.

By clarifying their identity and source of security, Childress and his congregation were able to more fully realize a lived ecclesiology of hospitality and became the only congregation in their city to implement a no-gun policy. The state-mandated signs are imposing but reinforce their sense of who they are: an inclusive congregation which welcomes all but excludes weapons.

Katie Day is a sociologist (PhD, Temple University), theologian (STM, Ethics, Union Theological Seminary), and the Schieren Professor Emerita of Church and Society at United Lutheran Seminary in Philadelphia. She has authored four books including *Faith on the Avenue: Religion on a City Street* (Oxford, 2014) and co-edited four volumes (most recently, *The Routledge Handbook of Religion and Cities* and *The Brill Companion to Public Theology*). In recent years, themes for research and publication have included: religious beliefs and practices around guns, the life and theology of Dietrich Bonhoeffer, religion and the shaping of urban space, public theology and ethics, and methodological approaches to the study of religion. She is ordained in the Presbyterian Church (USA) and currently lives in Maryland.

The Christian Handgun Owner and Just War

Michael R. Grigoni

SOCIOLOGISTS HAVE ESTABLISHED AN INTRICATE LINK between gun ownership and specific forms of Christianity, notably evangelical Protestantism, in US American life.[1] This finding prompts the question: Why do the followers of a crucified savior feel it necessary to have a gun in their lives? To explore this question, I undertook ethnographic fieldwork with evangelical Christian handgun owners in central North Carolina from 2017 to 2019.[2] I sought to develop a Christian ethical analysis of this issue that might be received by Christian handgun owners, making it imperative that I attend to the lived experience of such individuals. Ethnography enabled me to do so, facilitating engagement with a way of being in the world that I found "strange," yet which might, over time, become "familiar"—or at the very least, less strange.[3]

---

[1] See, for example, Stephen M. Merino, "God and Guns: Examining Religious Influences on Gun Control Attitudes in the United States," *Religions* 9, no. 6 (2018): 189; David Yamane, "Awash in a Sea of Faith and Firearms: Rediscovering the Connection between Religion and Gun Ownership in America," *Journal for the Scientific Study of Religion* 55, no. 3 (2016): 622–636. These studies correlate "white evangelical Protestants" (Merino) and "evangelical Protestant affiliation" (Yamane) with higher rates of gun ownership compared to other religious groups. See also Abigail Vegter and Kevin den Dulk, "Clinging to Guns and Religion? A Research Note Testing the Role of Protestantism in Shaping Gun Identity in the United States," *Politics and Religion* 14, no. 4 (2021): 809–824.

[2] During my fieldwork, I engaged in participant-observation and conducted qualitative interviews with twenty-five male Christian handgun owners, the majority of whom identify as white evangelical Protestants. In addition to my research in central North Carolina, I conducted site visits and qualitative interviews at two churches that employ armed church security in Colorado Springs, Colorado, and Dallas, Texas. I also attended the 2018 NRA Annual Meeting, held in Dallas that year. Duke University Campus IRB Protocol ID: 2018-0037 (E0361).

[3] I locate my use of ethnography within a broader turn by Christian theologians and ethicists who employ the method to ground theological reflection in concrete contexts and everyday life. On this turn, see Christian Scharen and Aana Marie Vigen, eds., *Ethnography as Christian Theology and Ethics* (London: Continuum, 2011); Todd Whitmore, "Crossing the Road: The Case for Ethnographic Fieldwork in Christian Ethics," *Journal of the Society of Christian Ethics* 27, no. 2 (2007): 273–294. The language of "strange" and "familiar" derives from the adage that anthropological

While attending a church security workshop at the outset of my research, I met Bill, a white Christian handgun owner and concealed carry instructor who provides armed security at his church on Sunday mornings. During our conversation, he told me he teaches concealed carry "from a Christian perspective" and invited me to take the course. Doing so, I thought, would help me shift from "learning about" to "learning from" an interlocutor—to begin to "know from the inside."[4] A few months later I took the course, journeying deeper into the form of life I sought to understand.

The course did not disappoint. For nearly ten hours one gloomy, wintry Saturday, Bill taught concealed carry in his living room to me and three other students. Framed by Bill's "Christian perspective," the course went beyond the requirements of North Carolina state law, describing how Christian identity and commitment should frame and limit the use of deadly force. This paper opens with a description of Bill's course and then turns to the just war tradition to illuminate what I encountered in Bill and other Christian handgun owners in my fieldwork. I argue that just war can assist Christian ethical reflection on guns as it moves from a descriptive to a normative register, while also helping to make sense of the lived experience of interlocutors like Bill. I then turn to the Deacons for Defense and Justice, an African American self-defense group founded in the mid-1960s that viewed firearms as integral to the advancement of civil rights. I use the Deacons for Defense as a contrastive case study to indicate the limits of just war for closing the gap between description and norm. This paper considers these cases together to advance Christian ethical reflection on guns in a manner that centers and speaks to the lived experience of actual handgun owners while also showing the benefits and limits of using an established Christian ethical paradigm (that is, just war) for doing so. It closes by indicating directions for future research.

A COURSE IN CHRISTIAN CONCEALED CARRY

Seated beneath a wall mounted flat-screen TV, Bill began his concealed carry course by directing our attention to 1 Corinthians 6:12 on a PowerPoint slide: "All things are lawful unto me, but all things are not expedient: all things are lawful for me, but I will not be brought under the power of any." Bill asked us to think about the first clause of the verse: "You may find yourself in a situation where the use of

---

inquiry renders the strange familiar and the familiar strange. See Matthew Engelke, *How to Think like an Anthropologist* (Princeton, NJ: Princeton University Press, 2018), 6.
[4] Tim Ingold, "Knowing from the Inside," in *Making: Anthropology, Archaeology, Art, and Architecture* (New York: Routledge, 2013), 1–15.

lethal force is lawful, but it may not be expedient for you to do so." He then turned to the second clause: "When carrying a concealed firearm, you must not be brought under the power of the bad guy. You cannot allow yourself to be provoked." A new slide appeared, which Bill identified as the course theme: "Your first priority is to not shoot. If you have to shoot, you shoot to stop, not to kill."

We then turned to North Carolina state law, reading portions selected by Bill in preparation for the test that would follow. Most of our time was spent on Article 14 of the North Carolina General Statutes which addresses the use of defensive force: "A person is justified in the use of deadly force and does not have a duty to retreat in any place he or she has the lawful right to be if … he or she reasonably believes that such force is necessary to prevent imminent death or great bodily harm to himself or herself or another."[5] Here Bill tutored us in North Carolina's version of Stand Your Ground, legislation present in some form or another in more than half of states. An extension of the logic of the Castle Doctrine, Stand Your Ground expands the justifiable use of deadly force from private to public space—from one's home to "any place you have the lawful right to be."[6] Prior to 2011, North Carolina state law required citizens to retreat if faced with an attack outside of their home; they are no longer required to do so.

As we read and discussed this statute, Bill offered commentary redirecting us to the course theme. "Don't fall into the trap of thinking that you're supposed to protect everyone," he would say. Or, "Stay out of it if you don't know the full picture," or, "Just because you can doesn't mean you should"—all the while rehearsing 1 Corinthians 6:12 to remind us not to confuse "lawfulness" with "expediency." He used the scriptural metaphor of wheat and chaff to distinguish between those who pursue a concealed carry license for "the right reasons" from those "legally seeking a thrill." His commentary served as a kind of midrash on North Carolina state law, instructing us that shooting to kill should always be a last resort for Christians.

Bill then led us in discussing a series of scenarios involving the use of deadly force drawn from various online news sources. An article headline and body text would flash onto the TV screen and Bill would read the news report in full, pausing to emphasize features such as

---

[5] North Carolina General Statutes, § 14–51.3.
[6] North Carolina General Statutes, § 14–51.3. The Castle Doctrine, rooted in common law, is a legal principle that allows individuals to use force, including deadly force, to defend their home or "castle" from unlawful intrusion, without a duty to retreat. For a discussion of the Castle Doctrine with reference to North Carolina, see Lawrence D. Graham, Jr., "Protecting the Home: Castle Doctrine in North Carolina," *Campbell Law Review* 43, no. 1 (2021): 137–154.

location, time of day, whether innocent bystanders were present, and the moments leading up to the use of deadly force by the intervening shooter. The articles presented a variety of scenarios: "Off Duty Cop Shoots Mall Attacker"; "Church Worker Uses Concealed Handgun to Stop Would-Be Robber"; "Man with AK-47 Targets Texas Waffle House. When Police Arrive, They Find Him Shot in Parking Lot." After each, Bill had us imagine ourselves as the intervening shooter, the supposed "good guy with a gun," asking not only whether we would be justified in shooting according to North Carolina state law, but whether we would be justified according to his principles for Christian concealed carry. The discussion became an exercise in phronesis in light of what we had learned. In most cases, the intervening shooter was not justified in taking the shot according to Bill's principles for Christian concealed carry, even if they were justified by law in doing so.

"What about Stephen Willeford?" I asked him. Just months before, Willeford had intervened with his AR-15 at the 2017 Sutherland Springs church shooting.[7] I was sufficiently familiar with Willeford's story to know that he likely stood as a moral exemplar for Christian handgun owners. "How did it end?" Bill asked me. I described how after firing on the shooter, Willeford pursued him in a high-speed chase which ended with the shooter dead in his vehicle from a self-inflicted gunshot. "Willeford was recently on the cover of an NRA magazine," I added to emphasize that he exemplified the NRA conviction that only a good guy with a gun stops a bad guy with a gun.[8]

Bill surprised me with his impassioned response. "The NRA doesn't get it," he said. "That man would have been in violation of North Carolina law. The shooter was in retreat; he was leaving the scene. And Willeford pursued him by driving above the speed limit, endangering the lives of others in doing so." Struggling to formulate a response, I resorted to jotting Bill's words in my field notebook as the next scenario flashed onto the TV screen.

On my drive home, I found myself equally fascinated and perplexed. Bill's recourse to scripture and his broader understanding of how a Christian should practice concealed carry limited what North Carolina state law declared to be lawful. It called into question NRA dogmatisms about "good" versus "bad guys."

---

[7] Saeed Ahmed, Doug Criss, and Emanuella Grinberg, "'Hero' Exchanged Fire with Gunman, then Helped Chase Him Down," *CNN*, November 7, 2017, www.cnn.com/2017/11/05/us/texas-church-shooting-resident-action/.

[8] See the cover of the January 2018 issue of *America's 1st Freedom* and the corresponding cover story: Mark Chesnut, "I Never, Ever Thought that I Would Be that Guy," *America's 1st Freedom*, January 2018, 32–37.

But perhaps more fascinating, latent within Bill's conception of Christian concealed carry was a form of everyday just war reasoning that emphasized the *jus ad bellum* conditions of just cause, right intention, and last resort. While he framed his course as providing instruction in "defense of the body," he explicitly limited this to "your body, your family's, and the body of Christ," capturing the condition of just cause.[9] His use of the metaphor of wheat and chaff to distinguish between proper and improper motivations for pursuing a concealed carry license reflected the condition of right intention. His repeated emphasis that one's "first priority is not to shoot," and, if possible, to avoid intervention mirrored the condition of last resort. Countering the logic of Stand Your Ground, Christian concealed carriers have a duty to retreat, if possible, when encountering a threat of "imminent death or great bodily harm." For Bill, 1 Corinthians 6:12 places a limit on Stand Your Ground.

In a later interview, Bill shared with me what his spouse and he would do in the case of a home invasion. Even in his home, Bill privileged the *jus ad bellum* condition of last resort. He told me that if an invader were to enter his home, his spouse and he would go into the room containing their gun safe and barricade the door with furniture. With their home alarm sounding, they would then use their landline to call 911. If the invader were to enter the bedroom, Bill would only take the shot as an absolute last resort—to protect his spouse's life or his own—even though North Carolina state law avers that he can do so lawfully as soon as the invader enters the home. Bill emphasized that if the invader were to ransack the home and not try to breach the barricaded room, he would not intervene. He would only defend life, not property. The many layers—physical and psychological—that Bill placed between himself and taking the shot fascinated me. His commitment to last resort limits not only what the law justifies under Stand Your Ground, but also under the Castle Doctrine. His dedication to practicing concealed carry and home security in a manner consistent with his faith leads him not to discriminate between public and private space. In both, Christianity places limits on his use of lethal force.[10]

---

[9] Here, the "body of Christ" refers to the gathered ecclesial body on Sunday morning.
[10] In refusing to discriminate between public and private space regarding his practice of armed self-defense, Bill renders the public-private distinction moot, a distinction presumed by liberal social thought and modern social life. He does so through recourse to divine law, which leads to an interesting—and unexpected—paradox. Against the expectation that he would not hesitate to use his firearms in public and private space and would view North Carolina state law as legally permitting this usage, Bill understands himself to be subject to a higher law, one which he aims to observe in his everyday practice as a religious believer. Theologically speaking, Bill's case is one in which divine law (his understanding of it, at least) trumps human or

CHRISTIAN HANDGUN OWNERSHIP AS STYLE

In Bill, I realized I had encountered something that might deserve to be called "Christian handgun ownership." By this I do not mean someone who is a Christian and owns handguns, but someone for whom Christianity shapes, qualifies, and limits the everyday practices constitutive of this way of being in the world. In Bill's case, this shaping and limiting corresponds to resources in the Christian tradition—namely, just war. But precisely how does Bill display a form of just war reasoning in his practices and self-conceptualizations? And what is the significance of this display? To address these questions, I begin by explaining why I describe Bill as employing an *everyday* form of just war reasoning, and how this generates a particular style of Christian handgun ownership characterized by moderation and reserve.

My use of the term *everyday* modifies what I identify as a form of just war reasoning in Bill's account of Christian concealed carry. In the just war tradition, *jus ad bellum* names conditions that must be satisfied for the resort to war to be just—typically the conditions of just cause, last resort, proportionality, legitimate authority, right intention, and probability of success. *Jus in bello* names conditions necessary for conduct in war to be just—typically the conditions of discrimination (noncombatant immunity) and proportionality.[11] As an everyday form of just war reasoning, Bill's account of Christian concealed carry, as described above, does not employ all of the criteria traditionally identified under the headings of *jus ad bellum* and *jus in bello*. Neither does his account involve a formal or formulaic application of the criteria. Indeed, to look for and expect to find a total or formal usage of such criteria in an everyday mode of just war reasoning is to miss the point. As my ethnographic vignette indicates, Bill's account of concealed carry is animated by a sensibility that emerges from his lived understanding of Christian commitment, and it is this sensibility that has resonances with certain *jus ad bellum* and *jus in bello* criteria. In other words, Bill is not a just war theorist, but a concealed carrier for whom Christianity places a check or limit on his practice in his everyday life.

---

civil law. As such, Bill is not quite the "repugnant cultural other" of left-wing cultural expectation, but something more complex. I draw the phrase "repugnant cultural other" from Susan Harding, who uses it to problematize "modernist presuppositions" regarding the study of particular kinds of cultural "others," such as fundamentalist Christians (on whom Harding has written). See Susan Harding, "Representing Fundamentalism: The Problem of the Repugnant Cultural Other," *Social Research* 58, no. 2 (1991): 373–393.

[11] See Helen Frowe, "The Just War Framework," in *Oxford Handbook of Ethics of War*, ed. Seth Lazar and Helen Frowe (Oxford: Oxford University Press, 2018), 44–58.

Bill's everyday mode of just war reasoning produces interesting—and unexpected—results, particularly in the aforementioned case of the Sutherland Spring church shooting. Bill there distinguished between justifiable and unjustifiable interventions on the part of Willeford. For Bill, Willeford was justified in taking the initial actions that led to the neutralization of the shooter, as the shooter constituted a threat to an ecclesial body at the time of his intervention. To draw on the language of 1 Corinthians 6:12, initially it was both lawful and expedient for Willeford to intervene in the situation with lethal force.

While Bill did not articulate this in terms of just war criteria, the way in which such criteria might be used to justify Willeford's engagement is fairly straightforward. Willeford's initial actions arguably satisfied the *jus ad bellum* conditions of just cause, right intention, proportionality, and last resort, providing partial justification for his decision to engage in the gunfight on just war grounds. Further, once engaged in the gunfight, Willeford satisfied the *jus in bello* conditions of discrimination and proportionality, taking the shot outside of the church rather than in the presence of noncombatants, and proportionally matching the firepower of the shooter with his AR-15.[12]

The remaining *jus ad bellum* conditions of legitimate authority and probability of success require more careful attention. The condition of legitimate authority must be considered in light of Willeford finding himself in a situation in which the police had not yet arrived, and in which he had sufficient reason to believe that death or great bodily harm had already been caused. As such, Willeford was justified in taking upon himself the police function of the state, serving as a legitimate authority given the absence of the state. Regarding the latter condition, it would have been nearly impossible for Willeford to determine his probability of success given the circumstances. His decision to intervene was based on limited information: sonic data (the sound of gunfire) and testimony (his daughter's description of seeing "a man wearing black tactical gear at the Baptist church").[13] He did not know whether the shooter was acting alone or with a partner or team, nor did he have a sense of the shooter's proficiency with firearms. All said, it is unlikely that one can ever achieve epistemic confidence about one's prospects for success in such a situation. The psychological and physiological pressures experienced by those

---

[12] Willeford's taking the shot outside of the church was more a matter of circumstance than intention, as the shooter "emerged from the church" as Willeford approached the building. Michael J. Mooney, "The Hero of the Sutherland Springs Shooting Is Still Reckoning with What Happened That Day," *Texas Monthly*, November 2018, www.texasmonthly.com/articles/stephen-willeford-sutherland-springs-mass-murder/.

[13] Mooney, "The Hero of the Sutherland Springs Shooting."

involved, combined with the need to respond quickly to mitigate injury and loss of life, do not accommodate making the kinds of calculations necessary for satisfying this particular *jus ad bellum* condition. Intellection must at some point give way to muscle memory and willful determination. Still, the scale tips toward Willeford's initial intervention being both lawful and expedient, all things considered.

For Bill, Willeford was not justified in carrying out the actions that followed—namely, pursuing the shooter in a high-speed chase. He cited three reasons for the unjustifiability of doing so: the shooter was in retreat and no longer constituted a threat; the pursuit required that Willeford, a civilian, break the law by driving well above the speed limit; and the pursuit could have harmed or killed innocent bystanders. In just war terms, the shooter no longer posed a threat, arguably dissolving the emergency that earlier gave Willeford just cause to use lethal force and take up the police function of the state. In threatening innocent bystanders during the chase, Willeford violated the *jus in bello* condition of discrimination.

Again, while Bill did not formally cite the criteria of *jus ad bellum* or *jus in bello* in his analysis of the Sutherland Springs church shooting, his analysis resonates with the just war tradition in terms of what I identify as an everyday form of just war reasoning. Bill arguably challenges a vision of handgun ownership marked by masculinist, heroic excess.[14] For Bill, there are limits on the degree to which the citizenry can take up the police function of the state. If one does so, preserving the ability to discriminate between an unjust aggressor and innocent noncombatants is of paramount importance. Further, Bill understands that the distinction between good guys with guns and bad guys with guns is not a Manichean one. Against the NRA dogmatism that only a good guy with a gun stops a bad guy with a gun, Bill exhibits a more sophisticated anthropology, one that is theologically-oriented, cognizant of the human potential for sin. Bill recognizes that good guys with guns have the potential to become bad

---

[14] This is not to say that Christian handgun owners do not participate in and reinforce patriarchal gender norms. In accord with the findings of sociologist Angela Stroud, many of my interlocutors described their reasons for engaging in concealed carry because of a responsibility they feel as husbands and fathers to protect their families, and others, more advanced in age, described firearms as a way of compensating for decreased physical ability, again in terms of this responsibility. For my interlocutors, guns can thus be understood as enabling the performance of a kind of "hegemonic masculinity," a culturally-recognized masculine ideal that, in virtue of its contrast to the gendered expectations of women and marginalized men, legitimizes patriarchy. See Angela Stroud, *Good Guys with Guns: The Appeal and Consequences of Concealed Carry* (Chapel Hill: University of North Carolina Press, 2016).

guys with guns absent the kinds of checks encapsulated in his usage of 1 Corinthians 6:12.

Theological anthropology aside, Bill's vision of Christian concealed carry is characterized by a sensibility of reservation and restraint. Recall the portion of the concealed carry course in which Bill led his students in a discussion of real-life cases drawn from various news sources of civilians using their guns to intervene in active shooter scenarios. While many of these uses were lawful according to North Carolina state law, Bill emphasized their inexpediency, concluding that non-intervention would have been a better choice more consistent with a Christian approach to concealed carry. For Bill, the threshold that must be satisfied for Christian concealed carriers to be justified in employing lethal force is high, not low. For him, Christian concealed carry is characterized by avoidance, moderation, and restraint.

CHRISTIAN HANDGUN OWNERS AS CHRISTIAN-PROTECTORS

Compared to my other interlocutors, Bill stands as the paragon of Christian handgun ownership as I have characterized it. But as my fieldwork came to reveal, many of my interlocutors enact modes of handgun ownership in which their Christian commitment places a check or limit on their practice—whether in terms of refusing to conceal carry in church despite feeling a desire to do so, choosing instead to trust in the efforts of the security team during worship; carrying a concealed firearm only when accompanying one's dependents; or refusing to see themselves as what sociologist Jennifer Dawn Carlson calls "citizen-protectors." In what follows, I characterize the citizen-protector model of handgun ownership and contrast it to that of my interlocutors, which I call the Christian-protector model.

Jennifer Dawn Carlson develops her account in *Citizen-Protectors: The Everyday Politics of Guns in an Age of Decline*, an ethnography of gun carriers conducted in the postindustrial contexts of Detroit and Flint, Michigan.[15] Through interviews and participant-observation with white and African American gun owners, Carlson describes how men employ guns in response to social precariousness and economic insecurity in ways that cut across racial divides. She argues that the use of guns in these contexts affects "the reformulation of citizenship to center on policing and protection," generating a class of citizens for whom "the act of killing to protect oneself and others [is] morally just, warranted, and respectable."[16] Combined with the liberalization of

---

[15] Jennifer Dawn Carlson, *Citizen-Protectors: The Everyday Politics of Guns in an Age of Decline* (New York: Oxford University Press, 2015).
[16] Carlson, *Citizen-Protectors*, 19.

firearm laws initiated by the lobbying efforts of the NRA—namely, the shift from may-issue to shall-issue systems for concealed carry licensing from the 1970s to the 2000s, to the more recent extension of the "No Duty to Retreat" doctrine from private to public space via Stand Your Ground laws[17]—the failure of the state to provide security for its citizens in Detroit and Flint generates a form of armed citizenship in which "gun carriers use firearms to actively assert their authority and relevance by embracing the duty to protect themselves and police others."[18]

The way in which this policing by civil initiative manifests among Carlson's interlocutors is, at times, dramatic and disturbing. Carlson opens *Citizen-Protectors* with two such examples. She tells the story of Corey, a white man who, while working the register at a corner store in Flint, shot and killed an African American man who brandished a weapon while demanding money of him; and Jason, an African American man who, while open carrying in Detroit at night as a means of deterring crime, was stopped by the police but eventually let go, leading bystanders to cheer and celebrate him.[19] These examples illustrate how a citizen-protector orientation to guns can take shape in everyday contexts. They also help indicate the similarities between my interlocutors and Carlson's subjects. Not unlike my interlocutors, Carlson's subjects turn to handguns in response to a felt ethical demand that extends beyond personal self-defense; they respond to this demand in an embodied way, cultivating a lived relationship between their bodies and their firearms; and they engage in armed practices as ordinary citizens in their everyday lives. The key difference, however, lies in the citizen-protector's embrace of policing as a civic duty—an embrace rejected by many of my interlocutors. Recalling Bill's usage of 1 Corinthians 6:12, even when lawful, policing as a generalized civic duty rarely presents itself as expedient.

How might we draw out this contrast further? If the armed embodiment of citizen-protectors is characterized by a civilian form of policing, we might say that citizen-protectors adopt a centrifugal orientation. Directed outward rather than inward, all of space serves as a theater for policing for them. Further, all bodies, not simply those to whom they stand in a relationship of familial or ecclesial kinship, can serve as an object of protection, as citizen-protectors do not discriminate between those bodies they are willing to defend. In contrast, my interlocutors eschew the policing orientation of citizen-protectors. Theirs is a centripetal orientation in which they discriminate between those bodies for whom they feel themselves to

---

[17] For a fuller discussion of these shifts, see Carlson, *Citizen-Protectors*, 5–6.
[18] Carlson, *Citizen-Protectors*, 10.
[19] Carlson, *Citizen-Protectors*, 1–4.

be responsible—their own, their family's, and their church's body—and those for whom they do not. This places constraints upon the kinds of spaces in which they engage in practices of protection. As described above, this posture is characterized by moderation and restraint, animated, at times, by what I call an everyday form of just war reasoning.

To press the contrast even further, it is worth reviewing an earlier article by Carlson, in which she draws on Foucault's account of governmentality and sovereign power to argue that citizen-protectors are best theorized as "sovereign subjects," exercising via guns "sovereign functions (particularly the execution of lethal and legitimate violence) that the state has typically monopolized."[20] Because of the state's inability to secure the common good of the citizenry in contexts of social decline (like Detroit), the sovereign subject finds itself legitimated *de facto* in taking up policing as civil initiative. Further, state-level legislative shifts establishing that citizens no longer have a duty to retreat in public space (Stand Your Ground Laws) legitimate *de jure* the exercise of this political subjectivity. Decentralized through processes of governmentality, sovereign power flows through these members of the citizenry, the full manifestation of which is disciplinary control over individual bodies according to a logic of "take life or let live" (as in the case of Corey).[21]

Again, my interlocutors reject the notion that their practice of concealed carry requires that they embrace a duty to protect or police others in general. Instead, they restrict this responsibility to their own bodies, the bodies of their family members, and their ecclesial body. Regarding their own body, even this is sometimes called into question: several interlocutors told me that if they were not fathers, they would not own firearms or conceal carry; they only do so to increase their chances of surviving a gunfight in order to stay alive and continue providing for their family. If they truly functioned as highly-localized manifestations of sovereign power, my interlocutors would not restrict the range of bodies they would be willing to defend. They recognize that the state continues to have a monopoly on violence. Put in just war terms, they recognize the state as the primary bearer of legitimate authority.

Further, in describing their motivations for practicing concealed carry or serving on their church's security team, my interlocutors often cited themes of protection, service, and care, linking these themes to their vocation as Christian men. A megachurch security team leader

---

[20] Jennifer Dawn Carlson, "States, Subjects, and Sovereign Power: Lessons from Global Gun Cultures," *Theoretical Criminology* 18, no. 3 (2014): 336.
[21] Michel Foucault, *"Society Must Be Defended": Lectures at the Collège de France, 1975–76* (New York: Picador, 1997), 241.

repeatedly used the phrase "protector" to describe himself during our interview, saying he has a "protector's heart" because God "designed" him that way. He described the challenges of keeping a volunteer security team in place: "It's boring as hell out here. You show up, drink your coffee, get bored and quit. It takes a particular individual to be a protector if that's who God created you to be." Regarding the familial body, many of my interlocutors told me that they see the protection of their families as integral to their role as fathers. Whether in relationship to their familial or ecclesial bodies, my interlocutors consistently frame their sense of obligation with reference to vocation and care.

For these reasons, I name the posture taken up by my interlocutors the Christian-protector model of handgun ownership in contrast to the citizen-protector model.[22] And if my interlocutors are best understood as Christian-protectors who see handgun ownership and concealed carry as a mode of care, and at times frame this mode of care in reference to an everyday form of just war reasoning, then further engagement with the just war tradition illuminates even more the practices and self-conceptions of my interlocutors. I turn now to a particular trajectory within the tradition as it manifests in the work of Augustine and Paul Ramsey—the trajectory that conceptualizes war, when justified, as an expression of charity. I argue that Augustine and Ramsey crystalize the resonances between my interlocutors and just war, as they and my interlocutors see justified violence as coterminous with charity.

CHRISTIAN-PROTECTORS AND THE JUST WAR TRADITION

Among Christian theologians, Augustine is one of the earliest to draw charity and rightly-intended violence together. He does so by granting the intentionality of the human person, expressed in the faculty of the will, paramount importance in his moral and political thought. For Augustine, rightly-ordered intention indicates a proper ordering of loves, evincing the presence of *caritas* in the individual. Alternatively, disordered intention indicates a disordered self whose loves are governed by *cupiditas*.[23] Love and intention cannot be disassociated in Augustine's anthropology, as love names that toward

---

[22] As described earlier, I engaged in participant-observation and conducted qualitative interviews with twenty-five male Christian handgun owners. Consequently, questions may emerge regarding the generalizability of my claims concerning the Christian-protector model of handgun ownership given my sample size. Nevertheless, it is important to recognize that this is a feature, not a bug, of qualitative research methodologies such as ethnography, which center long-term, relational modes of inquiry with human populations. I anticipate that my theoretical proposals will be tested and explored in other locales and within other communities of faith.

[23] Augustine, *On Christian Doctrine*, 3.16.

which the human person wills or intends, whether positive or negative.[24] As developed in *The City of God*, this applies to communities as well: if a society is ordered or disordered, it is because of what it loves.[25]

Because the human person is defined by its loves, intentionality serves as a linchpin in Augustine's moral theology. The moral valence of an action is, most fundamentally, a matter of the actor's intention.[26] Unsurprisingly, then, intention determinatively shapes how Augustine differentiates between just and unjust forms of violence. Following Ambrose, Augustine did not approve of killing in self-defense in private contexts, breaking with the Greco-Roman consensus that both individual and social bodies have the right to defend themselves via the principle of self-preservation.[27] For Augustine, intentionally killing in self-defense is driven by self-love and is thus disordered, as love of self rather than love of neighbor occupies the actor's intentionality under such circumstances. Intentionally killing in self-defense is thus never admissible under the scope of charitable action.

Yet Augustine held that soldiers participating in a just war kill without sin if they maintain right intention while doing so. While war is rendered just if the sovereign who wages it does so with right intention and for a just cause, the just participation of the soldier varies from individual to individual depending on whether he remains ordered by charity while soldiering. If he does so, abstaining from "the desire to do harm, cruelty in taking vengeance … fierceness in rebellion, the lust for domination, and anything else of the sort"—what Augustine calls the "things that are rightly blamed in war"—he serves as a rightly ordered instrument of the sovereign who, in waging a just war, does so in obedience to God.[28] Warring in this way, then, whether from the throne or the ground, renders killing coterminous with charity. As such, just wars serve as implements by which the earthly city sustains a degree of tranquility, keeping the *libido dominandi* in check through coercive love.

---

[24] "A righteous will, then, is a good love; and a perverted will is an evil love" (Augustine, *The City of God against the Pagans*, trans. R. W. Dyson [Cambridge: Cambridge University Press, 1988], 14.7).

[25] Augustine, *The City of God*, 19.24.

[26] See, for example, Augustine's discussion of pride and charity in *Ten Homilies on the First Epistle of John*, 8.9, or his treatment of the intent to deceive regarding lying in *The Enchiridion*, 18; *Against Lying*, 18. In the case of lying, the intent to deceive destroys the concord between the heart and the mouth required for truthful speech, rendering what is spoken duplicitous.

[27] See, for example, Augustine, "Letter 47 to Publicola."

[28] Augustine, *Answer to Faustus, a Manichean (Contra Faustum Manichaeum)*, trans. Roland Teske, SJ, in *The Works of Saint Augustine: A Translation for the 21st Century*, vol. I/20, ed. Boniface Ramsey (Hyde Park, NY: New City, 2007), 22.74; see also *The City of God*, 1.21.

Here, Augustine draws charity and war together, establishing what would become a central trajectory of the just war tradition, the leitmotif of which is that recourse to, and participation in, legitimate violence should be directed by and infused with love. While this generates a paradox for many modern readers of Augustine, it does not for my interlocutors, who would agree with Augustine that rightly-intended violence can be an expression of love. Just as Augustine centers the *jus ad bellum* criteria of right intention in his account of justifiable violence, so do my interlocutors in their self-descriptions. Bill, for example, privileged right intention during his concealed carry course, arguing that only those seeking to engage in practices of protection on behalf of the vulnerable should pursue a concealed carry license, not those "legally seeking a thrill." During an interview, a pastor told me the importance of having a vetting process when building a volunteer church security team, indicating that certain individuals may not be emotionally mature or stable enough to handle the responsibility. Only those whose intention is rightly oriented—or whose loves are properly ordered, to use Augustine's language—should be granted the responsibility of enacting care on behalf of one's familial and ecclesial bodies.

Among twentieth-century advocates of just war, Paul Ramsey best exemplifies this Augustinian linking of war and charity. Against Reinhold Niebuhr's Christian realism which sees love as an "impossible possibility," Ramsey sought to base Christian ethics wholly on love—specifically, the love command as it appears in scripture.[29] He does so by resourcing the notion of covenant—the relationship formed by God with humanity as manifested in the history of Israel and the ministry of Jesus.[30] Through this covenant, humanity is invited to respond to God's initiating expression of agape with love of neighbor. Contra Niebuhr's uncoupling of love and justice, covenant enables Ramsey to reconcile love and justice, as justice flows from the human community's adherence to God's covenant-making by following the love command.[31] With respect to war, the

---

[29] This is not to say that love is irrelevant for Niebuhr. As exemplified by Jesus, the "love ideal" remains "unattainable" yet "useful" insofar as it provides humanity with "an absolute standard by which to judge both personal and social righteousness," and a possibility toward which to "strive." See Reinhold Niebuhr, *Love and Justice: Selections from the Shorter Writings*, ed. R. B. Robertson (Louisville, KY: Westminster John Knox, 1957), 33, 38.

[30] Ramsey most prominently develops the notion of covenant in *Basic Christian Ethics* (New York: Scribner, 1950) and *Christian Ethics and the Sit-In* (New York: Association Press, 1961).

[31] In Ramsey's final words in *Basic Christian Ethics* the Niebuhrian friction between love and justice finds its synthesis and resolution: "These two are, in fact, the same

differences between Niebuhr and Ramsey on war could not be starker. For Niebuhr, war is justifiable insofar as it leads to the restoration of justice.[32] For Ramsey, war can be morally right in and of itself, not simply in terms of its ends, when waged in love of neighbor.[33]

Despite these differences, Ramsey remains a Niebuhrian regarding the unattainability of embodying Jesus's ideals. Ramsey understands Jesus's specific teachings, such as the Beatitudes, to be "thoroughly eschatological" in nature, not fully realizable prior to Christ's return.[34] In reference to Matthew 5:5 where Jesus says, "Blessed are the meek: for they shall inherit the earth," Ramsey writes:

> Jesus was not so *naïve* as to suppose that by the *power* of their meekness the meek would sooner or later inherit the earth. To be realistic about the forces which triumph in the present age, if the meek ever inherit the earth, the not-so-meek would promptly take it away from them. Meekness and inheriting the earth are entirely separate matters; only the approaching kingdom brings them into connection.[35]

Thus, while the "personal ethic" of Jesus might emphasize nonresistance and nonviolence, Ramsey diminishes the importance of this ethic for Christians today, classifying it as part of Jesus's "apocalyptically derived strenuous teachings."[36] He argues that Jesus's teachings and example can alternatively be understood as privileging a "preferential ethic of protection" for one's neighbor.[37] Further, when practiced on behalf of one's neighbor, this preferential ethic of protection accommodates coercive and violent forms of resistance. Protecting the innocent from harm, in other words, even to the point of killing an unjust aggressor, is not contrary to this alternative ethic for Ramsey; in fact, such interventions constitute one way of fulfilling the love command in the time of the *saeculum*,

---

thing: obeying the covenant and doing justice, love for neighbor and fulfilling the law" (388).

[32] For his classic articulation of this position, see Reinhold Niebuhr, "Why the Christian Church is Not Pacifist," in *Christianity and Power Politics* (New York: Scribner's, 1940), 1–32.

[33] Ramsey develops his critique of Niebuhr in *War and the Christian Conscience: How Shall Modern War Be Conducted Justly?* (Durham, NC: Duke University Press, 1961) where he states that the "technical political reason" of Christian realism has led Protestant ethics into a "wasteland of utility" (6).

[34] Ramsey, *Basic Christian Ethics*, 26.

[35] Ramsey, *Basic Christian Ethics*, 26.

[36] Ramsey, *Basic Christian Ethics*, 169–170.

[37] Ramsey, *Basic Christian Ethics*, 166–71.

whether in everyday interpersonal contexts or the theater of interstate war.[38]

Regarding interpersonal contexts, Ramsey—in contrast to Augustine—even permits that the use of lethal force for personal self-defense will, in certain cases, be congruent with the love command. Recall that for Augustine (and Ambrose), private self-defense is not admissible under the scope of charitable action as the use of lethal force to protect one's life is driven by love of self and thus disordered. Ramsey takes Augustine to task on this point, saying that "Ambrose and Augustine doubtless need to be criticized for their rather unqualified acceptance of public protection and also for their complete rejection of private self-defense."[39] He argues first that Augustine fails to recognize that the motivations governing interstate warfare is often likely driven by "collective egoism" and "self-interest."[40] To make a sharp distinction between personal and state-centric contexts in this regard is to fail to recognize that the disordering of loves runs up the scale, from individual persons to collectivized ones. Second, since love functions as an absolute moral norm for Ramsey, and since "a Christian does whatever love requires ... the possibility cannot be ruled out that on occasion defending himself may be a duty he owes to others."[41] Thus, while for Ramsey the love command does not sanction recourse to lethal force for personal self-defense in each and every case, neither does it propel him toward the opposite Augustinian extreme. As the servant of love, the Christian stands in an ambiguous space, one in which the Christian ethic of protection may justify such recourse under particular circumstances.

In short, Ramsey legitimates the use of force, coercive and lethal, according to his Christian ethic of protection. Such uses are most clearly expressive of love when exercised on behalf of the vulnerable in a manner proportionate to the threat, whether in the localized contexts of everyday life, or the global theater of international affairs. In doing so, Ramsey draws the use of force under the scope of love's actions. Herein lies the connection with my interlocutors, for whom the omnipresent threat of encountering an active shooter renders certain bodies particularly vulnerable within their phenomenal field—their familial and ecclesial bodies, as well as their own. Their firearms-related practices constitute a way of responding to the felt ethical demand to defend these bodies. In Ramsey's language, my

---

[38] See, for example, Ramsey, *Basic Christian Ethics*, 165. Ramsey develops this view more fully in *The Just War: Force and Political Responsibility* (New York: Scribners, 1968).
[39] Ramsey, *Basic Christian Ethics*, 175.
[40] Ramsey, *Basic Christian Ethics*, 175.
[41] Ramsey, *Basic Christian Ethics*, 176–77.

interlocutors understand themselves to be enacting a Christian ethic of protection as part of their vocation as husbands, fathers, and community members. Hence the security team leader who understands himself to be a protector, to be driven by a "protector's heart," or the pastor who views armed church security teams to be a necessary tool against potential threats to the gathered ecclesial body.

Further, just as for Ramsey the demands of neighbor love may at times legitimate the use of lethal force in personal self-defense, my interlocutors similarly frame their firearms-related practices with reference to the obligations they have toward their dependents. As one interlocutor described,

> I have to survive for my kids at my age. You know, it's imperative that I survive. It would be devastating for them if I died. But, if they were grown, then it's different. I can see myself not concealed carrying when they're grown. Because I don't care if I get killed. I'm going to heaven. I don't care.

We thus find, even here, clear echoes of Ramsey's sanction of private self-defense in light of the duties we have to others.

Let us review the ground covered. I have argued that my interlocutors are best characterized as Christian-protectors who take up a centripetally-oriented posture with their guns, rather than as citizen-protectors who adopt a centrifugally-oriented posture of policing. In doing so, I have resisted moves that would reduce my interlocutors to a class of "repugnant cultural others," characterizing them as modest regarding their firearms practices, tempering, in this way, their "strangeness." In arguing that they at times employ an everyday form of just war reasoning, I have woven them into the Christian theological tradition via just war, seeking also in this way to make them "familiar."[42] In identifying resonances between Augustine, Ramsey, and my interlocutors, I have tightened this weaving, showing that my interlocutors—and the Christian-protector orientation, more broadly—can be situated within the trajectory of the just war tradition that sees rightly intended violence as expressive of charity. In our politically polarized times, this framing takes seriously the lived moral experience of my interlocutors and those who turn to guns in response to such felt ethical demands.

Yet to stop here would be to leave several things unaddressed. To turn to these things and gesture toward the inability of the just war tradition to close the gap between description and norm regarding guns in the United States, I consider the manifestation of an ethic of

---

[42] On the "repugnant cultural other," see fn. 10. On the language of "strange" and "familiar," see fn. 3.

protection among African Americans during the civil rights era: the case of the Deacons for Defense and Justice, an African American self-defense group founded in the mid-1960s that viewed firearms as integral to the advancement of civil rights. Turning to this example enables me to highlight the similarities between my interlocutors and the Deacons for Defense and Justice through the prism of the just war tradition. Both forms of armed embodiment find justification under the just war trajectory considered above, particularly in terms of Ramsey's agapic-oriented preferential ethic of protection. Yet just war fails to account for the morally significant differences between my interlocutors and the Deacons for Defense and Justice, which suggests we must ultimately look beyond the just war tradition to develop a Christian ethics of the gun.

THE DEACONS FOR DEFENSE AND JUSTICE

As narrated by Nicholas Johnson in *Negroes and the Gun: The Black Tradition of Arms*, guns have served as a key implement in African American efforts at communal self-determination throughout US history.[43] The role played by firearms in such efforts, argues Johnson, is not so variant or haphazard to be beyond characterization; rather, it is constitutive of a tradition—a "black tradition of arms." Key to this tradition is the manner in which it "elevates and enshrines the distinction between self-defense against imminent threats and organized political violence seeking group advancement."[44] Broad in scope, Johnson's account discusses a multitude of figures and cases to show that, from the antebellum period to the civil rights era, the use of firearms by African Americans has privileged individual and communal self-defense rather than initiatory political violence.[45]

---

[43] Nicholas Johnson, *Negroes and the Gun: The Black Tradition of Arms* (Amherst, NY: Prometheus, 2014).

[44] Johnson, *Negroes and the Gun*, 58.

[45] Of course, the history Johnson narrates was not free from internal controversy regarding the tension between recourse to firearms for self-defense versus organized political violence. But this is precisely what is to be expected of tradition. Here I follow Alasdair MacIntyre, who defines tradition as "an argument extended through time in which certain fundamental agreements are defined and redefined in terms of two kinds of conflict: those with critics and enemies external to the tradition who reject all or at least key parts of those fundamental agreements, and those internal, interpretative debates through which the meaning and rationale of the fundamental agreements come to be expressed and by whose progress a tradition is constituted" (*Whose Justice? Which Rationality?* [Notre Dame, IN: University of Notre Dame Press, 1988], 12). In the black tradition of arms, African Americans negotiated their relationship to firearms (a set of social practices) in the context of a white supremacist society ("critics and enemies external to the tradition") and in relationship to each other ("internal, interpretative debates") in light of the goods toward which firearms-

Significantly, Johnson emphasizes that armed self-defense was not only essential for African Americans, given the ongoing threat of racialized violence, but often embraced by African Americans alongside "political nonviolence without any sense of contradicttion."[46] As such, *Negroes and the Gun* stands among recent efforts to contest accounts of the civil rights movement as strictly pacifist, arguing that the success of the movement depended, in part, upon the presence of and occasional recourse to firepower.[47]

Among the cases Johnson considers, The Deacons for Defense and Justice (DDJ) provide a key example for reframing the reflections developed thus far in this paper.[48] Founded in 1964 in Jonesboro, Louisiana, and spreading soon thereafter to Bogalusa, Louisiana, and later to Mississippi and Alabama, the DDJ was an African American armed community defense group that first emerged in response to the intimidation and terrorization of civil rights activists by the Ku Klux Klan, oftentimes with police support. Among its earliest efforts, the DDJ protected Congress of Racial Equality (CORE) activists who moved to Jonesboro in the summer of 1964 in order to "test" illegal segregation laws.

Shortly after their arrival, the CORE activists moved into a home—the Jonesboro "Freedom House"—quickly becoming a target of the Klan, which "regularly fired into the air around the house, shot through its windows, or drove by shouting threats."[49] Their organizing efforts were likewise met with Klan harassment. As a result, a coterie of African American men led by Earnest "Chilly Willy" Thomas began to guard the Freedom House and accompany CORE activists while they carried out their organizing work throughout Jonesboro. At first, Thomas and his group provided security without firearms, but that soon changed. As the summer progressed, "police and Klan harassment of CORE workers became routine," enflaming tensions between the Klan and Jonesboro's white police force, on the one hand,

---

related practices were oriented (whether survival, the advancement of civil rights, etc.).

[46] Johnson, *Negroes and the Gun*, 13.

[47] See also Charles E. Cobb, Jr., *This Nonviolent Stuff'll Get You Killed: How Guns Made the Civil Rights Movement Possible* (New York: Basic Books, 2014); Christopher B. Strain, *Pure Fire: Self-Defense as Activism in the Civil Rights Era* (Athens: University of Georgia Press, 2005); Lance Hill, *The Deacons for Defense: Armed Resistance and the Civil Rights Movement* (Chapel Hill: University of North Carolina Press, 2004). Like Johnson, Cobb also characterizes the role of "armed self-defense [in] black struggle" as a "tradition" in *This Nonviolent Stuff'll Get You Killed*, 1–2.

[48] In addition to Johnson, I also depend upon Cobb's account of the DDJ, which he develops in "Standing Our Ground," in *This Nonviolent Stuff'll Get You Killed*, 187–226, and Hill's *The Deacons for Defense*.

[49] Cobb, *This Nonviolent Stuff'll Get You Killed*, 196.

and CORE activists and the black community, on the other.[50] Concealed carry became a regular feature of the guardians' methods.

One evening in late July, an "assistant police chief led a fifty-car Ku Klux Klan caravan through [Jonesboro's] black neighborhood ... [which] threw leaflets denouncing the "outside agitators" and desegregation efforts in Jonesboro."[51] Following this, an armed white mob of more than one hundred men assembled at the jail where CORE organizers were being held. This brazen display by the Klan "convinced many folk of the need for something more systematic than the ad hoc decisions of black men," planting the "seed" for the DDJ.[52] With the encouragement of CORE's Charlie Fenton, the DDJ were "formally incorporated" in early January of 1965.[53]

As Johnson and Cobb describe, Fenton played a pivotal role in helping set the terms of the collaboration between CORE and the DDJ. Despite CORE's Christian pacifist roots and commitment to nonviolent direct action, the events of summer 1964 indicated to CORE activists the danger of living and carrying out their organizing efforts in Jonesboro without the support of armed security. Yet the DDJ could not adopt CORE's philosophy of nonviolent direct action. A compromise was struck, in which the two groups would remain distinct from each other but work side-by-side, with the DDJ "standing on the sidelines and stepping in if someone threatened to harm the nonviolent activists."[54] CORE activists thus continued with nonviolent direct action and the DDJ with practices of armed self-defense, providing security for CORE as they carried out their work, establishing a division of labor that benefitted both groups. While Fenton hoped that the DDJ would eventually relinquish their use of guns, he said, with regard to Jonesboro, "No one can tell what would have happened here if the Deacons hadn't formed their own ideas of protection."[55] The result was a "movement that combined nonviolent struggle and armed self-defense to protect that struggle."[56]

This said, Johnson argues that as the DDJ expanded their chapters and membership, their practices pressed deeper into the "boundary-land" between self-defense and organized political violence, generating fierce criticism from opponents to the civil rights movement, and ambivalence, as well as critique, from those within

---

[50] Cobb, *This Nonviolent Stuff'll Get You Killed*, 199.
[51] Cobb, *This Nonviolent Stuff'll Get You Killed*, 199.
[52] Johnson, *Negroes with Guns*, 271.
[53] Cobb, *This Nonviolent Stuff'll Get You Killed*, 201.
[54] Cobb, *This Nonviolent Stuff'll Get You Killed*, 197.
[55] Fenton in Cobb, *This Nonviolent Stuff'll Get You Killed*, 202.
[56] Cobb, *This Nonviolent Stuff'll Get You Killed*, 212.

it.[57] Aware that the DDJ threatened coalitional support for the civil rights movement, Martin Luther King, Jr., would aver in 1965 that

> The line of demarcation between aggressive and defensive violence is very slim. The Negro must have allies to win his struggle for equality. And our allies will not surround a violent movement. What protects us from the Klan is to expose its brutality. We can't outshoot the Klan. We would only alienate our allies and lose sympathy for our cause.[58]

The catalyst for this statement was the 1965 shooting of Alton Crowe, a white man, by Deacon Henry Austin during a protest march in Bogalusa, Louisiana—a case showing that "the boundary against political violence was not really a line so much as it was a minefield, a zone of dangerous decision making where individual exigencies crashed into the long-term strategies and aspirations of the group."[59] And yet King, as if to prove his initial point, had according to FBI reports the DDJ in his employ the following year while delivering a speech in Chicago.[60] If these reports are to be believed, then even King navigated these debates with the assistance of prudence rather than principle alone, recognizing that prudential judgment may sometimes side with armed self-defense given the goods which the civil rights movement aimed to secure.

Despite these tensions, the DDJ provide a compelling example of the black tradition of arms, one in which a communal recourse to guns privileged armed self-defense rather than organized political violence. Defensive rather than initiatory and retaliatory violence served as the Deacons' north star. In just war terms, the philosophy and practices of the Deacons emphasized right intention on the part of their members. Further, the Deacons aimed to serve the vulnerable neighbor in their midst. While the DDJ did not legitimate themselves in reference to the just war tradition, nor in reference to the Christian theological tradition more broadly, their practices find justification under the trajectory of just war reasoning considered in this paper, particularly in terms of Ramsey's preferential ethic of protection. Not unlike my interlocutors, the DDJ constitute a class of "protectors" or "just warriors," who, through a communally-oriented mode of armed embodiment, engaged in a form of care for the vulnerable neighbor.

---

[57] To draw again upon MacIntyre, this is to be expected of tradition—in this case, the black tradition of arms—which negotiates itself with reference to external critics and internal debates. See fn. 45.
[58] King in Johnson, *Negroes and the Gun*, 282.
[59] Johnson, *Negroes and the Gun*, 281.
[60] Johnson, *Negroes and the Gun*, 282; Hill, *The Deacons for Defense*, 231–32.

DISCRIMINATING BETWEEN TRADITIONS OF DEFENSE

If both the DDJ and my interlocutors find justification when considered through the lens of Ramsey's agapic-oriented account of just war, how might we make sense of the obvious differences between these two orientations? First, both the DDJ and my interlocutors engage in a traditioned mode of inquiry regarding the role of firearms in their everyday practices. While the forms of debate and discernment in the black tradition of arms, particularly during the civil rights era, were more centralized than the forms engaged in by my interlocutors, both can be understood as engaging in "an historically extended, socially embodied argument," one in which the goods constitutive of the tradition, and the practices and virtues necessary for achieving those goods, undergo recurring evaluation, negotiation, and adjustment.[61] The DDJ engaged in this work within their chapters and in relationship to broader national debates about the role armed self-defense should play in advancing civil rights, and the relationship of armed self-defense to nonviolent direct action. My interlocutors do so in the context of their churches and families, discerning communally—albeit in highly-localized contexts—the role firearms should play in their domestic and ecclesial environs. Further, one might discern structural similarities in the importance of figures like King and Williams, and the positions they embodied and inspired in the lives of everyday African American gun owners, with the role played by figures like Willeford in the lives of my interlocutors. Each of these figures represents the codification of a particular philosophy and posture regarding how to practice—or not to practice—armed embodiment in one's everyday life. As archetypes or moral exemplars, they direct how everyday subjects understand and negotiate their own practices within the tradition of armed embodiment they occupy, tradition here conceptualized as an historically extended and socially embodied process of discernment and negotiation.

Yet the historical antecedent of the black tradition of arms marks the key difference between these traditions. The original wound from which the black tradition of arms emerges, and to which it responds, is America's original sin: the wound of chattel slavery and its afterlives in the US American context. The black tradition of arms is preceded by a historical evil that made it practically impossible for the victims of chattel slavery to uphold a distinction between defensive and retaliatory violence. Regarding the kinds of violence engaged in by enslaved Africans against their masters, Johnson writes, "Many acts of resistance defy rigid boundaries, demonstrating both a personal fight against the immediate violence of slavery and a political

---

[61] Alasdair MacIntyre, *After Virtue: A Study in Moral Theory* (Notre Dame, IN: University of Notre Dame Press, 1981), 222.

resistance against the slave system. The black tradition of arms grows out of this milieu."[62] Accordingly, the distinction between armed self-defense and organized political violence prized by the tradition was hard-won. It could only emerge with slavery's abolition, as slavery itself constituted "a state of war."[63]

Beginning with the antebellum period, however, the constitution of African Americans as a people comes to have promise in the US. Under these circumstances the distinction between armed self-defense and organized political violence emerges and eventually becomes codified. Given the possibility of encountering racialized violence in their everyday lives, recourse to armed self-defense by African American individuals and communities becomes prudentially sound, as the state either would or could not intervene in time on behalf of African Americans, regardless of its claim to support the dignity and rights of its African American citizenry. Recourse to armed self-defense served as a way of responding to disparities in power given the legacies of oppression African Americans faced. As such, it served as one instance among many in which African Americans could engage in the practice of "forming a people as a response to powerlessness."[64] The black tradition of arms thus names a particular democratic practice by which African Americans have sought to form themselves into a "nation within a nation" in response to the white supremacist forces and legacies that seek to deny African Americans their individual and collective personhood.

The tradition and practices of my Christian handgun-owning interlocutors do not emerge from this kind of wound. Rather, my interlocutors take up a posture of armed embodiment in response to the specter of the active shooter—a potential future violence. This suggests it is worth contrasting these traditions of defense in terms of their temporal orientation. My interlocutors inhabit a temporal imaginary charged with the anticipation of violence, an imaginary directed toward a horizon that may one day be irrupted by an active shooter situation. The black tradition of arms, in contrast, is temporally hemmed in on both sides, emerging from racialized violence while ever-facing the possibility of encountering such violence again. It is a tradition and set of practices taken up in both the aftermath and anticipation of violence.

Further, while the specter of the active shooter gives the sense of precariousness felt by my interlocutors a certain omnipresence, as an active shooter can be encountered in any space at any time, throughout

---

[62] Johnson, *Negroes and the Gun*, 32.
[63] Johnson, *Negroes and the Gun*, 58.
[64] Luke Bretherton, *Christ and the Common Life: Political Theology and the Case for Democracy* (Grand Rapids, MI: Eerdmans, 2019), 82.

its history the black tradition of arms has had to respond to a threat exponentially more dangerous. Whether in terms of community-organized racial terror (e.g., the Ku Klux Klan) or state complicity with such terror (in which those charged with protecting citizens—the police—permit or assist in the carrying out of such terror), the black tradition of arms emerged in response to a living and actual omnipresent threat of racialized violence in every aspect of African American everyday life, not one more penumbral in quality. To render these traditions morally equivalent is to fail to attend to this set of crucial differences.

CONCLUSION

Here appear the shortcomings of the just war tradition: despite providing a language by which to describe the orientation of the DDJ and my interlocutors in terms of a preferential ethic of protection, just war fails to attend to contextually significant factors that must be considered when reflecting upon the moral import of these traditions, practices, and forms of life. In other words, while just war—particularly the trajectory that places justified violence under the scope of charitable action—assists in framing the lived experience of the DDJ and my interlocutors in a Christian ethical register, it cannot close the gap between description and norm regarding the place of guns in the United States. Other approaches are needed. Where do we go from here?

While several possibilities exist, I will name two which I aim to develop in future work on this topic: a liberationist approach that centers in its analysis those who suffer the brunt of firearm-caused death and injury in the United States; and an approach that turns to just peacemaking theory given the shortcomings identified here regarding just war. Ultimately, this paper has been ground-clearing in nature—to show that the just war tradition can assist Christian ethical reflection on guns as it seeks to render descriptive claims about Christian handgun owners in a Christian ethical register, one countering the stridency that marks the debate about guns in the United States by displaying the texture and complexity of my interlocutors' lived experience. Just war helps us attend to the moral dimensions of this lived experience and how my interlocutors use guns to respond to a felt ethical demand regarding those they perceive to be vulnerable to harm. But the discovery of faithful, hopeful, and loving judgments regarding guns in the United States requires that we ultimately look beyond the tradition in the ways intimated above. **M**

Michael R. Grigoni is Assistant Professor in the Department for the Study of Religions at Wake Forest University, where he teaches courses in religion, politics, and the history of Christianity. His current project explores the relationship of guns to American Christianity and is based on fieldwork he carried out with Christian handgun owners and Christian anti-gun violence activists in central North Carolina. He holds a PhD in Religion from Duke University.

Christian Arguments for Gun Violence Prevention: Reflections on Moral Claims in the Context of Advocacy

Ellen Ott Marshall

I AM STANDING OUTSIDE A MASSIVE WOODEN DOOR IN THE marble hallway of Georgia's state capitol building with four other women in red t-shirts. The woman in charge of our group is reading notes about the representative we are getting ready to visit during Advocacy Day for Moms Demand Action for Gun Sense in America. She tells us his party affiliation and what he has voted for and against recently, and then she says: "Oh, he's active in his church. He's … um … Methodist." Another woman in the group enthusiastically chimes in: "Well, Ellen should lead this one. She teaches at a Methodist seminary!" All heads swivel to me and nod their encouragement. Doubtful I could make the impact they hoped, I respond, "Well, given how conservative he is, I doubt a liberal female professor would be our strongest way to start." It was a persuasive point, and one of our more seasoned legislative advocates took the lead in speaking with the administrative assistant who graciously received our materials and told us that the representative was currently out of the office.

A few weeks after Advocacy Day, I was sitting in a Starbucks in midtown Atlanta with two women from our group and two other women who were joining us for the first time. We listened as a Moms Demand Action volunteer explained to us that this chapter of Moms is interested in developing an interfaith dimension. "We need to involve the religious community," she said. She told us a story about faith leaders in another state who took a visible stand against open carry legislation there. "The vote went through anyway, but it was important to have religious leaders speaking out against it." Together, we brainstormed a list of Jewish, Christian, and Muslim leaders vocal about gun reform who could be effective partners.

I have been an occasional volunteer with Moms Demand Action since 2014. I have attended meetings of two chapters in the Atlanta area, signed petitions, made phone calls, mailed postcards, sent emails, and participated in public events like Advocacy Day, demonstrations, and vigils. In 2018, I conducted text and web-based research for an article that explored Sara Ruddick's maternal thinking in connection with Moms Demand Action and Mothers of the Movement.[1] One of my observations was an apparent disconnect between the secular, policy-oriented language of the organization and the presence of spirituality and faith in the stories told by survivors and volunteer orientation. I had been considering a deeper dive into the religious worldviews of volunteers, but Advocacy Day and the Starbucks conversation prompted me to revise my plans.

I settled into my identity as a volunteer with expertise in Christian moral argumentation rather than a researcher gathering data on the religious views of others. That turn produced this article. The first part of the article describes two places where Christian moral arguments surface in the context of gun violence prevention advocacy. The second part of the article considers three dominant arguments that surface to varying degrees in these contexts of activism: the sacredness of all life, the sin of idolatry, and a call to nonviolence. Running through these arguments are references to vulnerability that, I argue, bring significant moral confusion. Is vulnerability something to be redressed as a social problem, accepted as existentially inevitable, or embraced as a sign of faithfulness? The third part of the article returns to the contexts of activism to introduce a third space, the vigil. In the vigil, the moral arguments continue to surface, but one also finds a practice that clarifies the moral confusion over vulnerability. When participants in the vigil read the names of victims and hear the stories of survivors, we are reminded that gun violence prevention necessitates a distinction between actual vulnerability to gun violence, existential vulnerability as finite creatures in a fragile creation, and a virtuous vulnerability that voluntarily assumes risk as a sign of faith in God. The vigil not only reminds participants of these distinctions, but holds those vulnerable to gun violence at the center of concern around which one organizes a moral and political response that approaches vulnerability as a problem to address and not a virtue to commend.

CHRISTIAN MORAL ARGUMENT FOR GUN VIOLENCE PREVENTION: CONVEYANCE AND CONTENT

This descriptive portion of the article considers Christian moral arguments for gun violence prevention that surface in two places. "The Presser" refers to public events in which high profile religious leaders lend their voice to the cause of gun violence prevention. "The PDF" refers to the many downloadable resources from denominational

---

[1] Ellen Ott Marshall, "Maternal Thinking in US Contexts of Gun Violence and Policy Brutality," *Journal of the Society of Christian Ethics* 40, no. 2 (2020): 363–379.

bodies and religious organizations intending to equip Christians to study, pray, and act. I offer one example of a press event and a few examples from the PDF category before turning to three arguments that run through them.

The Presser

On May 12, 2020, Everytown for Gun Safety issued a press release to announce an "initiative with faith leaders and faith organizations across the country who are pledging to mobilize faith communities to elect gun sense candidates up and down the ballot in the 2020 elections."[2] The press release included quotes from eighteen individuals described as available to speak to the press. The list included clergy well-known for activism related to gun violence and police brutality, prominent evangelical leaders, representatives of peace groups from the Protestant mainline and Catholic social justice traditions, and victims/survivors. They represent the wide-ranging coalition that organizations hope to achieve as leaders with different theological orientations find enough common ground to exercise their influence on behalf of the cause.[3]

The press release featured a variety of activist Christian clergy, ordained ministers from across the theological spectrum recognized as leaders in current social movements. Four of these clergy leaders represent Black church traditions. Reverend Michael McBride ("Pastor Mike") is the Lead Pastor of The Way Christian Center in Berkeley, California. As the Director of the Live Free Campaign of Faith in Action, he focuses on "addressing gun violence and mass incarceration of young people of color."[4] Reverend Traci Blackmon rose to national prominence during the Ferguson protests. Serving then as Senior Pastor of Christ the King United Church of Christ, she joined the protests, hosted and moderated meetings between activists and police, and remains a sought-after speaker for The Movement for Black Lives. In December 2020, she left Christ the King to serve full time as executive minister of Justice and Witness Ministries for the UCC.[5] Reverend Jason Carson Wilson is also a minister in the United Church of Christ. As founding director of the Bayard Rustin Liberation Initiative, he focuses on "angelic troublemaking that helps create a just world for same-gender loving people of color and

---

[2] Everytown for Gun Safety, "Everytown Announces New Initiative with Interfaith Leaders and Organizations to Mobilize People of Faith around Gun Safety in 2020," May 12, 2020, everytown.org/press/everytown-announces-new-initiative-with-interfaith-leaders-and-organizations-to-mobilize-people-of-faith-around-gun-safety-in-2020/.
[3] While the list also includes Jewish, Muslim, and Hindu leaders, I am only naming the Christians given the focus of this article on Christian activism and arguments.
[4] Pastor Mike McBride, "About," pastormikemcbride.com/about.
[5] Christ the King UCC, "Our Ministers," ctk-ucc.org/about-us.html.

LGBTQIA people of color."[6] Reverend Sharon Risher was serving Rice Chapel AME church as Associate Pastor for Congregational Care when she received the call that her mother, two cousins, and a childhood friend had been killed at Mother Emmanuel African Methodist Church in Charleston, South Carolina, on June 17, 2015.[7] She published a book about her experience and is an outspoken advocate for gun reform and against the death penalty.[8] She is one of the national spokespeople for Everytown USA and Moms Demand Action for Gun Sense in America.

Everytown's initiative also included three white men whose names regularly appear in materials and gatherings about gun violence prevention now: Shane Claiborne, Rob Schenck, and Michael Austin. I draw from the writing of Claiborne and Austin and will introduce them later in this article. Rob Schenck was an outspoken leader of the pro-life movement whose journey to extend his pro-life position to nonviolence and gun control is chronicled in the documentary *Armor of Light*. In the documentary and his speaking and writing, Schenck frames gun reform as the faithful and reasonable thing to do, given the sanctity of life and the data on gun violence. In his quote for the press release, he referenced Isaiah 1:18, saying, "God invites us to reason with Him" and "use our capability to develop reasonable policies and practices when it comes to firearms." He insisted that we "honor the Creator of us all" by identifying and pursuing "common-sense gun regulations."[9]

Everytown also included two people who represent long-standing peace groups in the mainline Protestant and Catholic social justice traditions. Reverend Deanna Hollis was ordained in the Presbyterian Church USA as a gun violence prevention minister in July 2019.[10] She serves as the Gun Violence Prevention Ministry Coordinator with Presbyterian Peace Fellowship, which produced one of the most robust PDF resources we will consider in the next section. Johnny Zokovitch became the executive director of Pax Christi in August 2019. Pax Christi is a fifty-year old peace, justice, and nonviolence organization "grounded in the Gospel and Catholic social teaching."[11] His quote for the press release integrated moral value and legislative

---

[6] Bayard Rustin Liberation Initiative, "Mission, Vision, and Purpose," angelictroublemakers.org.
[7] Sharon Risher, "Sharon Risher Speaks," sharonrisherspeaks.com/bio.
[8] Sharon Risher and Sherri Wood Emmons, *For Such a Time as This: Hope and Forgiveness after the Charleston Massacre* (Des Peres, MO: Chalice, 2019).
[9] Everytown, "Everytown Announces New Initiative."
[10] Leah Asmelash and Katherine Dillinger, "The Largest Presbyterian Denomination in the US Has Ordained a Minister of Gun Violence Prevention," *CNN*, July 30, 2019, cnn.com/2019/07/30/us/gun-violence-prevention-minister-deanna-hollis-trnd.
[11] Pax Christi, "Our Vision," paxchristiusa.org/about/our-vision/.

appeal: "At the heart of Catholic social teaching is the fundamental belief in the dignity of every human being—that each and every person is sacred, a creation of God. ... It's time we honor the dignity of our children by putting concrete action behind all those 'thoughts and prayers.'"[12]

Participating in this kind of initiative and the publicity surrounding it is not new for these Christian leaders. They are regularly in front of cameras, offering interviews and editorials, and speaking to fellow Christians through the lens of the media in order to advocate for this cause and others as well. In the context of "the Presser," their aim is to persuade fellow Christians to join the effort for legislative or electoral change. They do so by highlighting the alignment between core Christian values and the aims of the organization. The quotes confirm that reducing gun violence is a faithful expression of Christian commitments to uphold dignity, love the neighbor, exercise God-given reason, and affirm the value of human life. These leaders are performing the function that the Moms Demand Action volunteers in Starbucks hoped for: demonstrating Christian support for gun violence prevention and persuading more Christians that this legislative activity is the faithful and moral thing to do.

The PDF

I offer "The PDF" as the label for a second space where we find Christian moral arguments in the context of gun violence prevention. This space includes resources prepared by ecclesial bodies and faith-related organizations intended to help Christians study, pray, and act. There are many. "The Gun Violence Congregational Toolkit" prepared by Presbyterian Peace Fellowship (PPF) is a particularly robust example of this genre. Not a denominational entity, PPF is "a wide network of peacemakers" who strive to be "movers and shakers within the PCUSA and beyond."[13] The Toolkit is divided into three sections that reflect the study, pray, act approach. Section one, "Educational Resources," begins with pages of suggestions for documentaries, films, study group materials, articles, and books. It then provides a six-session study guide using *America and Its Guns* by Rev. James Atwood, a Presbyterian minister and long-time gun violence prevention advocate. This six-session study guide is followed by a five-session curriculum created by Reverend Margaret Leonard and revised by the PPF Gun Violence Prevention Working Group. This curriculum emphasizes basic knowledge about the availability of guns in US society, focuses on firearm-caused suicide, and concludes

---

[12] Everytown, "Everytown Announces New Initiative."
[13] Presbyterian Peace Fellowship, "Our Mission," presbypeacefellowship.org/about/.

with a review of gun violence prevention statements passed by the General Assembly of PCUSA.

The second section, "Pastoral Resources," begins with materials intended to help congregations and pastors deal with trauma and the aftermath of community violence. It then provides a list of "Scripture Passages for Addressing Gun Violence" and a list of "Hymns Relating to Gun Violence." Before listing additional worship resources, the Toolkit includes a link to a resource for dealing with conflict in the church. "Seeking to Be Faithful: Guidelines for Presbyterians in Times of Disagreement" was created by the Presbyterian Peacemaking Program (a denominational entity), adopted by the General Assembly in 1992, and has been available ever since as a resource for congregations experiencing conflict due to social issues or congregational processes. The Worship Resources begin with a "Sample Vigil to Comfort Those Who Grieve," created by Reverend Margaret Rossi and drawing on resources from the "God not Guns" program of the Brady Campaign to Prevent Gun Violence. The Toolkit also includes a "Litany on the Tragedy of Gun Violence" and pastoral care resources related to mental health, suicide, and "supporting those who grieve."

The third section, "Take Action," includes materials, suggestions, and concrete instructions for making public the church's gun violence prevention work. This includes signs that declare the church a gun-free zone, buttons, logos, prayer cards, and bookmarks listing action steps. The Toolkit also offers instructions for letter-writing campaigns, information about other forms of nonviolent direct action, and materials for voter education and election advocacy. Ten pages of this "Take Action" section include case studies from Presbyterian congregations describing the actions and programs taken to prevent gun violence in their local communities. The Toolkit concludes with another five pages listing state and national organizations that are part of the gun violence prevention network.

Other Protestant denominations have similar materials available online, and the US Conference of Catholic Bishops and Pax Christi have a number of statements and resources on their respective websites as well. For example, the USCCB created and posted a "Backgrounder on Gun Violence" in January 2020, titled "A Mercy and Peacebuilding Approach to Gun Violence," which references relevant pastoral letters and statements and lists legislation and programs the US Bishops have supported to reduce gun violence.[14]

---

[14] United States Conference of Catholic Bishops, Department of Justice, Peace, and Human Development, Office of Domestic Social Development, "A Mercy and Peacebuilding Approach to Gun Violence," January 2020, usccb.org/resources/backgrounder-gun-violence-mercy-and-peacebuilding-approach-gun-violence-january-2020.

One of the most oft-cited documents in the list is the 1994 Bishops Statement, "Confronting a Culture of Violence: A Catholic Framework for Action." In its six parts, this statement follows the pattern of other ecclesial materials. It describes the problem of violence at all levels of society, locates a foundational claim from the tradition in which to anchor the call for action ("respect for life"), puts forth a framework for action, recognizes the work being done, and calls the church to more. In keeping with the emphasis on the sacredness of life, the Bishops insist that "respect for human life is the starting point for confronting a culture of violence."[15]

"Confronting a Culture of Violence" was cited most recently in a statement to Congress from four US Bishops in the wake of the Uvalde School shooting in May 2022. In their June 3 letter, the Bishops write: "There is something deeply wrong with a culture where these acts of violence are increasingly common." Citing Pope Francis's call to "say 'no more' to the indiscriminate trafficking of weapons," the US Bishops call for background checks, extreme risk protection orders, a ban on assault weapons, and programs to strengthen mental health services.[16] This statement stands in a tradition of letters from US Catholic Bishops (at state and federal levels) calling for reasonable and effective legislative change to reduce gun violence. Indeed, the USCCB website, which houses all of these statements confirms an observation by Thomas Reese in a recent editorial: the US Catholic Bishops have a "strong and comprehensive position on gun control" and yet it remains a secret. "Bishops rarely talk about it. Catholics don't hear about it from the pulpit in church. The media does not report on it."[17]

While these statements provide ecclesial authority for gun violence prevention and place such activism in a broader context of theology and tradition, Pax Christi offers more concrete resources for training in nonviolence and nonviolent resistance. Pax Christi does not offer, however, resources solely focused on gun violence prevention. Rather, in keeping with the organization's historic focus on militarism, their materials address gun violence as part of a larger system of cultural

---

[15] United States Conference of Catholic Bishops, "Confronting a Culture of Violence: A Catholic Framework for Action," 1994, usccb.org/resources/confronting-culture-violence-catholic-framework-action-0.

[16] Paul S. Coakley, Salvatore J. Cordileone, Thomas A. Daly, and William E. Lori, "Letter to Congress on Gun Violence, June 3, 2022," United States Conference of Catholic Bishops, June 3, 2022, usccb.org/resources/letter-congress-gun-violence-june-3-2022.

[17] Thomas Reese, "The Catholic Bishops Support Gun Control. Why Don't We Hear More about it?," *National Catholic Reporter*, June 14, 2022, ncronline.org/news/opinion/catholic-bishops-support-gun-control-why-dont-we-hear-more-about-it.

and structural violence in the US. For example, the agenda for the 2022 National Conference celebrating the organization's fiftieth anniversary of Pax Christi does not include a workshop addressing gun violence, and the only item specifically addressing gun violence on the website points to the May 2020 press event cited earlier in this article. And yet, the workshop offerings and materials on the Pax Christi website provide a tradition and network for resisting violence and pursuing peace, which then inform education and activism related to gun violence.

These Catholic resources highlight a shared space between the PDF and the Presser in so far as documents on the websites might be intended for a public audience. And yet, even the Bishops' Statements explicitly intended for a public audience perform an important internal function: namely, to remind Catholics that a particular legislative appeal reflects a comprehensive ethic and tradition of respect for life. Similarly, the Protestant PDF materials have an internal focus, helping fellow Presbyterians (or Methodists or Mennonites) to understand the issue and the ways their faith tradition compels them to respond to it. The persuasive dimension is geared toward bringing fellow Christians and congregants into the cause, but is most often a soft sell inviting them to study, reflect, pray, and then act. Most of the Protestant online resources include materials for, or at least reference to, conflict in the congregation. They consistently note the divisive nature of the subject of guns and try to prepare participants for working constructively with those who disagree with them. I observed less mention of disagreement in the Catholic materials; rather, the consistent gesture to foundational commitments and ecclesial authority communicates shared tradition to the reader.

As this survey suggests, the PDF is a varied space that includes downloadable materials for learning, anchoring in tradition, addressing disagreement, integrating worship and social concern, and equipping for action. For this article, I surveyed sixteen different resources from seven different Protestant denominations, two Roman Catholic bodies, two ecumenical organizations, and one nondenominational group. Across these materials, my research assistant and I catalogued twenty-five different theological claims and thirty-two different scripture passages used to anchor arguments for gun violence prevention advocacy.[18] While the streamlined communication of the Presser encourages focused and succinct appeal using a few key claims, the PDF offers a dizzying array of concepts, texts, and traditions so that the study is thorough, the prayers well resourced, and the action well-grounded. The three themes I discuss below do not

---

[18] I remained indebted to Kathryn Harper-Spellings for organizing these findings.

capture all the variety within the PDF genre, but they do constitute dominant themes coursing through all the materials I examined. One of these three themes, the sacredness of life, is also prominent at press events like the one described above. The other two themes, idolatry and nonviolence, are equally prominent at public events when Christian leaders and clergy are speaking to fellow Christians, but less pronounced in pluralistic (interfaith) or explicitly political events.

Sacredness of Life

In the Presser and throughout the PDFs, one hears insistence on the sacredness of life. The particular theological language varies a bit, suggesting deeper differences below the surface, but the affirmation of life as sacred cuts across these different contexts of Christian argument and reflection. One important difference, which deserves mention even though examination is beyond the scope of this article, is the presence of pro-life and pro-choice advocates within the gun violence prevention activism space. As illustrated in the Everytown press event, some Christians understand gun violence prevention to be an extension of their pro-life position or comprehensive ethic of life stance. Joel Hunter, for example, introduces himself "as an evangelical leader who cares deeply about the value of life [and] a comprehensive pro-life view."[19] In the PDF materials, one finds resources for building on pro-life commitments as well. For example, several documents encourage participants to watch and discuss the documentary *Armor of Light* and discuss the question it raises: "Is it possible to be both pro-gun and pro-life?"[20] The 1994 Bishops' Statement includes abortion in its list of examples of violence along with proliferation of guns, rising crime, domestic abuse, and violence in media. Other speakers and materials affirm the gift of life or the dignity of the person as core convictions, but do not mention a broader pro-life, comprehensive ethic of life, or pacifist commitment. While these differences persist, public advocacy focuses on the shared argument that Christians who believe that life is sacred must also do whatever they can to stop gun violence.

Quotations from the press event insist that Christians who affirm the sacredness of life must also vote for officials who will pass common sense gun laws that save lives. The electoral activity is an extension of their theological conviction. One of the perhaps lesser-known speakers at the Everytown press event was Michael Austin, a philosophy professor at Eastern Kentucky University. His writing

---

[19] Everytown, "Everytown Announces New Initiative."
[20] Lindsey Long Joyce, "Gun Violence 101 Cheat Sheet: Responding to the Call to Prevent Gun Violence" (General Board of Church and Society, The United Methodist Church), 4.

surfaces frequently as a resource for Christians reflecting on gun violence. In the opening line of his recent book, *God and Guns in America*, Austin describes himself as "a Christian, a gun owner, and a professor ... concerned about violence."[21] Drawing on the range of moral sources in Christian ethics, scripture, tradition, reason, and experience, Austin makes a moral case for rethinking our "use of weapons, guns included" and a legislative case for reforming gun laws.[22] His quote for the press event reflects his sense of alignment between moral value and legislative change. "Common sense gun laws will reduce the level of gun violence, literally saving human lives. As Christians decide whom to cast our vote for, we must remember this fact." In the Presser, affirming the value, dignity, and sacredness of human life features prominently because it provides common ground across religious traditions and easily connects in a succinct and straightforward way to a legislative agenda designed to reduce killing and harm.

This conviction (or cluster of related assertions) also appears as an anchor point in the PDF, where it functions as a central conviction in which participants are invited to root their study, prayer, and action for gun violence prevention. For example, in materials prepared by the US Conference of Catholic Bishops, the detailed recommendations for gun violence legislation and programs consistently reference the sanctity of life. "As the Catechism of the Catholic Church notes, human life is sacred, and we need to address the threat to life posed by gun violence with the full strength of our tradition," insists Bishop Frank J. Dewane.[23] Especially in the pastoral resources included in the PDF category, references to the sacredness of life often open the prayers or litanies. For example, the "Pastoral Letter on Violence" issued by the bishops of the Evangelical Lutheran Church in America begins with the claim that "every person wounded or killed is a precious child of God."[24] The many liturgical resources created by the Episcopal Bishops United against Gun Violence also affirm those killed in gun violence as "precious children of God."[25] In his oft-cited book, *America and its Guns: A Theological Exposé*, James Atwood anchors his argument to this central assertion of the sacredness of life, as people created in the image of God and claimed as children of God.

---

[21] Michael Austin, *God and Guns in America* (Grand Rapids, MI: Eerdmans, 2020), xv.
[22] Austin, *God and Guns*, xvi.
[23] Frank J. Dewane, "Responses to the Plague of Gun Violence," General Assembly of Bishops, November 11, 2019, usccb.org/resources/responses-plague-gun-violence.
[24] Lutheran Peace Fellowship, "Pastoral Letter on Violence," March 11, 2013, lutheranpeace.org/pastoral-letter-on-violence/.
[25] Episcopal Bishops United against Gun Violence, "Litany in the Wake of a Mass Shooting," November 2018, bishopsagainstgunviolence.org/liturgical_resource/litany-in-the-wake-of-a-mass-shooting/.

Many of the PDF materials cite Atwood's work, including a guide first published in 2014 by the interfaith group "Faiths against Gun Violence." In the section offering a "theological basis for gun violence prevention," Atwood's writing takes the form of a list of theological assertions including: "Each of us is created in the image of God" and "Each of us is a child of God."[26] While the precise theological assertions vary across the materials (image of God, children of God, human dignity, sanctity of life), the shared point is that Christians should resist gun violence because all human life has sacred value.

Sin of Idolatry

References to the sin of idolatry are less prevalent in the public sphere of press events, but idolatry is a persistent theme in the materials that comprise the PDF category. Indeed, nearly every publication I collected cautions against the idolatry of guns. In our fear, these materials suggest, we turn to guns to make us feel safe. Like the anxious people at the base of Mount Sinai pleading with Aaron to make gods to go before them, people turn to weapons and pro-gun legislation to secure themselves (Exodus 32:1–6). They make an "idol of safety" and turn to guns to provide it.[27] For example, one of the suggestions offered in the Mennonite publication, "A Loaded Conversation: An Invitation to Talk about Guns," is to preach a sermon that "focuses directly on how one's desire for safety and the confidence we put in guns can be idolatrous."[28] As this invitation suggests, the materials do not necessarily claim that all guns are idols and all gun owners are idolatrous. Drawing on James Atwood, Michael Austin makes this distinction explicit in *God and Guns in America* arguing that guns become idolatrous when people believe they offer power and security. "If we *need* guns to make us believe that we are in control, to protect us from harm, to make us feel secure, then our guns have become idols." Guns become idols when people imbue them with power and treat gun rights as "sacrosanct and nonnegotiable."[29]

Other resources take the idolatry argument even deeper. For example, the United Church of Christ offers a five-part Bible study titled "Faith vs. Fear." Part Three, "The Gun as Idol," was contributed by Reverend Matthew Crebbin, senior minister of Newtown Congre-

---

[26] Faiths United to Prevent Gun Violence, "Gun Violence Prevention Faith Leaders Guide," September 2014, 9.
[27] Jon Huckins, "Worshiping the Idol of Safety," *Sojourners*, March 24, 2016, sojo.net/articles/worshiping-idol-safety.
[28] Mennonite Central Committee US Gun Violence Prevention Network, "A Loaded Conversation: An Invitation to Talk about Guns," 8, mcc.org/media/resources/8279.
[29] Austin, *God and Guns*, 109.

gational Church in Newtown, Connecticut, the site of the Sandy Hook Elementary School shooting in 2012. In his reflection on Exodus 20:4–5, Reverend Crebbin adapts a piece from Gary Willis that describes guns as more than idols in which we place our trust. They are also gods to which we sacrifice our children, he argues. The horror of Sandy Hook "was the sacrifice we as a culture made, and continually make, to our demonic god. ... The gun is not a mere tool, a bit of technology, a political issue, a point of debate. It is an object of reverence." Reverend Crebbin invites participants to reflect on the relationship between the second commandment and the second amendment, and closes the Bible study with a prayer, "O God, open our eyes to our hidden idolatry."[30]

In the PDF category, another oft-cited passage, Micah 4:1–4, constitutes a response to idolatry. When people awaken to the idolatry of the gun, they are able to see it as a weapon that can and should be transformed in a life dedicated to nonviolence and peace. Micah's call to beat swords into plowshares offers a metaphorical path forward in this journey from idolatry to faith. We give up reliance on weapons that destroy and take up tools of construction and creation. We relinquish the idolatrous reliance on weapons for safety and place our trust in God. In 2014, the United Methodist Church produced "Kingdom Dreams, Violent Realities," which integrates a study of Micah 4:1–4 with reflections on gun violence.[31] This text tells of a people struggling with threats inside, such as anxious awareness that they are separated from God, and threats outside from "powerful nations [that] lie in wait." In this context, Micah calls for repentance and offers a vision of "great promise."[32] "The transformation that occurs," insists this UMC resource, "is not only in the weapons but in those who wield them. It is a holistic and total transformation."[33] Turning away from idolatry involves much more than resistance to guns and the false security they provide; it is a call toward a new way of living.

Call to Nonviolence

The vision of transformation Micah describes has also inspired gun violence prevention activists to enact a literal practice of changing guns into tools. RAWTools, Inc., turns guns into gardening tools as a

---

[30] Matthew Crebbin, "Part Three: The Gun as Idol," in *Faith vs. Fear: A Faith Response to Gun Violence*, United Church of Christ, 6, uccfiles.com/pdf/faith-vs-fear-bible-study.pdf.

[31] Jeania Ree V. Moore, *Kingdom Dreams, Violent Realities*, revised edition (Washington, DC: General Board of Church and Society of The United Methodist Church, 2016).

[32] Moore, *Kingdom Dreams*, 11.

[33] Moore, *Kingdom Dreams*, 18.

central feature of its broader organizational focus on nonviolence training and community gun violence prevention.[34] Their work and the broader symbolism of transformation from destruction to construction shapes the book *Beating Guns*, co-authored by Shane Claiborne and Michael Martin, the founder of RAWtools. They open their book with Isaiah 2:4, which also offers the vision of beating "swords into iron plows and spears into pruning tools" (CEB). The transformation of weapons into garden tools is a concrete practice of nonviolent resistance and also a symbol of "transforming our way of life," they write. "We want to live in a way that moves the world toward love and away from fear. We want to live in patterns that generate life rather than exploit it, that see people and creatures as precious instead of disposable."[35]

This call to nonviolence persists through the PDF materials, grounded in a variety of claims and texts. "Blessed are the peacemakers" (Matthew 5:9) appears in nearly every resource I studied, as do references to other passages from the Sermon on the Mount (Matthew 5:1–12). Some resources center their call to nonviolence on love of neighbor (Matthew 5:43–44, Luke 6:27, John 13:31–35), not returning evil for evil, or turning the other cheek (1 Peter 3:9 or Matthew 5:38–40). Several cite Jesus's caution against living by the sword (Matthew 26:52b or Luke 22:51). While these sources may well anchor a comprehensive ethic of life or pacifist commitment, the PDF category offers them in a more focused way as theological and scriptural grounding for resisting gun violence. For example, "Engage: Lutherans for Gun Violence Prevention" cites Matthew 5:9 as the centering text for their mission: "to meditate on, educate about, and advocate for gun violence prevention in the nonviolent Spirit of Jesus."[36] In the document "Gun Violence: Faith and Facts," the United Methodist Church offers Micah 4:2–3 along with Matthew 5:9 and Matthew 5:43–44 as a response to the question, "What does the Bible say?"[37] While there are nuances and differences across these materials, there also is a common assertion that gun violence prevention is consistent with Jesus's call to a life of love and nonviolence. As Victoria Wilgocki writes in the "Faith versus Fear" Bible study, "Difficult as it may be to resist the way of the gun, we are

---

[34] Rawtools, Inc., rawtools.org.
[35] Shane Claiborne and Michael Martin, *Beating Guns: Hope for People Who Are Weary of Violence* (Grand Rapids, MI: Brazos, 2019), 22–23.
[36] Engage: Lutherans for Gun Violence Prevention, "Home," engageelca.org.
[37] General Board of Church and Society, "Gun Violence: Faith and Facts," umcjustice.org.

called to follow the way of Jesus: *love one another*."[38] This call to nonviolence reminds Christian activists that their resistance to gun violence is more than a policy position; it is a biblically informed way of life that transcends the particular context of any singular issue.

As suggested above, this emphasis on a nonviolent way of living is a central feature of *Beating Guns*, which has become a major resource for Christians in the contemporary gun violence prevention movement. It appears on resource lists in PDF materials, Claiborne is a sought-after speaker, and Martin's RAWTools organization is active and growing. Published in 2019, *Beating Guns* provides helpful overviews of data and history, includes "memorials to the lost" that draw attention to the victims of gun violence, and commends community violence prevention programs as well as legislative efforts. In addition to the call to nonviolence, it also contains the moral claims about idolatry and sacredness of life mentioned above. Indeed, Claiborne and Martin connect the sacredness of life, the sin of idolatry, and the call to nonviolence to an understanding of vulnerability as a mark of faith. That is, part of living a nonviolent life means eschewing the protection of a weapon and thus accepting vulnerability. In the context of gun violence, they argue that it is more faithful to resist nonviolently and suffer than to succumb to the temptation to take up guns for protection. Indeed, they insist that arming ourselves with weapons distances us from God. "When we are too strong and armed," they write, "we tend to lose our faith in God to deliver us. We rely on our guns and bombs, the idols that are easier to see and trust in than an invisible God who can at times feel distant. That's why living an unarmed life takes faith, and courage, and trust in God."[39] As in the earlier references, Claiborne and Martin understand reliance on weapons to be a form of idolatry, placing trust and faith in something other than God. Pulling on a thread deeply woven into Christian pacifism, they insist that vulnerability to violence is a mark of faith and brings us closer to God. In their words, following Jesus means choosing to be a "soft target" rather than a hard heart.[40]

Although this line of argument is more overt, it resonates with concerns about fear and idolatry in some of the materials discussed above. Like Claiborne and Martin, many of the materials in the PDF category construe protection and security as problematic and suggest that a willingness to be vulnerable to violence is thus a mark of faith. Rather than succumb to fear, Christians should place faith in God and

---

[38] Victoria Wilgocki, "Part One: Love One Another," in *Faith vs. Fear: A Faith Response to Gun Violence*, United Church of Christ, 1, uccfiles.com/pdf/faith-vs-fear-bible-study.pdf.
[39] Claiborne and Martin, *Beating Guns*, 169.
[40] Claiborne and Martin, *Beating Guns*, 158.

respond to the call to nonviolence. The materials conveyed through the Presser and the PDF persistently direct one's attention to fear. Indeed, fear of guns, fear of violence, fear of legislation, and fear of disagreement and conflict often occupy the center of moral concern. With attention directed toward fear, the materials counsel faithfulness. The faithful resist the temptation to make idols of guns and seek their own security. The faithful do not succumb to fear by taking up weapons. The faithful consent to vulnerability and commend it.

ANALYSIS AND RESPONSE

This line of thinking is a familiar groove for pacifists and nonviolent resisters, but it signals some moral confusion in the context of gun violence prevention advocacy. By moral confusion, I am not paternalistically suggesting that the activists themselves are confused. Rather, by moral confusion, I mean that in the materials and events where Christian moral arguments for gun violence prevention surface we find a tangle of meaning and value ascribed to forms of vulnerability. This is not a situation unique to gun violence prevention. Vulnerability is currently a rather contentious term that hosts a variety of meanings and values. My intention here is not to wade into the burgeoning and dynamic literature on vulnerability, but rather to highlight a kind of moral confusion that surrounds references to vulnerability in the context of gun violence prevention advocacy by Christians.[41]

First, one finds a mixture of descriptions of vulnerability. Particularly in the wake of mass shootings, press events communicate a sense of existential vulnerability. Mass shootings can (and do) happen anywhere: schools, grocery stores, workplaces, outdoor concerts, indoor movie theaters, houses of worship, small town parades. Given the intention of the press event, to mobilize for action, cultivating the feeling that the threat of gun violence is everywhere—that all are vulnerable—is strategic. It makes use of fear to build a sense of urgency and demand action. Public speakers and educational materials also regularly clarify that some are more vulnerable than others. 60 percent of gun deaths are suicides, primarily by white men.[42] Recent studies document a correspondence between prevalence of guns in the home in rural areas, gun stores in urban areas, poverty,

---

[41] I am particularly grateful to Jennifer Ayres and Gabrielle Thomas, whose work has brought clarity to these distinctions on vulnerability. Jennifer Ayres, "Embracing Vulnerability: Religious Education, Embodiment, and the Ecological Affections," *Religious Education* 115, no. 1 (2020): 15–26; Gabrielle Thomas, "The Status of Vulnerability in a Theology of the Christian Life: Gregory of Nyssa on the 'Wound of Love' in Conversation with Sarah Coakley," *Modern Theology* 38, no. 4 (2022): 1–19.

[42] Giffords Law Center, "Statistics," giffords.org/lawcenter/gun-violence-statistics/.

and mental health as contributing factors to firearm-caused suicide.[43] 35 percent of gun deaths result from homicide, and 50 percent of firearm-caused homicide victims are Black men.[44] According to Everytown, Black men and women combined constitute 68 percent of gun homicides.[45] Also according to Everytown, "gun homicides and assaults occur at high rates within cities, and have disproportionate impact in historically underfunded neighborhoods within our cities." The disparity increases along with the numbers when we consider non-lethal gun violence as well.[46] The category of firearm-caused homicide also includes killing by intimate partners, which increased 26 percent between 2010 and 2017.[47] Research published in the *American Journal of Preventive Medicine Studies* in 2019 documents a correspondence between firearm ownership and domestic violence homicide, meaning that the presence of guns in the home makes intimate partner homicide more likely. Dr. Aaron Kivesto, lead author of the study, puts it succinctly: "Guns are a real risk factor."[48]

Thus, in addition to a feeling of existential vulnerability related to the seeming randomness and pervasiveness of gun violence, one also finds statistics that make a distinction between this general awareness of vulnerability and particular circumstances that increase one's risk for gun violence. To these two forms of vulnerability, some who voice the call to nonviolence add a third, what Claiborne and Martin provocatively refer to as being a "soft target." Materials in the PDF category may not frame this argument so provocatively, but they too communicate the moral argument that the faithful Christian resists the idolatry of the gun by securing themselves in faith to God rather than taking up weapons. In refusing to take up arms, one chooses a form of vulnerability. In the familiar grooves of pacifism and nonviolent resistance, this form of vulnerability is virtuous.

The presence of these three different forms of vulnerability and the different values assigned to them contributes to moral confusion in the context of gun violence prevention. The materials and actors

---

[43] Erin Schumaker, "Prevalence of Gun Stores Linked to Higher Suicide Rates, Study Finds," *The Trace*, thetrace.org/2019/09/prevalence-of-gun-stores-linked-to-higher-suicide-rates-study-finds/.
[44] Giffords Law Center, "Statistics," giffords.org/lawcenter/gun-violence-statistics/.
[45] Everytown for Gun Safety, "Impact of Gun Violence on Black Americans," everytownresearch.org/issue/gun-violence-black-americans/.
[46] Everytown for Gun Safety, "Violence Intervention Programs," everytownresearch.org/solution/violence-intervention-programs/.
[47] Madeleine Carlisle and Melissa Chan, "Here's Why Domestic Violence Kills so Many Women and Children in America," *Time*, October 17, 2019, time.com/5702435/domestic-violence-gun-violence/.
[48] Sarah Mervosh, "Gun Ownership Rates Tied to Domestic Homicides, but Not Other Killings, Study Finds," *New York Times*, July 22, 2019, nytimes.com/2019/07/22/us/gun-ownership-violence-statistics.html.

themselves do not make clear distinctions between existential vulnerability, statistical vulnerability, and virtuous vulnerability. That is, references to these three wind through speeches and materials and become tangled up with different assessments of value. Is vulnerability a virtue to commend, an existential reality to accept, or a social problem to mitigate? In the mixture of public events, educational materials, and moral claims, it is all of these things, and that generates moral confusion.

Given the scope of gun violence prevention activism, a mixture of meaning and value is inevitable. However, the "soft target" argument crystallizes a concern about this mixture that must be addressed. This line of moral argument reflects a tradition that focuses attention on the character of the moral agent. How one responds to violence and the fear of violence is a matter of character. Does one succumb to the idolatry of the weapon or remain faithful to God? Firmly attached to this focus on character is an assumption that faithfulness may not be effective according to the metrics of culture. Resisting idolatrous violence puts one at risk. Refusing to take up arms renders oneself and others vulnerable to attack. The nonviolent choice may not be the effective choice, but it is faithful to the Gospel. This character-focused and dichotomous framing are deeply woven into the tradition of Christian pacifism and nonviolence.[49] There is nothing new about it, nor is it new for even fellow pacifists like me to be troubled by its implications for vulnerable people. Commending vulnerability as a mark of faith in the context of gun violence carries the same pastoral and ethical dangers as commending meekness to the marginalized and simplicity to the poor. It makes a virtue out of a situation instead of challenging the systemic and cultural realities that perpetuate it. When it surfaces in the context of gun violence prevention, two problems arise. First, the dichotomous framing of faithfulness and effectiveness is contextually inaccurate and unnecessarily limits the field of faithful responses to gun violence. Second, the false and unnecessary dichotomy not only keeps the focus on the moral character of the activist, but also pits the latter against the needs of those statistically vulnerable to gun violence.

The perception that the nonviolent alternative is ineffective in a violent society runs deep, and opponents to gun control lean heavily on it. However, as indicated by the statistics cited above, the prevalence of guns increases actual vulnerability to gun violence. The availability of guns makes mental illness, systemic racism, and domestic violence more deadly. The vulnerability of people struggling with mental illness, systemic racism, and domestic violence is

---

[49] I explore this dichotomy and challenge it in the article, "Pacifism and the Question of Responsibility," *Political Theology* 21, no. 3 (2020): 192–206.

increased when guns are readily available. Guns do not cause these problems, but they do make the circumstances more dangerous and deadly. Guns increase the vulnerability. They are a risk factor. This reality disrupts the faithfulness-effectiveness dichotomy. In the particular context of gun violence prevention activism, resisting the idolatry of the gun is both effective and faithful.

However, attention to actual vulnerability—the circumstances of those most at-risk for gun violence—also suggests that gun violence prevention requires much more than gun control. It also requires community-based programs to address intersecting forms of violence and provide comprehensive support for the vulnerable, wounded, and grieving. In other words, it requires a shift in attention from one's own moral claims about guns to the needs of those who have experienced and are most likely to experience gun violence.

I recognize that the line from data to argument is never straightforward. Differing viewpoints have their own studies to cite and people can come to different conclusions using the same evidence. However, I agree with Michael Austin's assertion that "there are many things we can and should do that are supported by research and experts from many fields, including law, medicine, public health, public safety, philosophy, and theology."[50] Keeping the needs of the vulnerable at the center of moral concern and action leads me to support legislation that requires background checks, restricts access to guns by persons deemed a danger to themselves and others, repeals stand-your-ground laws, funds research on gun violence and gun violence prevention, prohibits assault weapons and high-capacity magazines, and prevents guns on campuses. These proposals also align with my own commitments to pacifism and nonviolence. Because firearms are already in homes and communities, I also support firearm education and programs like "Be SMART," which educates families about gun storage.[51] As a pacifist, I feel some ambivalence about firearms remaining in homes and communities, but centering actual vulnerability to gun violence clarifies the need for firearm education given the data on gun violence caused by accidental shootings. It directs my attention to the victims and survivors and orients my action around responding to their needs, rather than debating about guns and focusing on moral character.

This intentional shift to center those most vulnerable to gun violence in moral reflection is not unique to me.[52] Indeed, it reflects an intentional and strategic effort in gun violence prevention activism

---

[50] Austin, *God and Guns*, 129.
[51] Be SMART, besmartforkids.org.
[52] Teal Rothschild, *An Ethnography of Gun Violence Prevention Activists: "We Are Thinking People"* (Lanham, MD: Lexington, 2019).

to focus on victims and survivors rather than guns. Centering survivors is a concrete expression of a development in gun violence prevention advocacy. Even in the years I have been volunteering with Moms Demand Action, I have noticed a change in language. Initially, the guidance from Moms was to use language of gun reform rather than gun control so that our advocacy would be less easily dismissed by gun rights supporters. They wanted to communicate an emphasis on reforming gun laws, not controlling the guns. In recent years, any reference to gun reform has also fallen out of messaging. Moms uses "gun violence prevention" language now in order to keep the focus on the victims and survivors rather than guns. Implemented by many advocacy groups, this change in language from gun control to gun reform to gun violence prevention is about changing the frame from a focus on guns to a focus on victims: "To enact policies that reduce gun violence, we are changing the issue 'frame' from one centered on taking guns away from people, to one centered on saving people's lives."[53]

This intentional re-framing of activism has been strengthened by regular practice of hearing from and supporting survivors. In 2015, Everytown for Gun Safety launched the Survivor Fellowship Program, which partners "with survivors as they share their stories with the public and give audiences a way to become involved in and connect with the gun violence prevention movement."[54] Fellows receive public speaking and media training and serve as resource people for two years for Everytown and their local Moms Demand chapter. After serving this term, they remain part of the Everytown Survivor Network. This is undoubtedly strategic, and not only because it helps to set a new frame. In the case of Moms Demand Action, foregrounding people who have experienced loss due to gun violence is also an important shift for an organization started by a white woman not personally affected by gun violence.[55] It has been crucial to their growth and mission to center survivors in their storytelling and

---

[53] Erika Soto Lamb, "Reframing the Gun Debate," *Stanford Social Innovation Review*, May 29, 2018, ssir.org/articles/entry/reframing_the_gun_debate. One finds similar advice in some of the PDF materials as well. For example, the United Methodist Church publication "Gun Violence 101 Cheat Sheet" advises participants to say "gun violence prevention" instead of "gun control" in order to "avoid trigger words." This same document also encourages people to use the word "violence" when starting the conversation in order to "focus on people who are impacted in your community" (Joyce, "Gun Violence 101 Cheat Sheet," 2, 4).
[54] Everytown for Gun Safety, "Everytown Survivor Network," everytownsupportfund.org/everytown-survivor-network/.
[55] Shannon Watts, *Fight Like a Mother: How a Grassroots Movement Took on the Gun Lobby and Why Women Will Change the World* (New York: Harper One, 2019), 3.

leadership. In Georgia, where I have attended events, this has also increased involvement from and leadership by women of color. For example, Sharmaine Brown is one of the religious leaders announced in the Everytown press event. Ms. Brown's son was killed by a stray bullet in 2015, and she is a member of the Everytown Survivor Network. She is also a leader in the Georgia chapter of Moms Demand Action and moderated the vigil for the Georgia chapter during Gun Violence Survivors Week.[56]

Centering victims, survivors, and those most vulnerable to gun violence is clearly strategic for advocacy groups like Moms Demand Action, but I also find it instructive for Christians involved in gun violence prevention advocacy. As noted above, there is considerable attention given in the PDF to internal debates about guns and helping individual Christians reflect on their moral stance on weapons. Such moral discernment and ecclesial dialogue are indeed important. But they need to be accompanied by experiences that bring us into regular contact with people who have suffered the forms of violence we are debating. Therefore, in addition to the Presser and the PDF, Christian gun violence prevention activists need experiences that routinely place those actually vulnerable to gun violence at the center of moral reflection.

Centering vulnerability, in this sense, means orienting reflection, concern, and action around responding to and addressing the needs of those vulnerable to gun violence. One does not disregard all the other texts, traditions, and arguments, but brings primary attention to vulnerability as a problem to address. Anchoring reflection and practice to texts like Matthew 25:34–40, Christians orient discipleship and pursuit of the kingdom around responding to need. The "least of these," those vulnerable to violence, remain the object of focus for moral concern and action. Centering on actual vulnerability also reflects a deliberative practice Sara Ruddick describes as maternal thinking. In Ruddick's philosophy, a mother is one "committed to meeting demands that define maternal work."[57] The preeminent demand is that of preservation or preservative growth. The distinctive feature of maternal thinking is that it understands "vulnerability as socially significant and as demanding care." Maternal thinking involves a practice of centering vulnerability and pursuing the deliberation and action required for preservation.[58]

---

[56] Sharmaine Brown, "In Memory of Jared," *Moments that Survive*, Everytown for Gun Safety, momentsthatsurvive.org/tribute/sharmaine-brown/.

[57] Sara Ruddick, *Maternal Thinking: Toward a Politics of Peace* (Boston: Beacon, 1995), 17.

[58] Ruddick, *Maternal Thinking*, 18.

It also centers vulnerability as something that demands a response, not as a virtue to commend. Maternal thinking, in Ruddick's philosophy, involves intentional deliberation to care for the one who is vulnerable. One practices maternal thinking not by commending vulnerability, but by enacting care that preserves, nurtures, and protects the vulnerable. Although Ruddick mentions her own Protestant Christian upbringing in passing, she writes as a philosopher drawing on reason and experience to make her arguments. As a Christian feminist ethicist, I integrate Ruddick's maternal thinking with Jesus's teaching to care for the least of these. In Jesus's parables, the least of these demands a response that meets their needs. The teaching is to respond to the one who is "hungry or thirsty or a stranger or naked or sick or in prison" by taking care of them, addressing their needs. The call is to see in the "least of these" a need that demands a response.

In the context of Christian gun violence prevention advocacy, this response must presume that vulnerability is a problem, not a virtue. But this requires intentional clarification of the ways we experience and value vulnerability. In the mix of actors, intentions, texts, and traditions that share the context of gun violence prevention activism, some mixture of meaning and value is inevitable. This particular area of confusion is something that can and should be clarified. While we experience different feelings of vulnerability in relationship to gun violence, the focus for Christian activists must remain on addressing the actual vulnerability of those most at risk.

In the final portion of this article, I develop this argument by describing a third space where Christian moral claims surface, namely the vigil. Like the Presser and the PDF, the vigil also communicates the affirmation of the sacredness of life and the call to be peacemakers and practice nonviolence. Like the Presser more so than the PDF, vigils are often hybrid spaces with a mix of religious traditions and an inclusion of ecclesial and political figures; thus, the language of idolatry recedes to the edges a bit. However, the purpose of the vigil is quite distinct. Where the Presser intends to persuade and enlist, and the PDF focuses on education and dialogue, the vigil aims to remember those who have died and comfort those who mourn. In a very explicit and embodied way, vigils center those actually vulnerable to gun violence.

CENTERING THOSE VULNERABLE TO GUN VIOLENCE: THE VIGIL

"The Vigil" refers to a particularly interesting hybrid space where participants remember the dead, support survivors, and pledge or re-commit themselves to action. These spaces often include a mix of liturgical and prayer practices from different traditions and participation from both political and religious leaders. They are sometimes public-facing events and sometimes semi-private circles of support. While the Presser and the PDF tend to unfold as one might expect, the vigil has become a rather varied and unpredictable space. I offer two examples that represent some of this variety.

In the summer of 2019, I sat holding a thick stack of 3x5 cards in the front seat of a priest's car on the way to a vigil near the capitol building in Atlanta. This priest, whom I call Catherine, had been organizing parishioners every month to read the names of fellow Georgians killed by gun violence. For two years, she stood in a circle with whomever showed up and used Episcopal liturgy and data from Gun Violence Archives to pray and read the names. They also prayed for the first responders, recognizing the toll gun violence takes on "their very being."[59] When I contacted Catherine for information about this vigil at the capitol, she offered to meet me at church and give me a ride.

When we arrived, the small treeless piece of lawn and scorching pavement were busy with Moms Demand Action volunteers in red shirts, people in religious vestments representing different traditions, two state representatives (Mary Margaret Oliver and Bee Nguyen), one US representative (Lucy McBath), and a few reporters and cameras. After prayers and comments from those on the platform, we attendees were instructed to form two lines so that we could take turns reading names of fellow Georgians killed by gun violence in 2018 and 2019. As we approached the platform, we were handed one of the 3x5 papers I had carried in Catherine's car. Each paper had five names or descriptions when names were unavailable (e.g., "unnamed 25 year-old man"). We stepped to the microphone and read the names, then returned to the end of the line to see if we needed to read a second time. Most of us did. Although I lost track of the time it took, news accounts report that we read names for thirty minutes.[60]

Reading the names of victims is a central practice of the vigil. For those grounded in liturgical traditions, it is an extension of prayer and a practice easily resourced by the church. Indeed, Bishops against Gun Violence, an organization of over one hundred Episcopal Bishops across the US, offers numerous liturgical resources on their website.[61] In their recent letter to President Biden and Vice-President Harris, the

---

[59] Catherine, interview with the author, May 18, 2020.
[60] Jill Nolin, "Lawmakers, Clergy Call for Gun Restrictions at Vigil near Capitol," *Georgia Recorder*, August 15, 2019, georgiarecorder.com/2019/08/15/lawmakers-clergy-call-for-gun-restrictions-at-vigil-near-capitol/; Ross Terrell, "'There Will Be More': Dire Warning Issued at Gun Violence Vigil," *GPB News*, August 14, 2019, gpb.org/news/2019/08/14/there-will-be-more-dire-warning-issued-at-gun-violence-vigil.
[61] Episcopal Bishops United against Gun Violence, "Liturgical Resources," bishopsagainstgunviolence.org/resources/liturgical-resources/.

Bishops pledge their support for policies that address "the unholy trinity of poverty, racism, and gun violence" and identify their contributions as champions of this cause. Among these contributions is: "We hold public liturgies—vigils, processions, and prayer services—to commemorate the dead and inspire the living."[62] For Catherine, a liturgist, reading the names is both a spiritual practice and a political act. It is one way she enacts and remembers one of her core convictions: "God resides within each and every human being." Reading the names of those lost to gun violence is one way she "holds all life as sacred." It is also a reminder and enactment of the responsibilities we have to one another, she says.[63]

Prayer vigils at church and interfaith vigils in public, political spaces are established traditions for ecclesial bodies and faith-related political organizations.[64] They have also become standard practice for gun violence prevention advocacy groups. As mentioned earlier, the Brady Campaign created a sample vigil as part of its "God not Guns" program. Moms Demand Action does not (yet) offer liturgical resources like this, but the organization does create space during in person and virtual gatherings to remember victims and hear the stories of survivors. During Gun Violence Survivors Awareness Week in February 2021, Moms Demand Action chapters organized virtual vigils throughout the week.[65] As summarized on the organization's website, these vigils were organized by state chapters and included prayers, survivor testimonies, music and spoken word performances, and guided meditations for healing. One member of the Everytown Survivor Network, Miami Knight, is a grief counselor and spiritual healer who offers guided meditations to gun violence survivors in the context of Moms Demand gatherings and through her own company. Her approach integrates guided meditation for relaxation with candle lighting rituals, and prayers for healing and comfort.[66] During the Gun Violence Survivors Week in 2021, Moms Demand Action also launched "Moments that Survive," "a year-round digital storytelling

---

[62] Episcopal News Service, "Bishops United against Gun Violence Pledge to Work with Biden and Harris on Gun Control," February 25, 2021, episcopalnewsservice.org/2021/02/25/bishops-united-against-gun-violence-pledge-to-work-with-biden-and-harris-on-gun-control/.

[63] Interview, May 18, 2020.

[64] For a robust analysis of protest liturgy, see Kyle Lambelet, ¡Presente!: Nonviolent Politics and the Resurrection of the Dead (Washington, DC: Georgetown University Press, 2019).

[65] Moms Demand Action, "Third Annual National Gun Violence Survivors Week," momsdemandaction.org/third-annual-national-gun-violence-survivors-week-concludes-with-thousands-of-powerful-stories-shared-across-the-country/. I attended the vigil for the Georgia chapter. However, given the intimate nature of the event, I chose to draw my description from materials available on the website.

[66] Miami Knight, miamiknightllc.com/.

site and campaign in which Americans across the country share defining details of their experiences with gun violence, in their own words."[67] Moments that Survive is intended to continue the practice of remembering victims and telling the stories of survivors; it is also a mechanism for connecting survivors to one another so that they can offer mutual support.

The vigil is a regular feature of gun violence prevention activism now, utilized in a variety of ways. Some gatherings are more traditionally liturgical, while others integrate a variety of spiritual practices. What I find consistent across them is that they hold a space for intentional reflection on experiences of loss and pain. Whether conducted by an Episcopal priest in the church courtyard or by a spiritual healer on Zoom, the vigil offers an embodied experience that centers those most vulnerable to gun violence. Participating in vigils orients us time and again to a kind of vulnerability that makes a demand on us. These activities focus attention on those actually at risk for gun violence and frames vulnerability as a problem to address, not a virtue to commend.

CONCLUSION

Gun Violence Prevention activism is a dynamic context in which Christians are participating as featured speakers at a press event, authors and consumers of materials intended to educate and motivate, and conveners and participants in vigils. In each of these spaces, Christians voice a variety of moral claims. This article focused on three: the sacredness of life, the sin of idolatry, and the call to nonviolence. In my analysis of these arguments in the context of gun violence prevention, I note a tangle of meaning and value ascribed to vulnerability. The pervasiveness of gun violence gives the sense that all are vulnerable anytime. The statistics around gun violence provide a more nuanced picture of increased vulnerability for some. And the familiar grooves that dichotomize faith and effectiveness in Christian nonviolence surface to suggest another form of voluntary vulnerability as a mark of faith. While a general feeling of vulnerability is understandable, it does not orient the activist properly toward the work that can and should be done. A more nuanced picture of vulnerability issues a moral demand and also clarifies the kinds of legislative and programmatic responses that can actually lower the numbers of gun deaths and injuries in the United States. Virtuous vulnerability warrants explicit challenge and re-direction. In the context of gun violence, vulnerability is a problem to address and not a virtue to

---

[67] Moms Demand Action, "Third Annual National Gun Violence Survivors Week," momsdemandaction.org/third-annual-national-gun-violence-survivors-week-concludes-with-thousands-of-powerful-stories-shared-across-the-country/.

commend. Vulnerability must be framed as issuing a moral demand, a response in the form of concrete actions to address the perceived need. The Presser and the PDF are filled with such concrete actions, and Christians are very busy undertaking them. In addition to those materials and actions, I underscore the value of the Vigil as a space that keeps activists properly oriented toward the vulnerable and the work they demand of us.🅜

Ellen Ott Marshall, PhD, is Professor of Christian Ethics and Conflict Transformation at Candler School of Theology, Emory University. She is also a faculty member in the Ethics and Society doctoral program and Director of the Graduate Division of Religion at Emory. She focuses on contemporary Christian ethics, with particular attention to violence, peacebuilding, conflict transformation, gender, and moral agency. She has edited three volumes and written three books including *Parenting for a Better World* (co-edited with Susanna Snyder, Chalice, 2022) and *An Introduction to Christian Ethics: Conflict, Faith, and Human Life* (Westminster John Knox, 2018).

Gun Culture, Free Riding, and Nothing Short of Conversion

Gerald W. Schlabach

MODERN PEOPLE WHO ARE WELL EDUCATED, DO WORK ON social policy, and read journals like this—more likely "liberals" of some kind—are not the sort who hand out tracts, buttonhole others, and press them to convert. They are more likely to denounce "proselytism" as a sin than denounce fornication or whatever else we picture the Puritans to have obsessed over. Boisterous talk of the need for conversion or concerted efforts to proselytize and win the world for Christ in our generation are considered disrespectful of other cultures. Yet here we are, dedicating pages to examining, perhaps denouncing, and probably trying to overturn something that many call—*nota bene*—"the gun culture" in the United States. What they have in mind might more precisely be labeled the "defensive gun culture" that has less and less to do with hunting or recreation but instead strives for personal self-protection.[1] Either way, what bears noting is that in this case, Christian gun control advocates who are more likely than not "liberal"

---

[1] "Defensive gun culture" as I am using the term corresponds with what sociologist David Yamane calls "Gun Culture 2.0." See David Yamane, "The Sociology of US Gun Culture," *Sociology Compass* 11, no. 7 (July 2017), doi:10.1111/soc4.12497. Some may wish to distinguish between different gun *cultures*: (1) the historic use of firearms primarily as a tool for economically-integral hunting, (2) later recreational use of firearms for sport and non-essential hunting, and now (3) the culture of gun ownership motivated by the desire for self-protection. I certainly recognize that the first of these is still possible apart from the others, though increasingly rare. My own father-in-law was a conscientious objector in World War II and a self-supported Mennonite pastor in a hard-scrabble region of the country; he depended on venison and fish to relieve pressure on the family budget, but as a pacifist would never have shot a gun at another human being to protect himself or his family. So for the sake of precision, as well as respect for hunters like my father-in-law, it seems wise to speak more narrowly of "defensive gun culture." Still, I do worry that any distinguishable gun *cultures* in the United States are but layers in what is becoming fused into a single gun culture. After all, the historical reality of the independent frontiersman hunting to feed himself or his family (#1) laid the basis for the culture of recreational hunting (#2) lingering long past subsistence economies. Together these have shaped the mythology of the gun-wielding protector (#3) who in the cinematic imagination might be a solitary lawman but can easily become a vigilante when necessary.

Christians, do want to change a culture. And that is as it should be. Indeed, Christians of the sort who advocate for gun control ought to put the righteous urgency of conversion back on the table.

Once we recognize and name what we are up against in the defensive gun culture of the contemporary United States, we may have to admit that it will remain insoluble without something approaching mass conversion. To be sure, gun control advocates offer many good reasons to regulate and reduce the presence of guns in the United States. Other articles in this issue will do so, and I expect them to be cogent. Generally, however, such reasons and the legal or policy alternatives they present address aggregates. In other words, most are collective reasons as to why more people in society would be safer and better off if there were fewer guns present and circulating in society. While it is impossible to determine the exact number of guns in private hands in the United States, what is indisputable is that there are by far more of them per capita than in any other country in the world.[2] Especially now that so many guns have been physically manufactured and dispersed throughout US society, any attempt to reverse course and reduce gun ownership will face a classic "collective action problem." Whether the relevant point of decision is selling back guns or willingly relinquishing them or maybe even just voting, the problem will be to convince individuals to work together for a solution that would benefit them *all*, when too many find incentives not only to hang back from collective action but actively to resist. After all, any *one* person or family can easily imagine a moment of extreme crisis that would give them reasons (of a sort), in that moment, to use a gun.

Now that so many guns are out there, current gun owners or gun-rights advocates perceive themselves to have even more compelling reasons to bear firearms. Even if they could somehow be brought to recognize that everyone would be safer if there were fewer guns in

---

[2] In their indispensable book *The Gun Debate: What Everyone Needs to Know*, 2nd ed. (New York: Oxford University Press, 2020), Philip J. Cook and Kristin A Goss explained the difficulty identifying a precise number of guns circulating in the United States (2–4), but landed conservatively on a "reasonable ballpark estimate" of three hundred million as of 2018. The Geneva-based Small Arms Survey arrived at a significantly higher number in 2017—393 million or 120.5 guns for every 100 persons in the United States (Aaron Karp, *Estimating Global Civilian-Held Firearms Numbers*, briefing paper [Geneva: Small Arms Survey, 2018], 4, www.smallarmssurvey.org/fileadmin/docs/T-Briefing-Papers/SAS-BP-Civilian-Firearms-Numbers.pdf). By comparison, the next-highest number per capita in the Small Arms Survey was 52.8 per 100 persons in Yemen—a country embroiled in a brutal civil war. Privately held guns in the United States are concentrated among a third of US citizens, according to the Pew Research Center, but fully 36 percent more were willing to consider owning a gun as of 2017 (Kim Parker, Juliana Horowitz, Ruth Igielnik, J. Baxter Oliphant, and Anna Brown, *America's Complex Relationship with Guns: An in-Depth Look at the Attitudes and Experiences of US Adults* [Pew Research Center, 2017], 4, www.pewresearch.org/social-trends/2017/06/22/americas-complex-relationship-with-guns/).

circulation, it may be too late. They will be free-riding on that social peace which comes from relying not on firearms or fear but on the oft-taken-for-granted web of mutual trust, agreed-upon norms, and patient conversation guiding human interaction among most people, even gun owners themselves, most of the time. Even if they are objectively free riders in that sense, they will see themselves as patriots protecting themselves in an increasingly dangerous society. Their own individual reasons for self-preservation will diverge from collective reasoning about what best serves the common good. Arguments about what happens to them or their loved ones when guns are so readily available—quicker and more efficient suicide attempts; accidental discharges, perhaps by children—may attempt to break through from collective to personal reasoning. Yet solid firearm training and responsible use of gun lockers and safeties by them and "people like them" provide reassurance that they can remain exceptions. And perhaps they are. Or perhaps many are wrong. Either way, the point is the same: this line of thinking and deciding will always remain available, ever enticing. And with it, the free-rider problem.

Unfortunately, philosophers, social scientists, and economists alike have shown that free-rider problems can at best be mitigated and may be well-nigh insoluble. If reasons for free riding can only be renounced, not argued down, we may have to admit—as an objective statement, not some kind of religious appeal—that gun control requires nothing short of conversion.

GOOD ARGUMENTS, THWARTED

The website of the Brady Center to Prevent Gun Violence—the most visible lobbying group for this purpose in the United States—provides us with a baseline of standard arguments for gun control. It identifies an accumulation of social and economic problems gun violence either creates or exacerbates, and gun control would hopefully reduce.[3] The indispensable and even-handed book by Philip J. Cook and Kristin Goss *The Gun Debate: What Everyone Needs to Know* cites additional arguments and helps fill out those from the Brady Center.[4] Negative effects of the defensive gun culture on individual gun owners and their families are among them, implying one kind of argument for gun control. Strikingly, however, even these are often stated as collective reasons to counter aggregate harms.

---

[3] Brady Center, "Our Resources," www.bradyunited.org/resources. Unless otherwise indicated, all citations from the Brady Center will be taken from pages that branch off from this one.

[4] Cook and Goss, *The Gun Debate*. Encyclopedic rather than a work of advocacy, this book provides arguments and facts favorable to both sides of the debate. I cite it simply to supplement what the Brady Center offers.

Standard Arguments for Gun Control

Indeed, the issues that the Brady Center listed as of early 2021 on a page explicitly entitled "Effects of Gun Violence" are all aggregates:

1. *Housing prices and local economy.* Neighborhoods associated with gun violence attract fewer businesses and thus offer fewer jobs. Housing prices are lower, along with credit scores and homeownership rates.

2. *Medical costs.* The Brady Center offered statistics from 2010, in which thirty-six thousand victims of firearms assaults went to emergency rooms, and twenty-five thousand of these were admitted to the hospital. Over half of the estimated $630 million in medical treatment for gun injuries was charged to publicly funded health insurance, and thus taxpayers.

3. *Public health.* Other health costs may be indirect yet constitute no less of a "public health crisis," as the American Medical Association has labeled it, and 87 percent of Americans agreed. As the Brady Center explained, "People who are impacted by gun violence may experience stress, depression, anxiety, and post-traumatic stress disorder (PTSD). The effects of this harm extend not just to survivors but also to witnesses, bystanders, neighbors, and all those who love them."

4. *Living in fear.* This effect of gun violence certainly has a very personal dimension. Teens fearful of school shootings and their parents stand out here, with students of color expressing the highest level of concern. Continuing to highlight public health, though, the Brady Center's comment is a generalized one: "Even living under the threat of gun violence affects our health."

Other issues around which the Brady Center organizes its advocacy can certainly be quite personal, not only in their effects but in the dimension upon which I am homing in—posing relevant decision points—yet they are most convincing in the aggregate:

5. *Risks to families.* The Brady Center has organized much of its educational work under the rubric of ending "family fire," defined as "a shooting involving an improperly stored or misused gun in the home that results in death or injury." Framing the issue this way has allowed the center to draw gun owners into conversation about ways to reduce gun violence through means short of legislated gun control—keeping firearms safely "locked, unloaded, separate from ammunition, and inaccessible to children."[5] Of course the argument that gun owners are, on balance, putting their families into greater

---

[5] Brady Center, "End Family Fire," www.bradyunited.org/program/end-family-fire. See also Brady Center, *A Comprehensive Approach to Preventing Gun Violence: 116th Congress* (Washington, DC: Brady Center to Prevent Gun Violence, 2019), 6, www.bradyunited.org/the-brady-plan.

danger of accidental death than they are preventing can also be a prominent argument for gun control.⁶ To be convinced, however, gun enthusiasts would have to accept that what holds "on balance" outweighs the individual circumstances they envision.

6. *Suicide*. Closely related is the increased risk that suicide attempts will be successful when the firepower of firearms is within reach. The gun owner him/herself may be the one to suffer this form of "family fire." The Brady Center cited findings published in the *Annals of Internal Medicine* according to which guns in the home increase the risk of completed suicides by 300 percent.⁷

As vivid as these dangers are—even or especially in the form of personal anecdotes—individuals deciding whether to purchase a gun or to vote to preserve an absolute right to gun ownership can still assure themselves that *they themselves* will remain responsible gun owners, well-trained in gun safety, and that other people outside of their social circles are the ones vulnerable to mental illness, for example. As compelling as a 300-percent statistical increase may be "overall," in the aggregate, it may scarcely influence them at their own points of decision. So too with two additional kinds of societal harms that surface in Cook and Goss and that argue for gun control:

7. *Violent crime rates*. Not only does the United States have more violent crime than other high-income countries, according to Cook and Goss, "where the US rates are really off the scale is with respect to homicide, and these high homicide rates are largely the product of America's outsized rates of *gun* homicide." Compared to Canada, for example, the gun homicide rate in the United States in 2017 was "a staggering 510% higher."⁸

8. *Intensification of violence*. Correlation is not causation, however, so Cook and Goss took pains to emphasize that the issue is not reducible to a simplistic claim such as "more guns, more crime." Rather, guns *intensify* violence:

> They take a bad situation and make it deadly. And because guns can be used to kill quickly, with little effort and from a distance, they give individuals who are so inclined the capacity to terrorize neighbor-

---

⁶ While recognizing the legitimate reasons that gun owners might want guns in their home, Cook and Goss note that "those who keep a loaded handgun accessible to fend off intruders buy their sense of security at a price of an increased chance of misuse by household members, especially if there are children at home, or violence-prone adults, or anyone who abuses drugs or is suicidal" (Cook and Goss, *The Gun Debate*, 23).

⁷ Andrew Anglemyer, Tara Horvath, and George Rutherford, "The Accessibility of Firearms and Risk for Suicide and Homicide Victimization among Household Members: A Systematic Review and Meta-Analysis," *Annals of Internal Medicine* 160, no. 2 (21 January 2014): 101–10, doi:10.7326/M13–1301.

⁸ Cook and Goss, *The Gun Debate*, 53.

hoods, assassinate even well-guarded public officials, and perpetrate one-man rampages in schools, workplaces, houses of worship, and other public places.[9]

Still, to a confident gun enthusiast for whom self-defense is the overbearing consideration, "quickly" and "deadly" may well be selling points, not alarm bells. While statistical studies pile up, the point of decision for a policymaker seeking to reduce aggregate harms remains quite distant from that of a gun owner envisioning an exceptionally immediate harm and hoping to counter it.

THE FREE-RIDER PROBLEM

One additional argument does begin to address the free-rider problem, insofar as it asks gun owners or potential gun owners to examine their assumptions about the dynamics at play in that narrow moment of immediate crisis in which they hope to act in an exceptional manner, whatever the overall statistics regarding the dangers of gun ownership. In this highly personal moment even social scientists spending their days thinking about policies that will serve the common good might nonetheless imagine a scenario wherein a loaded gun and the training to use it safely could make them and their families safer, not in the aggregate, but in the only available moment that matters *right then, right now*. However likely or unlikely to happen to any given person, this is the scenario around which gun debates pivot. As Cook and Goss put it,

> Personal safety is a vital matter, and self-protection is a more compelling rationale for owning guns than recreation. We can all conjure up the nightmare scenario of being defenseless in a violent confrontation with a burglar, mugger, carjacker, or rapist. For some people, the ready availability of a firearm brings peace of mind. Indeed, the predominant motivation for owning a gun is protection against other people.[10]

Will it work? Even-handed scholars that they are, Cook and Goss began their answer with a "qualified yes," though adding that: "Someone who is able to effectively deploy a firearm when attacked or seriously threatened may emerge from the encounter in better shape than if he or she had been unarmed." Yet the qualifiers to that "yes" are serious: "While it is surely possible to imagine instances in which having ready access to a firearm would be a lifesaver, it is also possible that it would make a bad situation worse."[11] This then could be a final

---

[9] Cook and Goss, *The Gun Debate*, 2, 63.
[10] Cook and Goss, *The Gun Debate*, 18.
[11] Cook and Goss, *The Gun Debate*, 19.

argument against owning guns for the purpose of self-protection—brandishing a gun will as often as not lead to an escalation by the very attacker one hopes to fend off.

9. *Escalation of immediate threats.* The statistics as to whether victims avoid bodily injury when they attempt to protect themselves with a gun turn out to be inconclusive.[12] While guns may help *some* to emerge unharmed, according to Cook and Goss,

> It is also true that introducing a firearm into the confrontation may escalate the level of violence and ultimately result in greater harm to the victim than would have been caused by alternative strategies—such as fleeing, reasoning with the assailant, or summoning help. And there is always the possibility that the "victim" will misunderstand the other person's intentions, in which case the gun can be the mechanism for a tragic mistake.[13]

Pointing a gun at an intruder attempts to induce fear in hopes that the adversary will back down, but also gives them a reason to pull their own trigger sooner rather than later. Rather than convincing the aggressor to stand down, one may simply be accelerating a vicious cycle of increasingly dangerous mimetic reaction. Cook and Goss summarized: "Common sense suggests that using a gun in response to a perceived threat could make things better or worse," but in either case what is certain is that gun use "tends to up the ante in the confrontation."[14]

---

[12] Cook and Goss, *The Gun Debate*, 18–19.

[13] Cook and Goss, *The Gun Debate*, 19. Although I am trying to give the benefit of the doubt to gun owners by stipulating good training and able marksmanship, note that we have now narrowed the scenario considerably. If we were to begin panning out from the exceptional to the average again, all kinds of things could go wrong. In her classic essay in favor of pacifism, the folk singer Joan Baez began her deconstruction of the situation in which she might hypothetically protect her grandmother from an attacker by making this point through humor:
"Say he had a gun, and he was about to shoot her. Would you shoot him first?"
"Do I have a gun?"
"Yes."
"No. I'm a pacifist, I don't have a gun."
"Well, say you do."
"All right. Am I a good shot?"
"Yes."
"I'd shoot the gun out of his hand."
"No, then you're not a good shot."
"I'd be afraid to shoot. Might kill Grandma."
Joan Baez, "What Would You Do If?," *Theology Today* 25, no. 4 (1969): 478. The essay first appeared in *Atlantic Monthly*, August 1968, 32–34, and later in Joan Baez, *Daybreak* (New York: Dial, 1968), 131–138.

[14] Cook and Goss, *The Gun Debate*, 20.

So where does that leave us? Gun advocates will undoubtedly marshal arguments to counter each of the nine points I have listed above, while gun-control advocates will then proffer counter-counterarguments. My purpose here is not to adjudicate but simply to drive home this point: even if arguments for gun control prove better and more convincing by the standards of social science, the free-rider problem will persist. At the point of decision indeed so often decisive—where enough people set society's agenda—we are at best at a stand-off.

Reading Cook and Goss, one can watch the free-rider problem snapping debates back toward sole consideration of what will happen to me or my loved ones in an imaginable, fear-inducing situation—back from aggregate considerations about what policies would be best for the common good to individual considerations gun owners find convincing. A single paragraph may illustrate:

> Perceptions of whether guns make "us" safer depend to some extent on whether the person asked, or someone else, has the weapon. Consider a fun survey experiment conducted in the mid-1990s. The first of two surveys asked whether "ordinary Americans" after "proper training" should be able to carry a gun on their person. In response, 65% of respondents said no. The second survey personalized the scenario by asking whether "average Americans, such as yourself" should be allowed to get a concealed-carry license "for self-protection." Here the result flipped: 60% now were in support.[15]

As people move imaginatively in from concentric social circles farther away from them to closer ones, and then to themselves, they become more confident that guns will do them good. Defensive gun culture thrives on fear of those who are "other," of course, but even if human beings were able to survey society without prejudice, it is almost a tautology that self-protection would remain a more proximate concern. No wonder Cook and Goss find that "the number-one reason for owning a firearm is personal security."[16]

Here, then, is how the free-rider problem works in the context of gun ownership: let us stipulate gun owners who are well-trained and consistently safety-conscious in a way that protects their family from accidental discharge. *I* may not be convinced that gun owners will be safer in high-pressured crisis situations where they imagine using a

---

[15] Cook and Goss, *The Gun Debate*, 29. The footnote to this paragraph reads: "Tarrance Group and Mellman, Lazarus & Lake/US News & World Report, May 16–18, 1994 (1,000 telephone interviews of a national adult sample); Tarrance Group/American Firearms Council, July 21–23, 1996 (1,004 telephone interviews of a national sample of registered voters)."
[16] Cook and Goss, *The Gun Debate*, 29.

gun for protection, given the accelerating unpredictability intrinsic to those very situations—but *they* are convinced. At least within the narrowed parameters of these scenarios alone, Cook and Goss have reported that the statistical findings about actual outcomes are inconclusive.[17] Even though something very visceral is inevitably part of the fearful scenario people are imagining,[18] a decision for gun ownership cannot simply be dismissed as irrational.

Nonetheless, let us also stipulate that a portion of gun owners might be able to compartmentalize the visceral and be open to evidence showing that in the aggregate, the presence of so many guns in the United States leads to more violence *overall*. As a matter of public policy—in the aggregate, again—it is arguably rational to discourage, regulate, reduce, and even work to eliminate individual gun ownership someday. We are thus in a stand-off between competing rationalities. In a society in which the best we can hope for is reasonable regulation of guns, gun control advocates gain little by denying a certain rationality to gun ownership. The very disjunction between the rationality of gun control and the simultaneous rationality of gun ownership marks an instantiation of the free-rider problem. What is rational for a larger community or society as a whole may not be rational for an individual or limited group, and vice versa.

There are other names for this kind of challenge or problem or dilemma as noticed in different disciplines. We have already mentioned what political scientists and sociologists call "*the collective action problem*"—how to get individuals to work together for a solution that would benefit all, when each has incentives to hang back. Philosophers and environmentalists have noted "*the tragedy of the commons*" by which we actually make things worse and despoil the shared resources we need to live productive lives precisely as we pursue our self-interests. Ethicists make their students think through "*the prisoner's dilemma*" in order to help them recognize how important though hard it is to identify what actually might be in our *enlightened self-interest* if only we could find a way to cooperate. Meanwhile, as climate change becomes increasingly ominous, the

---

[17] Cook and Goss, *The Gun Debate*, 18–19.
[18] Even an essay arguing for an ethic of nonviolence in situations of personal threat that would seem to call for violent self-defense recognizes this dimension: "This question ... is troubling precisely because of its personal specificity and because of the visceral reaction it evokes. You are present as one of your own loved ones is being attacked. And you are being asked to respond as you would, or as you hope that you would, in that moment of crisis. It carries within it so much particularity" (Amy Laura Hall and Kara Slade, "What Would You Do If Someone Were Attacking a Loved One?," in *A Faith not Worth Fighting for: Addressing Commonly Asked Questions about Christian Nonviolence*, ed. Tripp York and Justin Bronson Barringer [Eugene, OR: Cascade, 2012], 31).

free-rider problem itself seems to be getting increased attention at the juncture between economics and environmentalism. From small businesses to entire nations, there are perverse incentives to continue drawing on the shared resources of both natural and built environments while emitting carbon dioxide and other pollutants without paying for "externalities"—the costs of doing business that accrue to others without ever appearing on one's own ledger. The challenge is that there seem to be insufficient incentives to clean up or change one's own practices unless everyone else does so simultaneously. Free riders thus ride gamely on.

As one surveys these different but overlapping disciplines, it is hard to avoid the conclusion that the free-rider problem as variously named may well be insoluble.[19] The Nobel-winning economist Ronald Coase attempted to defend the strength and capacity of free markets by showing how they could account for externalities—avoiding one kind of free-riding—but his defense of what came to be known as the Coase Theorem relied on highly delimited cases involving only two parties.[20] Other economists debating the Coase Theorem eventually demonstrated why the free-rider problem resurfaces as soon as theorists introduce just one more party into their scenarios[21]—underscoring the difficulty of blocking out free-riders amid the boundless network of those who have any kind of stake in environmental degradation or the proliferation of gun ownership for self-defense, especially given unequal power.[22] Garrett Hardin, who penned the famous essay "The Tragedy of the Commons," warning of environmental catastrophe due to population explosion, did offer possible solutions but they were so grim and coercive that the essay is most often remembered as a counsel of despair.[23] The so-called "prisoner's dilemma" (in which either one of two prisoners in separate cells can go free if he alone betrays the other, but doesn't know what the other is doing) has been a classic not only among game theorists but among ethicists and moral philosophers for over half a century

---

[19] The field of Christian ethics seems mainly to have addressed the free-rider problem and its cognates indirectly. Note however the emerging work of Mary Nickel in her paper at the 2021 meeting of the Society of Christian Ethics entitled "Blessed Assurance: A Theological Ethics of Collective Action Problems."

[20] R. H. Coase, "Problem of Social Cost," *Journal of Law and Economics* 3 (October 1960): 1–44.

[21] Tore Ellingsen and Elena Paltseva, "Confining the Coase Theorem: Contracting, Ownership, and Free-Riding," *Review of Economic Studies* 83, no. 2 (April 2016): 547–586.

[22] Stéphane Gonzalez, Alain Marciano, and Philippe Solal, "The Social Cost Problem, Rights, and the (Non)Empty Core," *Journal of Public Economic Theory* 21, no. 2 (April 2019): 347–365.

[23] Garrett Hardin, "The Tragedy of the Commons," *Science* 162 (13 December 1968): 1243–1248.

precisely because it allows no neat way to break through even to enlightened self-interest.

Sociologists and political scientists do keep working at ways to build up enough social capital or critical mass to break through to the other side of the collective action problem,[24] and some have traced how this has happened in other times and cultures.[25] American individualism certainly makes this harder insofar as it "undermines civic charity by reaping the benefits of civic relationships while denying any concomitant responsibilities," as Christopher Jones and Conor Kelly noted, even as they held out hope that structural as well as cultural remedies could offset this free-riding tendency.[26] A mixed but in-this-regard-hopeful case study of social mobilization among poor white South Africans in a neighborhood of Cape Town suggests that at least on a local level it is possible to initiate collective action, building up trust and social capital even among strangers in a way that will make further collective action easier next time.[27] It may be a bug or a feature, but mobilization to break through the collective-action problem proved most viable locally. That is a clue to which I will return.

We are left to conclude that the free-rider problem and its cognates can never be eliminated wholesale. The best we may be able to hope for is to mitigate them. The question then is how, at what level, at which social locations, and by whom. Even if change is possible at the level of law and policy, there must be people to do the changing—people of a certain character and formation.

NOTHING SHORT OF CONVERSION?

---

[24] Michael W. Macy, "Learning Theory and the Logic of Critical Mass," *American Sociological Review* 55, no. 6 (December 1990): 809–826; Michael Laver, "Political Solutions to the Collective Action Problem," *Political Studies* 28, no. 2 (June 1980): 195–209.

[25] Dominic D. P. Johnson, "God's Punishment and Public Goods," *Human Nature* 16, no. 4 (December 2005): 410–446; Courtney Jung, "Breaking the Cycle: Producing Trust out of Thin Air and Resentment," *Social Movement Studies* 2, no. 2 (October 2003): 147–175.

[26] Christopher D. Jones and Conor M. Kelly, "Sloth: America's Ironic Structural Vice," *Journal of the Society of Christian Ethics* 37, no. 2 (Fall 2017): 117–134; quotation from 117.

[27] Jung, "Breaking the Cycle." What makes this case study mixed is that there were some racial undercurrents in the mobilization it found possible. On the one hand, residents of the neighborhood mobilized to protest the bussing of hundreds of black students into their school. On the other hand, they had legitimate complaints that their school had been so underfunded and neglected that it could not host more students of *any* color. Jung also provides evidence that racial tensions, though present, were not a dominant factor: "Some mixed-race couples we interviewed claimed in fact that they had moved to Ruyterwacht because it was less racially hostile than other areas where they had lived" (154).

To recognize the challenge of gun-control as a free-rider problem hardly is original. Kristin Goss's *Disarmed: The Missing Movement for Gun Control in America* is a sustained effort to chart ways to organize sufficient collective action to overcome it.[28] As the subtitle suggests, what prompted Goss's book was the paradox that has puzzled many—why there is no real movement for gun control in the United States even though a strong majority of Americans favor it.[29] The "traditional" or "textbook" answer is that while political support for gun control is widespread, it is also diffuse, whereas support for gun rights is intense and focused through one-issue voting.[30] But why is *that* the case? Goss wanted to go deeper. To answer she examined "an array of structural constraints, historical developments, and organizational choices," in which the success of gun-control opponents' use of American federalism has been a through-line.[31] Still, the divergent intensity on opposite sides of the gun debate itself reflects a free-rider disjunction, and the problem surfaces even as analysis moves from the passion that drives individual agency to the dynamics of movement organization. The National Rifle Association can offer its members both concrete benefits and focused lobbying that channels a deeply-felt sense of identity, while organizations advocating for gun control struggle to offer more than a generalized prospect of greater public safety.[32] Naming this itself as a free-rider problem, Goss studied the success of other movements which "have found ways around that problem."[33]

Although the very goal of "securing a public good" leaves gun control "inherently vulnerable to the free-rider problem," Goss held out hope that "the free-rider problem can be overcome under certain circumstances"[34] and explored how. Together, three core social-movement strategies might turn the free-rider problem inside out by distributing or "socializing" the costs of gun control individuals otherwise try to avoid, while bringing home, "personalizing," or "individualizing" the otherwise diffuse and generalized social benefits of freedom from gun violence.[35] Citing historical examples from other

---

[28] For explicit discussions of free-rider dynamics see Kristin A. Goss, *Disarmed: The Missing Movement for Gun Control in America* (Princeton, NJ: Princeton University Press, 2006), 26–28, 50, 60, 108, 174, 190–191.
[29] Goss, *Disarmed*, 3.
[30] Goss, *Disarmed*, 6–7.
[31] Goss, *Disarmed*, 3.
[32] This is my own summary of points in Goss, *Disarmed*, 90–91.
[33] Goss, *Disarmed*, 91.
[34] Goss, *Disarmed*, 50, 27.
[35] Goss, *Disarmed*, 108. For additional summaries of this overarching strategic principle of reversal, see also 50–51; 72. The three subsidiary strategies are: (1) "Socializing the costs of participation" (51–60, further developed in chapter 3); (2) "Personalizing the

social movements, Goss argued that gun-control advocates should (1) *socialize the costs of participation* by attaining the patronage of larger institutions (philanthropic or even governmental); (2) *personalize the benefits of participation* by identifying "compelling, actionable self-interest" that shows sympathizers what they will have to gain through greater movement participation; and (3) *boost the participation payoff* by aiming for incremental, achievable localized policy wins that cement participants' sense of empowerment and personal identity. As a result, "individuals can see a benefit to participating in social reform and recognize the cost of doing nothing. When issues are so personalized, intensity rises. Even though free-rider problems are still present, they are greatly reduced."[36]

Goss did not characterize this flipping of the logic of free-riding as "conversion," religious or otherwise. The obvious reason is that she is a social scientist who uses the terminology of her discipline. One might also anticipate that such language—like a certain kind of disempowering Evangelical discourse—implies that there is no use working for social justice without transforming individual hearts through personal salvation. Making a sustained argument against centralized, top-down approaches to political changes and in favor of "modest measures" achievable through "incrementalism,"[37] her contention was still about how to achieve legislative and policy change, not to distract from them as goals. Along the way she drew both on examples of other movements in US history that have had some measure of success at "champion[ing] policy proposals that would regulate individual behavior and hence restrict liberty,"[38] and sociological analysis of social movement dynamics. Since the free-rider problem names a stand-off between individual self-interest and collective goods (or at least enlightened self-interest), Goss's strategies necessarily pivoted around shifts in decisions and agency by individual citizens, who must come to identify more intensely with the gun-control cause and join, and then participate energetically, in voluntary organizations if there is to be a social movement at all.

In a sense, one should hardly need to argue that gun-control advocates ought to put the theme of conversion on the table: gun enthusiasts have already done so. James Atwood, a Presbyterian pastor who is both a hunter and a gun-control activist, has described much of the work of the National Rifle Association and gun manufacturers as

---

benefits of participation" (60–65, further developed in chapter 4); and (3) "Boosting the participation payoff" (65–72, further developed in chapter 5).
[36] Goss, *Disarmed*, 127.
[37] Goss, *Disarmed*, 145–189.
[38] Goss, *Disarmed*, 51.

"vigorous evangelizing."³⁹ To the degree that gun ownership has arguably taken on religious dimensions, such terminology becomes simple description, not metaphor. Atwood has not shied away from proposing that for at least some in the United States, guns have become idols.⁴⁰ For a Christian minister or theologian, "idolatry" can have a precise and technical meaning. For believers in *any* of the three Abrahamic traditions, trust that some competitor to God will secure our lives is precisely what constitutes idolatry. Catholic Bishop Michael William Warfel illustrated how this works when he told of a woman who hesitated to be baptized because she heard parishioners speaking in favor of gun control:

> She was speaking of the Second Amendment as if it were the second commandment of the Decalogue from the Bible. She had elevated the Bill of Rights to the level of a holiness code. For her, the right to own and bear arms, and to do so with minimal limitations, were God-given rights and therefore sacred.⁴¹

Though it is tempting—and for some people accurate—to describe gun ownership as "a religion" in and of itself, it is analytically safer to see it as a cross-cutting religious phenomenon or movement (by analogy, in a class more like Fundamentalism, the Charismatic Movement, or an ancient heresy rather than constituting a denomination or religion *per se*). Atwood has offered the provocative term "Gundamentalism" as a way to name the quasi-theological and mystical belief in the power of guns.⁴²

Social scientists may want to be more cautious and precise, but clearly the right to own and use firearms to protect oneself and one's family has for many become an article of faith alongside other beliefs. With the help of a qualitative study conducted in northeastern Kansas, Abigail Vegter and Margaret Kelley have shown how beliefs about guns can correlate with a cluster of other beliefs about the supernatural character of evil, Armageddon, Hell, and the demonic.⁴³ Another correlative set of beliefs defines what sociologists Andrew Whitehead

---

³⁹ James E. Atwood, *America and Its Guns: A Theological Exposé* (Eugene, OR: Cascade, 2012), 203.
⁴⁰ Atwood, *America and Its Guns*, 19–21. Also note the titles to chapters 3, and 9–13.
⁴¹ Michael William Warfel, "Why Gun Control?," *America* 182 (15 April 2000): 18.
⁴² In addition to *America and Its Guns*, see James E. Atwood, *Collateral Damage: Changing the Conversation about Firearms and Faith* (Harrisonburg, VA: Herald, 2019) and James E. Atwood and Jan Orr-Harter, *Gundamentalism and Where It is Taking America*, including discussion questions by Jan Orr-Harter (Eugene, OR: Cascade, 2017).
⁴³ Abigail Vegter and Margaret Kelley, "The Protestant Ethic and the Spirit of Gun Ownership," *Journal for the Scientific Study of Religion* 59, no. 3 (September 2020): 526–540.

and Samuel Perry have called "Christian nationalism"—"a collection of myths, traditions, symbols, narratives, and value systems ... that idealizes and advocates a fusion of Christianity with American civic life."[44] In Whitehead and Perry's analysis, Christian nationalism overlaps with but is distinguishable from white Evangelicalism.[45] Christian nationalists are "least likely to support federal gun control legislation," while "those who attend church more often, pray more often, or read their Bible more frequently are more likely to support gun control."[46]

One lesson moral theologians can draw from Whitehead and Perry, then, is that conversion, formation, and transformation really do make a difference. The question is whether gun-control advocates and other progressives will recover an appetite for framing their message as a call to conversion away from faith in the power of guns. Whitehead, Perry, or Goss cannot be expected to talk and frame the issue in religious terms. As theologians, I and other contributors to this issue should put aside any such scruples.

To be sure, the pull of those scruples is unmistakable. Martin Marty—for many decades one of the most prolific representatives of mainstream Protestantism in the United States—has noted that even thinkers who try to distinguish coercive and disrespectful "proselytism" from responsible and dialogical efforts at "conversion" have to exercise great care. For they are deeply aware

> that in the present-day cultures in which most readers of this book reside, the sound of the word has pejorative overtones and undertones. In these cultures it is ordinarily not considered good to proselytize. Those who speak positively about doing so on any scale have to know that they are inviting complex criticism or even simple dismissal.[47]

---

[44] Andrew L. Whitehead and Samuel L. Perry, *Taking America Back for God: Christian Nationalism in the United States* (New York: Oxford University Press, 2020), 10.

[45] Whitehead and Perry, *Taking America Back for God*, x, 20–21, 84–87. On page 153 they add: "Christian nationalism is significant because calls to 'take America back for God' are not primarily about mobilizing the faithful toward religious ends. Some social scientists have argued that when Evangelicals appeal to the religious heritage of the United States or work toward privileging Christianity in the public sphere they are focused on encouraging greater religious devotion. We disagree. They are instead seeking to retain or gain power in the public sphere—whether political, social, or religious. Christian nationalism is, therefore, ultimately about privilege. It co-opts Christian language and iconography in order to cloak particular political or social ends in moral and religious symbolism."

[46] Whitehead and Perry, *Taking America Back for God*, 155.

[47] Martin E. Marty, "Proselytizers and Proselytizees on the Sharp Arete of Modernity," in *Sharing the Book: Religious Perspectives on the Rights and Wrongs of Proselytism*, ed. John Witte, Jr. and Richard C. Martin (Maryknoll, NY: Orbis Books, 1999), 2.

The intellectual atmosphere of post-Enlightenment modernity gives general reasons for this caution, which Marty went on to list: the modern celebration of freedom and autonomy, the requirements of pluralism, sensitivity about the insecure identities that come along with freedom and pluralism, and an ensuing struggle between relativism and potentially violent absolutisms.[48] Post-Conquest, post-Holocaust, and post-colonialization, the legacy of centuries of efforts to force conversion means that violence is no mere specter; in ecumenical circles, the Holocaust and the centuries of Christian anti-Semitism that prepared for it serve as a regular reminder.[49]

A glance across the ocean might serve to remind those anxious about rhetorics of conversion to beware of what they wish for, lest protestation against proselytism serve to insulate nationalism from critique. Since 1989, efforts to distinguish proper evangelism from proselytism have become especially heated in the context of Central and Eastern Europe, where Orthodox churches protest the incursion of Evangelical and Pentecostal groups from the West. The threat these groups represent is not only to the ecclesiological turf of older churches but to the cohesion of national identities for which Orthodoxy has claimed to be the glue.[50] Whether such protestation is legitimate and when[51] probably depends on how one evaluates specific forms of patriotism, nationalism, and efforts to preserve a specific cohesion that has historically relied on religion. The point here is not to discredit legitimate concerns of Eastern Orthodox leaders, but to issue a reality check back on the American side of the Atlantic. At a time when many are sounding warnings not only about Christian

---

[48] Marty, "Proselytizers and Proselytizees," 2–3.

[49] See Marc H. Tanenbaum, Marvin R. Wilson, and A. James Rudin, eds., *Evangelicals and Jews in an Age of Pluralism* (Grand Rapids, MI: Baker Book House, 1984); John Witte, Jr. and Richard C. Martin, eds., *Sharing the Book: Religious Perspectives on the Rights and Wrongs of Proselytism* (Maryknoll, NY: Orbis Books, 1999).

[50] See John Witte, Jr. and Michael Bourdeaux, *Proselytism and Orthodoxy in Russia: The New War for Souls* (Maryknoll, NY: Orbis Books, 1999); Miroslav Volf, "Fishing in the Neighbor's Pond: Mission and Proselytism in Eastern Europe," *International Bulletin of Missionary Research* 20, no. 1 (January 1996): 26–31; Darrell Richard Jackson, "Proselytism in a Central and Eastern European Perspective," *Journal of European Baptist Studies* 8, no. 2 (January 2008): 18–36; Tim Noble, "Proselytism and the Ethics of Mission," *Acta Missiologiae* 6 (2018): 47–63.

[51] As Tim Noble has noted, "In practice, the debate is hard to even get started. I presume that just about everyone will agree that it is wrong to tell lies, to manipulate or to use psychological, physical or social force to persuade people to change their religious confession. That is not the problem. The problem is, as so often, with how we name what we see. In English the verb seems to be conjugated 'I evangelise, you proselytise'" (Noble, "Proselytism and the Ethics of Mission," 56).

nationalism but also more extreme forms of white nationalism, gun-control advocates who join them are already distinguishing among and critiquing at least some forms of nationalism. Not all US gun owners are nationalists, of course, much less white nationalists, but protecting the Second Amendment is a particularly impassioned tenet that unites disparate movements and helps them recruit regular gun owners to their cause.[52] When "God, guns, and country" falls easily off the tongue and onto the placard, one kind of conversion has already been happening for a long time. To counter it, progressives may need preachers more than they need policy wonks.

To point out the many ways guns already constitute a religious issue might seem akin to "whataboutism"—the fallacious rhetorical tactic of deflecting criticism of one's own position or practice by claiming that one's opponents are doing the same. Kristen Goss's *Disarmed* makes clear why more than that is going on. Identity issues are a thread running throughout her analysis of social movements and strategic proposals. No social movement can be effective unless otherwise disaffected individuals come to recognize themselves as part of a group and begin to act collectively; agency comes by way of identity, Goss has observed.[53] Two of her three top-level strategies thus aim to personalize general social benefits, and then deepen and intensify those persons' participation.[54] The process addresses values as it moves people to define their identity according to "purposive benefits" that "appeal to people's sense of altruism."[55] After all,

> to understand mass mobilization we must first understand what causes people to care enough to overcome the natural free-rider impulse. Economic interest is one answer but many of the most salient policy debates in America revolve around noneconomic considerations such as identity, justice, morality, or security.[56]

For activists on the ground, the key to all this is "reframing" the gun issue in order to change the scope of individuals' assessment of their interests: "What frames do is legitimize the involvement of

---

[52] Evidence here must probably be journalistic. For such evidence see, for example, Mike Giglio, "'Civil War is Here, Right Now': The President's Supporters on the Militant Right Are Bracing for Conflict," *The Atlantic* 326, no. 4 (November 2020): 68–69.

[53] Goss, *Disarmed*, 32. See also her further elaboration of this point on page 116, and her comments on page 33 on how leaders of the Civil Rights Movement drew upon "black group identity forged through centuries of repression and group agency," expressed and solidified through "historically black colleges and churches" that provided "volunteers, money, leadership, and other movement resources."

[54] Goss, *Disarmed*, 60–72.

[55] Goss, *Disarmed*, 57.

[56] Goss, *Disarmed*, 60.

interested individuals by creating a 'we.' Thus, effective frames expand the scope of conflict by linking personal identity to collective action."[57]

Even if we are talking about shifts and transformations of identity on the purely secular terms of social science, then, we are talking about some kind of "conversion." As we have seen, Goss's social movement strategies together aim to turn the free-rider problem inside out by "socializing" the costs of gun control while "personalizing" its otherwise diffuse or aggregate social benefits. My own point is this: insofar as the free-rider problem represents a stand-off between competing rationalities, more than reason is needed to jump from limited to enlightened self-interest—to say nothing of crossing the threshold to altruism and a generalized concern for the common good. It would thus be foolish and short-sighted for those working for freedom from gun violence to be too chary or polite that they keep the need for conversion off the table.

JUST-PEACE ETHICS AS AN OFFER OF "GOOD NEWS"

Additional objections to this claim may linger. One such objection might be that Evangelicalism has so entrapped and impoverished the language of conversion as to render it irretrievable. Closely related, another might be that even if retrievable—as available in the common heritage of Christianity—the language of conversion is intrinsically too individualistic to be helpful for social policy. Third, for moral theology to speak to social policy in a pluralistic society requires argumentation that appeals to non-particularized reasons and motivations, such that religious overtones in the word "conversion" could prove distracting. Finally, even if all of these objections are met—a skeptic might say—to affect public policy would require not just conversion but many conversions and indeed mass conversion, so that if mass conversion is our only hope our situation may indeed be hopeless.

Some of these objections can be met with brief historical reminders. Not only does Evangelicalism not hold a trademark on "conversion" but the tradition and historical precursors that prepared for its emergence in the twentieth century have played a greater role in liberative social movements than its contemporary reputation would allow.[58] The questions of how much hope we dare place in conversion,

---

[57] Goss, *Disarmed*, 107.
[58] See Donald W. Dayton, *Rediscovering an Evangelical Heritage: A Tradition and Trajectory of Integrating Piety and Justice*, with Douglas M. Strong, foreword by Jim Wallis (Grand Rapids, MI: Baker Academic, 2014). Adjacent both in issues and tradition is the work of Paul Alexander on Pentecostalism and peace witness: *Peace to War: Shifting Allegiances in the Assemblies of God*, foreword by Glen Stassen

however, and whether its religious overtones are necessarily distracting, hinge on what we envision when we hear the term.

As long as believers heed the insistence of Pope Paul VI that they must *propose* not *impose* their message,[59] then putting conversion back on the table could certainly involve preaching, apologetics, or outright evangelism—but this is secondary. What is crucial is the shape of the gospel being proclaimed, and whether it invites transformation to the fullness of love for God *and love for neighbor as oneself.* This is a love that curves not in on itself but outward in the expectation that the self will find fulfillment only through reconciled relationships that reach out even to enemies. Differing theories of atonement in the Christian tradition may set the stage for such proclamation with lesser or greater clarity. In a way, however, any conception of atonement will do, so long as it recognizes God's gracious initiative and expects our response to issue in active gratitude.[60] It is altogether biblical and orthodox to insist that however forgiveness happens, the only rightful response by us who once made ourselves God's enemies through sin (Romans 5:8–10) is to reciprocate gratefully with a corresponding grace toward others, even our enemies. This is the lesson of the Parable of the Ungrateful Servant in Matthew 18:23–32. And then, to those with ears to hear and eyes to see, a whole new, wholly creative dynamic is being released into the world—thus revealing a new world for those "in Christ" (2 Cor 5:17), and with it a new worldview: *God's grace. Our gratitude. Issuing in graciousness toward others.* The unfurling of grace corresponds to the furling of fear.

"Who's on first?" is an old comedy routine by Abbott and Costello but also an ancient and deadly serious question for humanity. Who will make the first move to break the vicious cycles that ensnare us in accelerating patterns of violence? Christians believe—or at least claim to believe—that in Jesus Christ, none less than the God who created the universe has reached out first, taken the initiative, the ultimate risk,

---

(Scottdale, PA: Herald, 2009); *Pentecostals and Nonviolence: Reclaiming a Heritage*, foreword by Stanley Hauerwas (Eugene, OR: Pickwick, 2012).

[59] Pope Paul VI, *Evangelii Nuntiandi [Evangelization in the Modern World]*, apostolic letter (1975), no. 80.

[60] While my argument here does not require choosing among the several Christian theories of atonement, I do expect that the most adequate would reflect insights akin to those of René Girard. I refer especially to the way the French literary critic and philosopher connected the death of Jesus as innocent victim to patterns of mimesis and the breaking of cycles of violence and injustice not only in the biblical drama but through the arch of history. For a helpful introduction to Girard's wide-ranging and visionary work see Rowan Williams, "Foreword," in *Can We Survive Our Origins?: Readings in René Girard's Theory of Violence and the Sacred*, ed. Pierpaolo Antonello and Paul Gifford (East Lansing: Michigan State University Press, 2015), xi–xvi.

and broken humanity's cycle of recriminating, mimetic, self-protecting violence. To respond violently even when one does so with just cause may fuel vicious cycles by inflicting new injustices and inviting recrimination. The *kenosis* (self-emptying) of Jesus Christ that the hymn embedded in Philippians 2 charts is God's decisive inversion of the free-rider problem. And it should also be ours. To identify through any kind of gratitude with the faith or logic or aesthetic of this drama is—in the vision of Saint Paul—to start becoming "of the same mind," looking increasingly to the interests of others and not just one's own self-interest (Phil 2:2–5). That means I might be the one called to risk being the next to "go first"—do the unexpected for the sake of others. With that, *behold, a new creation!* Those who accept the reconciliation "all" from God are drawn into God's own ministry of reconciliation (2 Cor 5:17–20). The Jesus of St. Paul or of the Creed is not different from the Jesus of the Gospels and the Sermon on the Mount; my "personal salvation" is wholly of a piece with the salvation of the world. To recognize the dynamic power of "going first" that stretches from the cosmic to the salvation-historical to the daily personal is key to keeping Jesus our Savior theologically indivisible from Jesus our Lord and Teacher; it highlights the ethical import in naming him none less than the second person of the Trinity and provides the ultimate grounding—both biblical and metaphysical—for a just-peace ethic.

Nomenclature has varied somewhat as a "just-peace ethic" has developed in continuity with the "just-peacemaking theory" the late Baptist ethicist Glen Stassen and others have championed, while benefiting from the maturing field of peace studies and an increasingly professional field of strategic peacebuilding.[61] Calls for a just-peace ethic have gained new attention thanks to an "Appeal to the Catholic Church to Recommit to Gospel Nonviolence" at a meeting in Rome in April 2016 organized by Pax Christi International and the Pontifical Council for Justice and Peace,[62] but also from mainstream Protestant

---

[61] Eli S. McCarthy, ed., *A Just Peace Ethic Primer: Building Sustainable Peace and Breaking Cycles of Violence* (Washington, DC: Georgetown University Press, 2020); Glen H. Stassen, ed., *Just Peacemaking: The New Paradigm for the Ethics of Peace and War*, 3rd edition (Cleveland, OH: Pilgrim, 2008); Daniel Philpott and Gerard F. Powers, eds., *Strategies of Peace: Transforming Conflict in a Violent World* (New York: Oxford University Press, 2010). For a summary of just-peace norms, criteria, and practices, see Gerald W. Schlabach, "What is 'Just Peace'?," March 2, 2018, www.geraldschlabach.net/2018/03/02/what-is-just-peace.

[62] Pax Christi International, "An Appeal to the Catholic Church to Re-Commit to the Centrality of Gospel Nonviolence," final document of the conference "Nonviolence and Just Peace: Contributing to the Catholic Understanding of and Commitment to Nonviolence," hosted by the Pontifical Council for Justice and Peace in Rome, April 2016, nonviolencejustpeace.net/appeal-to-the-catholic-church. For an account of the development of this initiative, see Marie Dennis, ed., *Choosing Peace: The Catholic*

efforts in recent decades to break through the centuries-old impasse between pacifist and just-war traditions in order to reach a new consensus,[63] as well as from ecumenical dialogue between paradigmatic representatives of those traditions—Mennonites on the historic peace church side, and Roman Catholics delegated by the Vatican.[64]

What has driven much of this decades-long initiative and shaped the emerging just-peace ethic is—as the name implies—the hope for a synthesis or Hegelian *Aufhebung* that simultaneously transcends yet preserves the best of both elements.[65] Whatever the terminology, the work of just peacebuilding seeks to hold on to the best-intentioned end of just-war tradition—achieving the most effective justice realistically possible in this fallen world—while also holding on to the moral vision of pacifist traditions by insisting that means to the end of justice must themselves be just, specifically as they respect the dignity of all by avoiding new harms. If such a synthesis can realign means and ends in what Eli McCarthy has called the principle or norm of "reflexivity,"[66] then the limitations and dangers of both just-war and

---

Church Returns to Gospel Nonviolence (Maryknoll, NY: Orbis Books, 2018). For a fuller and more seasoned articulation of the implications of the 2016 appeal, see Catholic Nonviolence Initiative, *Advancing Nonviolence and Integral Peace in the Church and the World: Biblical, Theological, Ethical, Pastoral, and Strategic Dimensions of Nonviolence*, ed. Rose Marie Berger, Ken Butigan, Judy Coode, and Marie Dennis (Brussels: Pax Christi International, 2020).

[63] World Council of Churches, *Overcoming Violence: The Ecumenical Decade 2001–2010* (Geneva: World Council of Churches, 2011), www.overcomingviolence.org/file admin/dov/files/OvercomingViolence.pdf; World Council of Churches, *An Ecumenical Call to Just Peace*, received, endorsed, and commended for study, reflection, collaboration, and common action during the Central Committee meetings in February 2011 (Geneva: World Council of Churches, 2011), www.overcoming violence.org/en/resources-dov/wcc-resources/documents/declarations-on-just-peace/ecumenical-call-to-just-peace.html.

[64] Mennonite World Conference and Pontifical Council for Promoting Church Unity, "Called Together to Be Peacemakers: Report of the International Dialogue between the Catholic Church and Mennonite World Conference, 1998–2003," *Information Service* 2003-II/III, no. 113 (2004): 111–148, www.christianunity.va/content/unitacristiani/it/dialoghi/sezione-occidentale/conferenza-mennonita-mondiale/documenti-di-dialogo/2003-called-together-to-be-peacemakers-/en.html; Mennonite World Conference and Pontifical Council for Promoting Church Unity, "A Mennonite and Catholic Contribution to the World Council of Churches' *Decade to Overcome Violence*," Report from Mennonite–Catholic Conference, Rome, 23–25 October 2007 (2007), www.overcomingviolence.org/fileadmin/dov/files/iepc/Mennonite_and_Catholic_contribution_to_DOV.pdf.

[65] The best way to understand the difficult German word "*Aufhebung*" in the Hegelian sense but also as used by theologian Karl Barth, is to compare it to the process of pickling. A cucumber that has become a pickle has been destroyed *qua* cucumber, yet preserved.

[66] McCarthy, *A Just Peace Ethic Primer*, 67–68, drawing upon Jarem Sawatsky, *Justpeace Ethics: A Guide to Restorative Justice and Peacebuilding*, foreword by Howard Zehr (Eugene, OR: Cascade, 2009), 12–15.

pacifist approaches might be left behind even while preserving their insights and aspirations.

Though Jesus's Sermon on the Mount (Matthew 5–7) has long been an arena of contention between historic peace churches and just-war affirming churches, fresh exegesis has in fact shifted the debate and reinforced new insights into the contemporary dynamics of just peacemaking. The tireless work of Glen Stassen is evident on both counts.[67] In the wake of the 1989 Revolution that peacefully brought down the Iron Curtain, Stassen led a group of Christian ethicists and political scientists from both just-war and peace-church traditions in studying what really—realistically—had led to the long-unimaginable end of the Cold War between the Soviet bloc and the alliance of Western countries. The group identified ten "normative practices" for just peacemaking that ethicists from both traditions could agree upon even if they did so out of somewhat different starting principles. Simultaneously, Stassen was reexamining the Sermon on the Mount, convincing New Testament scholars of the validity of his exegesis, and showing that Jesus's ethic was not mere idealism, but practicable and politically potent.[68] The pattern he discerned in the Sermon on the Mount lay just under the surface when the just-peacemaking working group published the first edition of its findings in 1998.[69]

---

[67] I provide footnotes to the most important books and articles by Stassen and others but the reader may also want to consult my own summaries both of Stassen's exegesis of the Sermon on the Mount and how it plays out in the contemporary "transforming initiatives" of just peacemaking theory. See Gerald W. Schlabach, "A 'Manual' for Escaping Our Vicious Cycles: The Political Relevance of Enemy-Love," *Modern Theology* 36, no. 3 (July 2020): 478–500; chapters 8–9 of *A Pilgrim People: Becoming a Catholic Peace Church* (Collegeville, MN: Liturgical Press, 2019), 236–294; or the shorter preliminary installment of this work in this journal: "A 'Manual' for Escaping Our Vicious Cycles," *Journal of Moral Theology* 7, no. 2 (June 2018): 86–91.

[68] For a detailed presentation of Stassen's exegesis aimed at an audience of New Testament scholars, see Glen H. Stassen, "The Fourteen Triads of the Sermon on the Mount (Matthew 5:21–7:12)," *Journal of Biblical Literature* 122, no. 2 (Summer 2003): 267–308. For a more pedagogically accessible version aimed at a popular audience, see Glen H. Stassen, *Living the Sermon on the Mount: A Practical Hope for Grace and Deliverance* (San Francisco: Jossey-Bass, 2006). For related resources see Glen H. Stassen and David P. Gushee, *Kingdom Ethics: Following Jesus in Contemporary Context* (Downers Grove, IL: InterVarsity, 2003); Glen H. Stassen, "The Sermon on the Mount as Realistic Disclosure of Solid Ground," *Studies in Christian Ethics* 22, no. 1 (2009): 57–75; and chapters 10–11 of Glen H. Stassen, *A Thicker Jesus: Incarnational Discipleship in a Secular Age* (Louisville, KY: Westminster John Knox, 2012).

[69] First published as *Just Peacemaking: Ten Practices for Abolishing War*, the subtitle for the second and third editions has been more circumspect. See Glen H. Stassen, ed., *Just Peacemaking: The New Paradigm for the Ethics of Peace and War*, 3rd ed. (Cleveland, OH: Pilgrim, 2008). Stassen was already laying the basis for this

What simultaneously discloses the practicability of Jesus's teachings and propels the peacemaking in a just-peace ethic are what Stassen called "transforming initiatives"—actions and practices that "go first" by acting in unanticipated ways, thus changing power dynamics and social configurations amid oppression or potentially violent conflict. For centuries, biblical interpreters had jumped to conclusions when Jesus repeatedly taught, "You have heard it said ... but I say unto you" in Matthew 5, assuming that Jesus's teachings only had two parts—first naming the inadequacy of traditional morality derived from the Old Testament, then setting the high bar of God's true and perfectly loving ideals. This left some Christians striving for unattainable moral perfection and others despairing as they turned elsewhere for moral guidance and political effectiveness in the face of humanity's most intractable moral dilemmas. Through careful literary analysis that might look almost abstruse at first—but that issues in sharp social insight—Stassen showed the heart of the Sermon on the Mount to be organized around a series of triads, not dyads or binaries. The upshot is that what exegetes and preachers alike had long called Jesus's "hard sayings"—and implicitly or explicitly dismissed as such—are not the focus in Jesus's teachings, nor high-bar standards, but interim diagnoses of why "traditional righteousness" never seems to liberate us from our vicious cycles. The climax of each teaching comes in a third part that points to the practical liberation we need.

Consistently, Jesus's moral imperatives in the third part of each respective teaching in Matthew 5–7[70] offer creativity and hope. In the passage often interpreted to mean "Don't ever get angry!" (Matthew 5:21–26), for example, the real lesson is to be quick to seek out reconciliation. Part 1 names the *traditional righteousness*—don't murder. Part 2 *diagnoses the vicious cycles* by which angry accusatory words provoke more in return and invite community judgment for doing the same thing one is accusing others of. Part 3 then offers guidance that is at once grace-filled, practical, and imperative—a *transforming initiative* to lay aside pride and even piety to reach out "first" through gestures that heal relationships. This is the threefold pattern throughout the entire series of fourteen teachings in the Sermon. Coinciding with the work of biblical scholars Clarence

---

integration of exegesis and ethics in *Just Peacemaking: Transforming Initiatives for Justice and Peace* (Louisville, KY: Westminster John Knox, 1992).

[70] More precisely, in the long middle section that stretches from Matthew 5:17 through 7:12.

Jordan[71] and Walter Wink,[72] Stassen showed that the key paragraphs at the end of Matthew 5 on retaliation and love of enemies are also practicable in ways mainstream Christian traditions have long missed or dismissed. Translating the Greek in Matthew 5:39 more carefully, we see that Jesus does not say never to resist evil (which hardly squares with other biblical injunctions anyway) but rather, "not to retaliate revengefully by evil means."[73] Examined closely and in historical context, to turn the other cheek, give up one's cloak as well as one's coat, and go the second mile all emerge as paradigmatic strategies of nonviolent direct action that turn the tables on oppressors and equalize social power. They are transforming initiatives that break out of vicious cycles by responding to violence and injustice—but not in kind.

They not only resist the temptation to free ride; they begin to reverse the sociology of free riding. They resolve to act first, at risk to oneself, for the good of the whole. But that starts to make it imaginable for less heroic actors to act in similar ways. The point is not to approach gun owners nicely in order to convince them to change their minds—though patient dialogue should certainly be part of the practice of active nonviolence. Rather, the point is to begin by demonstrating the courage to renounce recourse to violence oneself, individually and as Christian communities, and practice in public the skills of nonviolent accompaniment, active listening, and trust-building that exhibit alternative forms of security. As more people do so, they change permission and support structures; they gather a critical mass and make a movement possible. Vis-à-vis gun ownership for the purpose of self-protection despite the aggregate dangers that come when more and more people own guns, therefore, a just-peace ethic offers at least three responses or layers to one integrated response to defensive gun culture:

1. As already noted, it is worth examining the assumption that readily accessible guns will actually serve the purpose of self-protection well, even in the fearful scenario being imagined. As Eli McCarthy has insisted, a just-peace ethic will be a virtue ethic. That is, it expects to open up new and creative ways to respond to difficult moral situations by beginning sooner rather than later to develop the skillsets, virtues, moral motor skills, and community support that prepare moral agents to improvise well when a crisis comes. To be as

---

[71] Clarence Jordan, *The Substance of Faith and Other Cotton Patch Sermons* (New York: Association Press, 1972), 69, cited by Stassen, "The Fourteen Triads," 281.
[72] Walter Wink, *Engaging the Powers: Discernment and Resistance in a World of Domination* (Minneapolis, MN: Fortress, 1992), 175–194; Walter Wink, *The Powers That Be: Theology for a New Millennium* (New York: Doubleday, 1998), 98–111.
[73] Stassen, *Living the Sermon on the Mount*, 91.

responsible as they claim to be, gun owners must invest hours upon hours at gun clubs learning safety and marksmanship. So if someone does have a legitimate fear of some kind of violent intruder (say because they live in an isolated rural area or an area that truly is a conflict zone), it is not too much to ask that we (first) and others (in turn) spend a comparable amount of time training in nonviolent direct action, bystander protection, and crisis response in order to hone the reflexes for creative responses to danger that depend on social not physical force. To do so might not just make society safer in the aggregate, but actually for everyone on the scene.

2. Note that none of this requires discounting the legitimacy of personal self-defense. A just-peace ethic will not deny just causes and ends, but rather will say "Yes, and ..." by holding out for nonviolent means both because they are right and because they are effective. Once we follow Stassen in recognizing the dynamic of transforming initiatives in Jesus's ethic we can, like him and his colleagues in the just-peacemaking project, begin to see them at work in the realism of contemporary affairs. Though just-peacemaking theory has focused on social and political conflict, others have gathered examples of creative responses to personal threats that have defused violence nonviolently.[74] The point is not that anecdotal evidence from either side is adequate, but that accounts of nonviolent and nonlethal defusing of threat will help pique, then form, the imagination that is one of the resources upon which the practices of active nonviolence depend.

3. Can a nonviolence trainer or just-peace ethicist promise success every time? No, but neither can gun vendors. The Christian tradition, which sees power in suffering and even martyrdom, should be altering a Christian's calculation of risk, if not the very definition of what constitutes a salient risk. Since we are anticipating how to bring cultural and legal change to a society that cannot be expected to share the worldview of committed Christian disciples, we may do well to bracket these variables. What a frank acknowledgement of risks on all sides should finally open up is a reasoned conversation about aggregates and free-riding exceptions, short-term safety and long-term security, narrow and enlightened self-interest. Simply to have such a conversation will have begun to neutralize the free-rider problem.

---

[74] See part three of John Howard Yoder, *What Would You Do?: A Serious Answer to a Standard Question*, expanded ed., with Joan Baez, Tom Skinner, Leo Tolstoy, and others (Scottdale, PA: Herald, 1992). I have not made use of Yoder's own title essay in this book in the present article because the record of Yoder's theologically rationalized sexual abuse will require the work of at least a generation of feminist scholars to determine what can be retrieved from Yoder's thought. The collection of essays and accounts he gathered from others in parts 2 and 3 of *What Would You Do?*, however, remains a valuable resource.

Conclusion

Those who claim to be "in Christ" (2 Cor 5:17), coming to share the mind of Christ (Philippians 2:1–5), and thus inviting God's conversion—whether sudden or lifelong or both—are not the only ones who can be changed. *Vicious* cycles can spiral out of control, but *virtuous* cycles spiral outward too, in opposite directions. The "going first" Christians see God doing in Jesus Christ is but the climax to the plot of salvation history discernible already in the call of Abraham (Gen 12:1–3). The context of Abraham's calling is the downward spiral of humanity as a whole in Genesis 1–11, which God seeks to reverse. When God chooses and calls out one particular family, God has not given up on "all the families of the earth," but rather God has discovered the only social change strategy that ever seems to work—to move outward from the particular to the whole through the blessing that defines an identity that cannot be hoarded. The blessed are to become a blessing to other families and ultimately all the families of the earth or they are not who they were called and claim to be. The grammar of this exquisite paradox plays itself out throughout the biblical drama and in church history.[75]

While the very nature of my thesis has required that I not shy away from using quite Christian language in the previous section, the argument does not require sectarian retreat, nor does it give up hope of social transformation. Other faiths and secular movements are altogether welcome to learn, perhaps be inspired, mine their own traditions and sacred texts for the resources to transform the self-interested into the benevolent, to begin inverting the logic of the free-rider problem, and so encourage the collective action needed to build a movement for freedom from gun violence. The lessons here apply to all movement organizers, regardless of religious affiliation. The "Abrahamic" model of social transformation affirms the kind of local grassroots work Kristin Goss implicitly and explicitly advocated in *Disarmed: The Missing Movement for Gun Control in America* in order to supply the missing movement: local work is never lost, for indeed, local incremental change is often the key to empowering the people needed for widening social movements. The insight of just-peace ethics into the power of "going first," wherever we are, should remind Christian activists that we dare not skip past our own local communities and churches.

That is arguably true at all times and for all social issues, but it is especially and obviously true when some of the strongest opponents of gun control claim to be fellow Christians. I would think that even quite secular gun-control advocates would welcome encouragement

---

[75] For a thorough exposition of the claims in this paragraph, see chapter 3 of Schlabach, *A Pilgrim People*, 133–161.

for Christians to recognize that the gospel we claim to proclaim matters and is not something to set aside in working for social justice and violence prevention. As part of this effort, the discipline of theology can contribute to that work by clarifying the gospel—exposing nationalistic and idolatrous accretions and helping strip them away. As a Christian believer and a theologian, it is hardly surprising that I believe that attending to how Christian faith communities articulate and live out the gospel can further rather than postpone work for the common good in partnership with others. At a time and place when the idolatry of trust in guns for security has taken so many captive under the banner of "God, guns, and country," this should be especially manifest. The work of fraternal correction Christians need to do among themselves may be the single most important thing we can do for the social order. As Pope Paul VI noted in his apostolic exhortation on evangelization, sometimes Christians themselves must be the first to be converted.[76]

Gerald W. Schlabach, PhD, is Emeritus Professor of Theology at the University of St. Thomas in Minnesota, where he has also chaired the Department of Justice and Peace Studies. Among his books are *A Pilgrim People: Becoming a Catholic Peace Church* (Liturgical Press, 2019), *Just Policing, Not War: An Alternative Response to World Violence* (Liturgical Press, 2007), and *At Peace and Unafraid: Public Order, Security, and the Wisdom of the Cross* (co-edited with Duane K. Friesen, Herald Press, 2005).

---

76. Paul VI, *Evangelii Nuntiandi*, nos. 15 and 21.

Firearms and Moral Theology: A Response

Tobias Winright

"THERE IS A LOCKDOWN RIGHT NOW. IT'S NOT A DRILL, I DON'T think. I hear yelling. I love you all so much." My wife and I received this text message from our seventeen-year-old daughter at 9:12 a.m. (CST) on Monday, October 24, 2022. At the time, she was a senior at Collegiate School of Medicine and Bioscience, which shares a building and facilities with Central Visual & Performing Arts, both of which are magnet schools within the public school system in St. Louis, Missouri. It was 3:12 p.m. for my wife and me, though, because two months earlier, on August 21st, we had moved 3,897 miles away to Maynooth, Ireland. However, we hadn't noticed the text message until 3:25, so thirteen minutes had already transpired before my wife texted our daughter back: "I love you!!! ... Text me asap. Where are you???" We panicked, worried that the worst might have already happened to her, but our daughter immediately replied, "We're in AP Lit. In the basement. The door is barricaded." She added, "Lots of yelling and screaming but no gunfire." We felt relieved she was still alive, but our fear increased as we again typed back how much we love her.

Our daughter had chosen to stay in St. Louis during the fall semester to finish high school in December, rather than being required to spend two more years in secondary school in Maynooth. We didn't wish to leave her behind, but supported her decision to stay, especially since it was for only four months, plus she was staying with the family of one of her best friends from school. Admittedly, my family occasionally heard gunfire during our seventeen years living in St. Louis—almost daily the last two years when we lived downtown, where most of our neighbors were Black persons disproportionately impacted by gun violence.[1] For two years straight, St. Louis has been identified as the most dangerous city in the United States.[2] I sometimes

---

[1] Monica Obradovic, "Missouri's Black Homicide Victimization Rate Again Highest in US," *Riverfront Times*, April 27, 2023, www.riverfronttimes.com/news/missouris-black-homicide-victimization-rate-again-highest-in-us-39941072.

[2] Laura Begley Bloom, "Report Ranks America's 15 Safest (and Most Dangerous) Cities for 2023," *Forbes*, January 31, 2023, www.forbes.com/sites/laurabegleybloom/2023/01/31/report-ranks-americas-15-safest-and-most-dangerous-cities-for-2023/.

videoed gunfights on the streets several floors below our apartment and photographed bullet casings I saw on the streets and sidewalks during my daily runs, occasionally posting these on social media. In fact, a decade ago, while I was running on the sidewalk, as an oncoming car approached on the street, a passenger quickly aimed a gun out his window and shot me in the chest; keeling over, worried I wasn't going to see my family again, I was relieved to realize the liquid on me wasn't blood but paint. So, although we were concerned about the safety of our two daughters, including when they went to school (one once told us about how a boy along the street pointed a gun at her bus as it passed by), we never really thought an active-shooter situation would happen. Indeed, our older daughter's school is one of the most secure buildings in the city's system, with locked doors, metal detectors, and security officers. We later learned that a 19-year-old male, a recent alumnus, shot his way through the entrance.

We continued texting over the next three minutes. Everything seemed to be moving in slow motion. At 3:29, our daughter wrote, "I can see police through the window. Four shots just went off." I asked if she had a desk or something to hide behind and whether she had anything to throw at the shooter. I wondered if she could escape through a window, but she replied that the windows were barred. She then heard the police yelling at the shooter. It was now 9:33 in St. Louis, 3:33 in Ireland. A minute later, our daughter updated us, "The police are coming door to door to evacuate kids." Three long and uncomfortably silent minutes later, we finally read the welcome words, "We're out."

We felt a wave of relief, but our daughter then reported that as she exited her classroom and entered the hallway, she had to step past a dead student. She couldn't recognize her, though. Months later I happened to meet the Bureau of Alcohol, Tobacco, Firearms, and Explosives (commonly called "ATF") agent, coincidentally a member of our former parish in St. Louis, one of the two law enforcement officers first on scene. He informed me that he had stood next to the deceased girl's body as my daughter and her classmates escaped. A brave 61-year-old teacher, Jean Kuczka, was also murdered in another location inside the school.

The shooter used an AR-15 (Armalite) style rifle and had six hundred rounds of ammunition. The devastation and disfigurement caused by this type of weapon, invented during the Vietnam war and intended for military—not civilian—use,[3] was why my daughter did not recognize her fellow student who had been murdered. A note left behind in his car said he intended to kill more students, faculty, and

---

[3] Sam Frizell, "AR-15 Inventor's Family: This Was Meant to Be a Military Weapon," *Time*, June 16, 2016, time.com/4371452/orlando-shooting-ar-15-military-civilian-family/.

staff than were murdered in other schools in Columbine, Colorado, in 1999, and Parkland, Florida, in 2018. This was one of 305 school shooting incidents in 2022.[4] It is expected that the number will be even greater in 2023. As I write this, tears well up in my eyes. Almost every time I speak or write about it, the emotions from that day resurface. Each new day my daughter, her younger sister, her mother, and I dread hearing about another school or mass shooting happening. Even with counseling, our daughter is not the same. She has been traumatized. The sound of sirens, loud firecrackers, backfire from the exhaust of a car, even loud music in a pub all cause her trauma to resurface. One of our common loves, watching Marvel Universe superhero movies, is now a thing of the past. Any film or television show likely to feature bloodshed is more than she can handle.

My own experiences of violence enable me to understand to a certain extent. As a former reserve police officer, I have seen gunshot victims. I have entered houses where someone has been shot. I have viewed dead bodies and blood-soaked furniture, floors, and walls. I have observed loved ones as they wail and try to grasp what has happened. As a former corrections officer, I have booked alleged perpetrators, or did hospital duty monitoring inmates who had gunshot wounds. Decades later, these images, branded in my mind's eye, resurface—and I lament that our daughter, so young, will never forget what she heard and saw on that crisp autumn morning in her school. I also feel sorrowful for all others indelibly impacted by what happened: the loved ones of the two who were murdered; the other students, teachers, and staff who were there and their families, too; the first responders, including the ATF agent who shared with me how it has traumatized him as well; and the family of the shooter, also shot and killed that day.

Several months later, the Peace and Justice Commission of the Archdiocese of St. Louis contacted me and asked if I might recommend someone who could provide a Catholic theological-ethical perspective on gun violence at a summit on July 29, 2023. The archdiocesan staff knew I had published some opinion pieces on the question, including one about my daughter and her school.[5] A decade ago, in the wake of the massacre of twenty children and six staff members at Sandy Hook Elementary School in 2012, I was also among

---

[4] For more on school shootings, see the K-12 School Shooting Database, k12ssdb.org/all-shootings.

[5] Tobias Winright, "A Parent's Worst Nightmare: An Active Shooter at My Daughter's School," *National Catholic Reporter*, November 2, 2022, www.ncronline.org/opinion/guest-voices/parents-worst-nightmare-active-shooter-my-daughters-school. For an earlier piece, see Tobias Winright, "What St. John XXIII Has to Say about Gun Rights," *America*, February 23, 2018, www.americamagazine.org/politics-society/2018/02/23/what-st-john-xxiii-has-say-about-gun-rights.

the sixty scholars, priests, nuns, and two former ambassadors to the Vatican who issued a letter, in connection with the annual March for Life in Washington, DC, calling for "common-sense reforms to address the epidemic of gun violence in our nation."[6] Yet, few, if any, other moral theologians have addressed this issue, so I agreed to return and speak at the summit, which also included other presentations and workshops, with over 350 laity, religious, clergy, and other persons in attendance.[7] Similarly, a couple of years ago, when staff at *America* magazine emailed me and requested names of Catholic moral theologians who might speak on the topic of gun violence, I was able to suggest only two of my peers, who had presented papers on the subject at professional conferences I had attended.[8]

Since then I have learned that two other Catholic moral theologians, William P. George and Richard C. Sparks, CSP, wrote about firearms, both published in 1996, the latter in two succinct pages and the former in an article that in retrospect seems very prescient and still helpful today.[9] There is also a chapter in *Catholic Bioethics and Social Justice*, edited by M. Therese Lysaught and Michael McCarthy, on "Health Care Providers on the Frontline: Responding to the Gun

---

[6] Laurie Goodstein, "In Fight over Life, a New Call by Catholics," *New York Times*, January 25, 2013, www.nytimes.com/2013/01/26/us/politics/catholics-raise-issue-of-guns-amid-call-to-end-abortion.html.

[7] Tony Messenger, "I Went to a Gun Safety Talk. I Ran into an Even Bigger Moral Problem," *St. Louis Post-Dispatch*, August 3, 2023, www.stltoday.com/news/local/column/tony-messenger/messenger-i-went-to-a-gun-safety-talk-i-ran-into-an-even-bigger-moral/article_5a74ba6c-3161-11ee-a7be-d7932f7faa3c.html?fbclid=IwAR1y3FvECm_OgXwYSzk2t1ihv4563CDGAQ4_p-1nD3A7xAE_pIYY9PTTJek; Valerie Schremp Hahn, "Hundreds Gather for Gun Violence Summit Hosted by St. Louis Archdiocese," *Catholic Health World*, September 1, 2023, www.chausa.org/publications/catholic-health-world/archive/article/september-1-2023/hundreds-gather-for-gun-violence-summit-hosted-by-st.-louis-archdiocese.

[8] Patrick T. McCormick presented a paper, "Addressing the Structural Causes of America's Unique Epidemic of Firearm Suicide," at the 2017 Annual Meeting of the Society of Christian Ethics in New Orleans, and earlier he published a short column piece also on firearms and suicide, "Weapons of Self-destruction," *US Catholic* 74, no. 1 (January 2009): 42–43. For an interview of McCormick by Sebastian Gomes, Executive Editor at *America* and host of the podcast *Voting Catholic*, see Robert David Sullivan, "Voting Catholic: Is There a Catholic Approach to Gun Policy?," www.americamagazine.org/politics-society/2022/10/31/voting-catholic-2022-guns-244037. Krista Stevens Inman presented a paper, "The Barbarian at Our Gate: A Common Good Argument for Stricter Gun Control," for the Catholic Social Thought Topic Session at the 74th Annual Convention of the Catholic Theological Society of America in Pittsburgh, which is noted in Patrick Flanigan's report in the *Proceedings of the Catholic Theological Society of America* 74 (2019): 108–109.

[9] William P. George, "Guns and the Catholic Conscience," *Chicago Studies* 35, no. 1 (April 1996): 82–95; Richard C. Sparks, CSP, *Contemporary Christian Morality: Real Questions, Candid Responses* (New York: Crossroad, 1996), 136–137.

Violence Epidemic," that applies principles of Catholic social teaching to this public health problem; however, its four coauthors are health care professionals, not moral theologians or bioethicists.[10] As for non-Roman Catholic theological ethicists, two of my teachers—pacifists John Howard Yoder and Stanley Hauerwas—concentrated on the problem of wars between nations, giving minimal attention to the gun violence on our streets and in our homes, schools, churches, cinemas, workplaces, concert venues, and shopping centers.[11] If, as Hauerwas claims, "The question of violence is the central issue for any Christian social ethic,"[12] it is striking that gun violence has garnered such lack of scrutiny from theologians. Otherwise, most of the extant literature offering a Christian ethical perspective, as noted by Michael Grigoni in the introduction to this special issue of the *Journal of Moral Theology*, is from pastors and activists, or from bishops and church leaders, rather than moral theologians.[13]

---

[10] Michelle Byrne, Virginia McCarthy, Abigail Silva, and Sharon Homan, "Health Care Providers on the Frontline: Responding to the Gun Violence Epidemic," in *Catholic Bioethics and Social Justice: The Praxis of US Health Care in a Globalized World*, ed. M. Therese Lysaught and Michael McCarthy (Collegeville, MN: Liturgical Press Academic, 2018), 31–45. See also Alexander Garza, MD, "Guns, Germs, and Health Care: Lessons Observed and Learned," *Health Progress* 100, no. 6 (November-December 2019): 9–13.

[11] John Howard Yoder, *What Would You Do? A Serious Answer to a Standard Question*, expanded ed. (Scottdale, PA: Herald, 1992), 20–42; Stanley Hauerwas, *A Community of Character: Toward a Constructive Christian Social Ethic* (Notre Dame: University of Notre Dame Press, 1981), 145–147, where he recalls when, while he was a student at Yale Divinity School and visiting his family back home in Texas, his father crafted a deer rifle and gave it to him. Hauerwas retells this story in his foreword to *God and Guns: The Bible against American Gun Culture*, ed. Christopher B. Hays and C. L. Crouch (Louisville, KY: Westminster John Knox, 2021), ix–xi.

[12] Stanley Hauerwas, *The Peaceable Kingdom: A Primer in Christian Ethics* (Notre Dame: University of Notre Dame Press, 1983), 114. An exception is Episcopalian priest and theologian Lyndon Shakespeare, "Friendship, Love, and Mass Shootings: Toward a Theological Response for Gun Control," *Anglican Theological Review* 95, no. 4 (November 2013): 607–625.

[13] I should note, too, that Catholic moral theologians have published blog posts about the problem of gun violence: Andrew Kuzma, "The Children of God: The Catholic Response to Gun Violence," *Catholic Moral Theology*, May 1, 2018, catholicmoraltheology.com/ the-children-of-god-the-catholic-response-to-gun-violence/; Tom Bushlack, "Guns, God, and Rights," *Catholic Moral Theology*, December 20, 2012, catholicmoraltheology.com/guns-god-and-rights/; Shawnee M. Daniels-Sykes, "Environmental Racism, Gun Violence Homicides, and the Construction of Memorial Acclamations," *Catholic Moral Theology*, June 21, 2015, catholicmoraltheology.com/ guest-post-as-environmental-racism-gun-violent-homicides-and-the-construction-of-memorial-acclamations/; David Cloutier, "A March for Peaceableness," *Catholic Moral Theology*, March 24, 2018, catholicmoraltheology.com/a-march-for-peaceableness/; Marcus Mescher, "Guns in America: Ideology or Idolatry?," *Millennial*, August 31, 2015, millennialjournal.com/2015/08/31/guns-in-america-ideology-or-idolatry/; and Tobias Winright, "*Pacem in Terris*, The US Gun

So, I was pleased when the editors invited me to write a response to these thoughtful and timely articles on this question of "special urgency" today.[14] I am grateful to the authors, whose essays help fill a curious lacuna, one that the Board of the College Theology Society, in a recent statement on gun violence, has called on theologians to study and address.[15] Each contributor tackles the issue of guns in the United States, drawing on their respective areas of expertise while analyzing different facets of the problem. In this way, redundancy and repetition are avoided—this special issue of the *Journal* is not beating a dead horse—and the articles complement one another so that an overarching argument is constructed and reinforced. In what follows, I offer a few thoughts prompted by these articles, with the hope that this conversation shall continue and, most importantly, bolster efforts to curtail gun violence.

In his article, "Gun Laws and Gun Deaths: An Empirical Analysis and Theological Assessment," Conor Kelly, who has written extensively in the area of Catholic health care ethics, culls from empirical data on firearms deaths to establish persuasive reasons why Catholics should endorse policies that further restrict (not ban completely) access to firearms. These fatalities, which disproportionately impact the vulnerable in society, are preventable. Throughout his article, Kelly notes relevant themes and concepts from Catholic social teaching and theological ethics: common good, structural sin, preferential option for the poor, and neighbor love.

The statistics Kelly highlights should speak for themselves, but he anticipates skepticism that might arise about whether such information can move people to advocate change from the status quo. Indeed, I must confess my own doubt, at first, because on other questions in recent years—climate change and COVID-19 vaccines, for example—many Americans have been in denial even when given the empirical and scientific data. Kelly persuasively shares evidence that laws limiting access to guns can and do impact the inequitable distribution of firearm mortality. At the same time, I appreciate his

---

Legislation Debate, and Rights," *Catholic Moral Theology*, April 11, 2013, catholicmoraltheology.com/pacem-in-terris-the-us-gun-legislation-debate-and-rights/.

[14] Vatican II's *Gaudium et Spes* ("Pastoral Constitution on the Church in the Modern World") addressed certain "questions of special urgency": marriage, culture, socioeconomics, politics, and peace. Although gun violence—such as school and mass shootings—was not treated, I think it warrants the attention of more moral theologians, especially in the United States. See Judith A. Dwyer, SSJ, ed., *"Questions of Special Urgency":* The Church in the Modern World *Two Decades after Vatican II* (Washington, DC: Georgetown University Press, 1986).

[15] A link to a pdf of the statement, adopted on June 1, 2023, is available on the website of the College Theology Society, www.collegetheology.org/.

exercise of the virtue of epistemic humility, recognizing possible limitations to the studies on which he relies, as well as the conundrum of determining causality in these connections. His proposals for public policy are reasonable even as he observes that connecting the dots between the empirical data and public policy recommendations is not easy. In addition, Kelly does not shy away from responding to likely objections, such as from those who allege that easier access to guns or "stand your ground laws" will deter and decrease firearms fatalities. As he notes, the overall empirical evidence shows otherwise, although I still hear from Catholics and others that they are not convinced by this. At the summit in St. Louis, during a break after my presentation, one woman continued to refer to a 2013 study by the Centers for Disease Control and Prevention (CDC) and conducted by The National Academies' Institute of Medicine and National Research Council that reported, "Defensive use of guns by crime victims is a common occurrence," with survey results from the 1990s, which was unpublished, leading her and others to hold onto the view that defensive gun use saves lives.[16] Still, such a position at best maintains the status quo, though the statistics about rising suicides, accidental killings, and gun homicides reflect that the "status quo" is actually worsening over time. In the end, Kelly rightly calls for the virtue of prudence, and on Catholics to guard themselves against a callous disregard for the human lives lost from gun violence, recommit themselves to the common good, and accept their responsibilities for making sure a right to keep and bear arms does not undermine it, points I too have made elsewhere.[17]

In "Natural Law's Return: Uncovering the Roots of Intractability on Guns as a Prelude to New Growth," John E. Carter meticulously brings his expertise in theology and jurisprudence to bear regarding the right to self-defense and the Second Amendment "right of the people to keep and bear Arms." An impressive contribution to the growing scholarship on this controversial amendment in the Bill of Rights and recent Supreme Court opinion related to it, Carter's article attempts to clarify the history and legal issues surrounding gun rights to carve out space for the possibility for moral deliberation and discourse rather than intractability and intransigence. Although as an undergraduate I took two semesters of Constitutional Law, and have read elsewhere treatments of the Second Amendment, Carter took me

---

[16] See, for example, Paul Hsieh, "That Time the CDC Asked about Defensive Gun Uses," *Forbes*, April 30, 2018, www.forbes.com/sites/paulhsieh/2018/04/30/that-time-the-cdc-asked-about-defensive-gun-uses/?sh=4d4b9a5f299a.

[17] Winright, "A Parent's Worst Nightmare."

to school on the subject.[18] I share his hope that a retrieval of the natural law tradition, which moral theologians across the supposed conservative/liberal spectrum are reviving in various ways, may help address the problem of gun violence. May Carter's erudite article be read widely by legal scholars and theological ethicists.

Luis Vera's article, "Guns, Agency, and Attention in a Technocratic Context," inspired by Pope Francis's critique in *Laudato Si'* of the "technocratic paradigm," offers a more comprehensive vantage point for analysis of guns as technologies. In particular, Vera engages seriously those who justify their gun ownership to protect oneself and others, and interrogates their assumptions about agency and responsibility.[19] I found especially insightful the section in which Vera examines "situational awareness," something I learned while in law enforcement (e.g., sitting in a restaurant against a wall with a clear view of the entrance and everyone in the room) and only now, while living in Ireland, where there are no guns (most police officers are not armed), I notice that I do not need to practice such alert attentiveness. While Vera is correct that most US citizens "live in relative safety from gun violence," my family and I did not while we lived in St. Louis. Of course, he rightly observes that the risk is higher for people who are young, urban, Black, and poor. I agree that many armed white men may be "disconnected from reality" with regard to their assessment of threats, but what to do for non-white citizens whose reality truly is dangerous on a daily basis? Indeed, increasingly Black, LGBTQIA, and other minority persons are arming themselves for self-defense.[20] If their situational awareness is more connected to reality, is it also captured by the technocratic paradigm and a myth of autonomous choice? Questions such as these, I trust, will not be

---

[18] See relevant chapters in, for example, Adam Winkler, *Gunfight: The Battle over the Right to Bear Arms in America* (New York: W. W. Norton, 2013); Firmin DeBrabander, *Do Guns Make Us Free? Democracy and the Armed Society* (New Haven, CT: Yale University Press, 2015); and Hugh LaFollette, *In Defense of Gun Control* (New York: Oxford University Press, 2018).

[19] The question of guns as technologies was also considered more, I think, succinctly, clearly, and helpfully in George, "Guns and the Catholic Conscience," 91–93. Like George, who persuasively argues that "technologies have intentions built into them" (92), Shakespeare writes, "Guns may not have agency, but they do have a purpose" ("Friendship, Love, and Mass Shootings," 615). Indeed, assault weapons, for instance, "are built to guarantee maximum destruction" (614), as my daughter saw in the hallway at her school. See also Mark Ryan, "Guns and Practical Reason: An Ethical Exploration of Guns and Language," *Journal of Moral Theology* 11, no. 1 (2022): 85–106.

[20] See, for example, Ryan Young, Dakin And one, and Pamela Kirkland, "Gun Sales Rise among Black People as They Look for Firearm Training and Education," *CNN*, June 23, 2021, edition.cnn.com/2021/06/23/us/black-gun-owners-sales-rising/index.html.

neglected by moral theologians who respond to Vera's call to "engage gun owners with regard to how their best concerns could be done better justice through fully ecological reflection."

Presbyterian pastor and public theologian Katie Day considers shootings in recent years at mosques, synagogues, gurdwaras, and churches, including Black churches such as Mother Emanuel African Methodist Episcopal Church in Charleston, South Carolina, and the impact that this threat—rare as it may actually be—has on how these communities view the world and make meaningful sense of, or narrate, their identity (their "lived ecclesiology"). Her study of how congregations have responded to a growing sense of the threat of gun violence (e.g., active shooter training, security teams) is very useful. When I worked in law enforcement, it disturbed me whenever a fellow officer told me he or she had a firearm on them in a sanctuary during worship. Now even pastors and parishioners are carrying guns. I worry about this trend. A highlight during the summit in St. Louis was my former parish, St. Margaret of Scotland, in which was formed a group that seeks to steer clear of a fortress mentality to instead foster an ecclesiology of hospitality in such a way that, as Day suggests, "security is uncoupled from physical safety and takes on a deeper meaning, rooted in the community of Christ."[21]

I believe I first met Michael Grigoni in person when I convened the session in which he presented his paper "Just War Theory, Handgun Ownership, and Everyday Life" during the 2019 Annual Meeting of the Society of Christian Ethics in Louisville, Kentucky. His present article, "The Christian Handgun Owner and Just War," also the subject of his doctoral research and dissertation, further develops his train of thought. His work resonates with my own in many respects, both intellectually and experientially. Although my lived experience as an actual gun owner was not as much due to choice, especially a decision to study it—I became a law enforcement officer to work my way through undergraduate study, being the only person in my working class family of farmers, factory workers, and cops to go to university—I appreciate Grigoni's choice to undertake an ethnographic study of gun ownership, not only by interviewing Christians with guns but by sharing in their experience by taking Bill's course on concealed carry.[22] Likewise, although my scholarly interest

---

[21] See www.stmargaretstl.org/parish/get-involved/ministry/gun-sense-for-the-common-good/.

[22] Ryan also claims to use an ethnographic approach by threading throughout his article reflections on his experiences with his gun-owning brother-in-law "Joe." Although indeed insightful, what he shares is more anecdotal and narrative in content and style rather than ethnographic (see Ryan, "Guns and Practical Reason"). Grigoni notes the work of Todd David Whitmore, a Catholic theological ethicist who has done pioneering work on ethnographic fieldwork and Christian ethics. My PhD

in just war theory evolved from my experiences as a law enforcement officer (and as an Army ROTC student) and my concerns about justifying and constraining the use of force, I welcome Grigoni's utilization of just war reasoning for possible normative guidance on the question of gun ownership and use.[23]

Because most Christians, at this time, are not pacifists or have not yet centralized nonviolent practices for responding to violent threats, Grigoni's effort to uncover their moral reasoning for firearms ownership and use, I think, is noteworthy. In my presentation at the archdiocesan summit, I used his point that the "everyday form of just war reasoning" that surfaces amongst the Christian gun owners he encounters goes beyond the requirements of the law, such as stand-your-ground laws. When I showed PowerPoint slides with Tertullian and other early church pacifists, followed by Ambrose and Augustine, who provided criteria for the use of force by soldiers and magistrates but not for private self-defense, the strict criteria Aquinas provided for self-defense, and then the strict guidelines for "legitimate defense" in the Catechism (nos. 2263–2267), attendees recognized how a Catholic perspective on gun ownership and use differs from the stand-your-ground mentality. In short, although nonviolence, de-escalation, and other practices should be prioritized in our churches and their institutions (schools, universities, hospitals, etc.), for those who do not "voluntarily set aside our rights" to gun ownership, as Cardinal Joseph W. Tobin, CSsR recently urged,[24] this everyday form of just war reasoning still should voluntarily moderate and limit these weapons and their use.

I am less persuaded, though, by the apparent distinction between Christian handgun owners ("Christian-protectors") and "citizen-protectors," whereby the former hold "a centripetally-oriented posture with their guns" and the latter possess "a centrifugally-oriented posture of policing." I am surprised that the Christian-protectors from Grigoni's sample would not try to protect another citizen, who is not a biological or ecclesial family member, from lethal harm. Perhaps

---

dissertation, "The Challenge of Policing: An Analysis in Christian Social Ethics" (University of Notre Dame, 2002), was directed by Whitmore.

[23] For a popular op-ed by a lawyer that suggests, inspired by just war reasoning, the formulation of a theory on firearms, force, and self-defense, see Marvin Lim, "The Church Has a Stance on War, but Needs a Stance on Guns," *National Catholic Reporter*, December 1, 2016, www.ncronline.org/church-has-stance-war-needs-stance-guns. See also Tobias Winright, "What Does Catholic Teaching Say about Using Guns for Defense?," *National Catholic Reporter*, August 2, 2023, www.ncronline.org/opinion/guest-voices/what-does-catholic-teaching-say-about-using-guns-defense.

[24] Cardinal Joseph W. Tobin, CSsR, "Rejoice in the Lord," May 26, 2023, rcan.org/pray-end-all-instances-violence/.

this is because these Christian-protectors are evangelical Protestants, rather than Roman Catholics and mainline Protestants for whom just war theory has been articulated and taught (even if many members are unfamiliar with it in these traditions, too). Although Grigoni claims that Paul Ramsey's ethic of just war and self-defense has a connection with the Christian ethic of protection espoused by his interlocutors from his ethnographic study, Ramsey does not limit this ethic to personal, familial, and ecclesial bodies. For Ramsey, the same mode of moral reasoning applies to all uses of force, including policing and, as Grigoni rightly notes, sit-ins and civil disobedience.[25] To illustrate "the *logic*, the heart and soul, of such protective love," Ramsey asked what would Jesus have had the good Samaritan do had he "come upon the scene while the robbers were still at their fell work?"[26] For Ramsey, whenever a choice must be made between an attacker and an innocent victim, circumstances dictate that the latter is to be preferred—a sort of preferential option for the victim, one might say—so that armed force may be justifiably used against the former, though such force will be employed in accordance with rules formulated to govern it out of respect for the enemy. As Grigoni correctly notes, Ramsey—in contrast to Augustine—permits the use of lethal force for personal self-defense, too. Accordingly, Christian-protectors should be able to assume the responsibility to protect anyone anywhere as citizen-protectors (if no police are present or able to respond in time), and their use of armed force should still be moderate and limited.

Similarly, while I recognize the parallels between Grigoni's Christian-protector interlocuters and the Black tradition of armed defense exhibited by the Deacons for Defense and Justice (DDJ), I am still not persuaded that either of these—descriptively or normatively—fully subscribe or adhere to Ramsey's (or most Roman Catholic and mainline accounts of) just war. Grigoni's account teasing out the differences between his Christian-protector interlocuters and the DDJ seems more on target, especially with regard to how African

---

[25] Other theologians and ethicists have written about how the moral reasoning is similar in just war, just policing, and legitimate defense—whether armed or unarmed. See Tobias Winright, *Serve and Protect: Selected Essays on Just Policing* (Eugene, OR: Cascade, 2020); and "A Just Mining Framework for the Ethics of Extraction of Natural Resources and Integral Peace," in *Catholic Peacebuilding and Mining: Integral Peace, Development, and Ecology*, ed. Gerard F. Powers and Caesar A. Montevecchio (London: Routledge, 2022), 95–116. Grigoni notes, too, Paul Ramsey's *Christian Ethics and the Sit-In* (New York: Association Press, 1961).

[26] Paul Ramsey, *The Just War: Force and Political Responsibility* (New York: Charles Scribner's Sons, 1968), 142–43. See also Paul Ramsey, *Basic Christian Ethics* (Louisville, KY: Westminster John Knox, 1950, 1993), 165, 169–71; and *War and the Christian Conscience: How Shall Modern War Be Conducted Justly?* (Durham, NC: Duke University Press, 1961), xvi–xvii.

Americans have had to respond to the "original wound" of slavery and racism, and the violent threats to their lives that are "exponentially more dangerous." I agree with Grigoni that the just war theory "cannot close the gap between description and norm regarding the place of guns in the United States," but I would insert the word "alone" at the beginning of that observation. With Grigoni, I recommend more ethnographic and historical research here, as well as engagement with recent scholarship on just war, just revolution, just policing, and just peacemaking/peacebuilding.[27]

In my view, "Christian Arguments for Gun Violence Prevention: Reflections on Moral Claims in the Context of Advocacy," by Ellen Ott Marshall, a United Methodist theological ethicist, does us service by providing a critical survey of the Christian moral arguments that arise in gun violence prevention advocacy ("the Presser" and "the PDF"), the main arguments found in Christian activism (sanctity of life, sin of idolatry, a call to nonviolence), and the place of the vigil. At the summit in St. Louis, I witnessed everything she examines and, for my part, I tried (having read her essay, which offers an important corrective on this) to avoid any confusion over vulnerability. To do so, while I highlighted the same three arguments, I added attention to the preferential option for the poor and vulnerable, trying "to center those most vulnerable to gun violence in moral reflection," as Ott Marshall urges. I also made sure I focused on gun violence prevention and reduction—as she recommends, gun reform rather than gun control. I appreciate how Ott Marshall, a pacifist, acknowledges the confusion and reservations Christians, especially people on the margins and truly at risk in US society, may have about nonviolence and vulnerability. I, too, believe that the vigil centers on those actually vulnerable to gun violence, focusing on actual persons and their story. Such vigils are powerful and empowering experiences.

Finally, in "Gun Culture, Free Riding, and Nothing Short of Conversion," Gerald W. Schlabach attempts to take "defensive gun culture" and its reasons justifying gun ownership seriously even as he notes how gun ownership tends to do exactly the opposite of what they claim (e.g., instead of protecting family, gun owners are putting their

---

[27] Some that I recommend: Ryan P. Cumming, *The African American Challenge to Just War Theory: A Christian Approach* (New York: Palgrave MacMillan, 2013); Therese Feiler, *Logics of War: The Use of Force and the Problem of Mediation* (London: Bloomsbury/T&T Clark, 2020), especially the chapter on Paul Ramsey, 117–149; Anna Floerke Scheid, *Just Revolution: A Christian Ethic of Political Resistance and Social Transformation* (Lanham, MD: Lexington, 2015); Gerald W. Schlabach, ed., *Just Policing, Not War: An Alternative Response to World Violence* (Collegeville, MN: Liturgical Press, 2007); and Eli Sasaran McCarthy, *Becoming Nonviolent Peacemakers: A Virtue Ethic for Catholic Social Teaching and US Policy* (Eugene, OR: Pickwick, 2012).

families in greater danger of accidental death or suicide; instead of stopping a threat, guns escalate it and intensify the violence). He recognizes that some will nevertheless consider themselves to be exceptions, "whatever the overall statistics regarding the dangers of gun ownership," what Schlabach calls "the free-rider problem." This rings true to my experience, including for myself (although at least I had much more training, while in law enforcement, with firearms than most citizens—but police sometimes err, too, of course). Likewise, Schlabach's recognition that there is "a certain rationality," albeit "very visceral" regarding supposed threats, seems right to me. Like Ott Marshall he focuses on mitigation rather than elimination of gun violence. Also similar to her, when she emphasizes the formative role of local vigils, he highlights local mobilization efforts to address "the collective-action problem." Like Ott Marshall and Grigoni, Schlabach concludes by recommending nonviolence and a just peace approach, the latter of which possibly is moving toward a synthesis of the best practices and principles of the pacifist and just war traditions—what I have called an "integral peace" approach.[28] At the end of the day, with Schlabach, I worry that "the free-rider problem will persist." I know that, as a Christian, I should have the virtue of hope, including for the conversion that Schlabach rightly encourages (starting with Christians), but I confess I wrestle with despair about reducing gun violence in the United States, which is one of the reasons why my family and I decided to move to Ireland, where such madness (even if there is a rationality to it) is much less likely to occur.

Before concluding, I wish again to express my gratitude to these contributors. Their articles will inform any further work of mine on this urgent moral problem, and I hope theological ethicists and other scholars find them stimulating and useful. That these articles are available online makes it easier for our peers to gain access to them, which is a good thing.

However, availability and accessibility are not necessarily the same thing when it comes to usefulness for other audiences. In saying this, I have in mind what James F. Keenan, SJ, has referred to as "more public, less academic audiences" in his plenary address on "Impasse and Solidarity in Theological Ethics" at the 2009 annual convention of the Catholic Theological Society of America in Halifax, Nova

---

[28] Tobias Winright, "Ukraine and the Ethics of War: The Possibility of a Just War," *Commonweal* 150, no. 5 (May 2023): 24–28. I have suggested this in a number of places in recent years, first doing so in Tobias Winright, "Your 'Just Peace' Reading List," *National Catholic Reporter*, December 21, 2016, www.ncronline.org/books/2022/10/your-just-peace-reading-list.

Scotia.[29] Especially concerning urgent issues having to do with injustice and the need for solidarity, Keenan counsels theological ethicists "to expand our circle of readers" and "move other audiences to understand within our societies and within our churches the need for an affective solidarity that leads to practices of justice."[30] While acknowledging that doing so may be difficult "when we do not resonate with the public audience" (he notes, e.g., immigration reform and similar issues; obviously, we can add gun violence reduction to the list), he suggests we "develop more embodied, relational, practical, and narrative-based arguments to offer effective ways of addressing impasse in the world, the church, and the academy today."[31] Keenan even recommends that "we could learn to write more appealingly not only for others, but even for one another."[32] *At times*—and this may be attributable to my own lack of intellect—*some* of these otherwise fine essays, or portions within them, seemed more abstruse than necessary, at least for me. On this life-and-death matter, accessibility is vital.

The issue of gun violence divides citizens, including Christians, in the United States, and the need for what Keenan encourages of us is great. I urge the contributors here and their professional peers who read these articles to write more about this issue, not only for our discipline, but for undergraduates and seminarians, pastors and politicians, the person in the pew and the person on the street, all the while keeping in view those most vulnerable and thus most in need of gun reform and gun violence reduction.🅼

Tobias Winright, PhD, is Professor of Moral Theology at St. Patrick's Pontifical University in Maynooth, Ireland. He is also Associate Member of the Las Casas Institute for Social Justice, Blackfriars Hall, University of Oxford. Prior academic appointments include Saint Louis University (2005–2022), Walsh University (2003–2005) and Simpson College (1998–2003). Among his recent publications he edited the *T&T Clark Handbook of Christian Ethics* (Bloomsbury/T&T Clark, 2021). With Mark Allman he co-edited the *Journal of the Society of Christian Ethics* (2013–2017).

---

[29] James F. Keenan, SJ, "Impasse and Solidarity in Theological Ethics," *Proceedings of the Catholic Theological Society of America* 64 (2009): 53, ejournals.bc.edu/index.php/ctsa/article/view/4925.
[30] Keenan, "Impasse and Solidarity," 53.
[31] Keenan, "Impasse and Solidarity," 54–55.
[32] Keenan, "Impasse and Solidarity," 55.